Inverness

Historic City

And

Highland Capital

by

Duncan MacDonald

In memory of my parents,
who always encouraged
me to do what I wanted to,
and to do it well;
and to my wife, Jean,
with love.

Printed and Published by
For The Right Reasons
60 Grant St
Inverness
IV3 8BS

fortherightreasons@rocketmail.com

Acknowledgements

If I were being truthful, I would have to say that there are more than enough people to thank, for help given to me, than would fill a book in itself. Some who told me tales of this and that over the years, and others who clarified various points which I asked them about and put me right when I wandered off the truth of a story or historic fact. It is not possible, therefore, to name all of them – much though I would have liked to do so. Instead I will simply acknowledge the fact that much help and support was given to me in the gathering of facts and writing of this book.

I must, however, thank my wife, Jean, for putting up with my endless hours of background reading, working on the computer, flying into a strop when things just wouldn't go right, visiting the Library and the Archive Centres – in Inverness and Edinburgh - and all the other things I got up to whilst she sat on her own without complaint – I am not so sure that I could have done the same thing had the pen been in the other hand (so to speak).

Contents

Introduction

Although Inverness only gained its "City" status with the new Millennium, it has a long and well-established history, going back much further in time than one might imagine. As well as being the chief town for the north of Scotland, at various times in its history it has also been a market town, a seaport, a royal burgh, the county town of Inverness-shire, and has long been known as the Capital of the Highlands. By virtue of its geographical position, it is a natural route centre for travel throughout the north of Scotland, and all who venture into the Highlands will surely pass through Inverness at some stage in their journey. It has, therefore, by virtue of its situation, always been destined to be a place of significance. Over the centuries, the City has developed a proud cultural heritage, which continues to this day with language, music, poetry and dance, along with drama and entertainment in Eden Court Theatre and other venues throughout the city. Inverness people have a reputation for being welcoming and friendly, always willing to help out if needed; and the City has a convivial atmosphere which makes its visitors feel at home, whether they are shopping, sightseeing, dining, or enjoying the nightlife in the City centre pubs and clubs. It is this benevolence which gives it a growing, impressive reputation as a short break and holiday destination, not just within the UK, but also worldwide. It is also true to say that the environs of the city are very beautiful, and in some instances, if one is positioned in the right place, it is possible to see views of the scenery beyond the city boundaries which are exceedingly fine.

I have lived in Inverness for over 70 years and have always harboured a special interest in the local history of the City and its people. As for the City itself, or town as it was in my younger day, one could not wish for a more beautiful situation - on the Moray Firth coast, with the tree lined River Ness threading its way through the Islands and past the Cathedral and the Castle, before meandering through the City centre on its way to the sea. Nestling at the mouth of the river Ness, Inverness enjoys a pleasant climate (with the exception of an occasional cold east wind) considering its northerly situation, and is within an easy drive of some of the most beautiful scenery in Britain, if not in the world. One can stand on the Castle Hill and look out over the roof tops and along the path of the river towards the hills in the distance, sometimes with a dusting of snow on their peaks, and wonder where on earth can be seen its like. Although I have travelled far and wide throughout the 'globe' I have found few places (if one discounts the sunshine in foreign parts and some of the scenery in New Zealand), which can match the diversity of attraction, scenery, and lifestyle offered to the Invernessian. Perhaps that is why the City is growing at such an alarming rate and why so many people are keen to settle here and raise a family.

The people of Inverness have always been an interesting "cosmopolitan" mix, and at one time (in my younger days) I knew a significant percentage of the population. Nowadays, however, with the City the size it is that percentage is far less, and is ever decreasing. Initially, I knew those whom my parents were friendly with, or told me about, and those I grew up with; then there were those I taught (first in the High School and then in Charleston Academy) and the friends I gathered as I travelled through life. When they are all added up it comes to a considerable number of individuals – which is why my daughter once remarked as we walked through the town saying "hello" to those I knew, "Do you know everyone in this town, dad?" I firmly believe that it is the experiences we have in life, and the people we meet and mix with, that colour the way we live and determine our outlook in life, as well as our future. Which is why a wide assortment of good friends and a sound education are so important for young people – I was very lucky in my youth, in that I had the advantage of both. In the past I sometimes thought that I should have left the town and plied my trade elsewhere, but on reflection, I am pleased that I did not. I would not change a single thing about any of the time I have spent in Inverness, and indeed, can honestly say that I have enjoyed every single minute of it.

Having spent many years reading numerous books about Inverness and the surrounding area, and often spent time browsing through papers and articles relating to its people, places and events, I felt compelled to note down the knowledge I had accumulated over the years, before the passage of time gradually faded those treasured memories. I was pleasantly surprised by the quantity of information on this topic which I was carrying about in my head (and even more pleased that I could remember it), and so began to marshal it into some kind of formality, of which you see the end result in this volume. As to the quality of the information, well, that is for the reader to decide. In the writing of this book there is no pretence, on my part, to any literary merit, nor do I possess any kind of historical background, either of which, I am sure, would have improved the quality of the book no end.

Some of the material I have used has inevitably been commented on in other books and papers about Inverness, and to that end I have deliberately tried to put my own stamp on it, but without purposely changing either the meaning or the historical facts surrounding the information used. Of course I am as slanted in my reporting of events as any other non-historical writer, but would suggest that the slant lies in the direction which any locals, proud of their heritage, will recognise and, hopefully, accept and understand. All I have reported on is as factual as I can make it, according to my research, and I have attempted not to alter or embellish it in any way whatsoever. That said, during my research I occasionally came across slight differences in the dating of events and occurrences and was initially confused as to why this should be so. Later I realised that prior to 1600 the New Year started on 25th March, but on that year it changed to 1st January, except in England where the change did not take place until 1752. This meant that anything taking place in January, February or March between these years was probably dated differently in Scotland and England. In addition, prior to 1752 the calendar was out of synchronisation with the sun through lack of leap years, and in order to rectify the situation it was agreed that September 3rd would become the 14th hence the loss of 11 days in that year.

I started to write this book with a clear idea of what I wanted to say, but as the book progressed I found that, occasionally, it took on the power to speak for itself and portray events in its own way, sometimes despite my own efforts to outline various facts and happenings. The people and the activities often took hold of me and I found myself caught up in their lives, tragedies, and fortunes only to be gently brought back to reality at the end of a story, book, or article. Researching the historical facts for the book was occasionally tedious but more often than not extremely interesting, and sometimes enthralling to the point of obsession, as my wife will no doubt bear witness to. There can be no better way to gain a sense of history and heritage than to research into the kind of documents I am referring to, and no better way to build a sense of pride in one's own heritage and Nationality than a clear understanding of one's historical background. Oh that more local and Scottish history was taught in our schools so that our youngsters could take more of a pride in their Scottish heritage.

Inverness has been populated over the centuries with real Highland people as well as a plethora of incomers from places near and far, both at home and abroad. The people's story is often one of a bitter struggle with life but, thankfully, it is mostly one of a race of people who are well suited to cope with their time and place in history. Initially, the people overcame the geographical and climatological disadvantages of this area exceptionally well, and eventually their tenacity and inventiveness turned them into a community that was renowned in many parts of the world for all sorts of different reasons, and still is today. They were strong, proud, reliable and adaptable, with a smattering of good Highland hospitality always present in whatever they did. These are some of the people who gave this country its backbone and helped form the Nation we are today, although they were seldom given the credit they deserved in history. Thankfully, with the passage of time, life became easier for most people in the Highlands, as improvements in communications brought increased wealth and development to the town. Those who were blessed with wealth, or were lucky enough to gain a good education, prospered well at home and abroad, whilst those who were poor and without education struggled to overcome the hardships life threw at them – much as it is today, but without the benefits of the welfare state. Many of those who left the town to seek their fortune abroad did extremely well, as we shall see later – which is why there is hardly a corner on this earth where you will not find something Scottish, or where a Scot has exerted some kind of influence.

Much has been said, and even written, about the "English" influence in Inverness, and undoubtedly, if one reads into history it is there to be seen as plainly as the words on this page; but delve deeper and one finds a slightly different slant to the story. That the town was an "English speaking colony" supporting the ruling monarch and situated in the midst of a Gaelic speaking hinterland was very much an exaggeration of the reality of the town's population, but it is a view which has been put forward on more than one occasion. One must bear in mind that much of what was written in the past was done so by English speaking travellers passing through the Highlands and writing accounts of their travels, and also by Officers stationed here with the English army, writing to their friends and loved ones in England. The first group would not have had much contact, if any, with the "common man", mixing and conversing with other English speaking people wherever possible. The second group would have been in much the same position and would have dealt largely with the Magistrates and Town Council officials, many of whom were well educated and spoke English fluently as well as Gaelic. No wonder, therefore, that some of these accounts report that there was little evidence of Gaelic being spoken in Inverness, since the writers would only have spoken English to those they came in contact with. Virtually all the "indigenous" Highlanders would have been Gaelic speaking only, with perhaps a few words of English to cover any need that arose or when they chose to use them. Since many of them would not have been able to write in Gaelic, nor would they have seen any need to, little is recorded therefore, in that language, of their true situation – although much is written in English about their perceived circumstances. In addition, from the middle of the 18th century the Gaelic language and traditions were outlawed by the occupying English forces, and Highlanders were forced to adopt a new way of life which was quite alien to them. Even in some schools the teacher (especially if he had been taken from the Lowland areas of Scotland) would punish children for speaking their native Gaelic. One teacher in the Glenurquhart area was so determined to stamp out the language that he would give any child heard using the Gaelic a "tessara" which was a small piece of carved wood. The child held on to it until he heard another using the language to whom he would then pass it on, and so on until the end of the day when the poor unfortunate holding the "tessara" would be severely beaten and asked to give it to the one he had received it from. The beatings would continue until all who had spoken Gaelic were punished.

Those who left the countryside and moved into the town of Inverness to seek employment were forced to learn the English language, although most also retained their Gaelic language and traditions. I strongly suspect that it is in the learning of "English" from a "Gaelic" base that enabled Invernessians to speak "good" English, rather than from any idea that they were taught by the English soldiers, since most of them would not have been "good" English speakers anyway. Census records show, however, that as late as the end of the 19th century almost one third of the townspeople still spoke Gaelic although it is likely that the majority of them did not hold positions of influence within the town. It is very likely that many of them spoke English when they had to, but spoke Gaelic at home, thus giving the impression to any traveller they may meet that they were "English speaking" instead of bilingual. That said, it is important to note that the history of any town does not depend solely on its civic leaders, but rather on the wider population and the influence they have in shaping its culture and heritage. One only has to look at the local landmarks and place names to see the influence Gaelic has had on Inverness in the past.

If anything of the charm of 'Old Inverness' and its people comes over in this book then I shall have achieved as much as I set out to do, for it is not a task I found easy to accomplish. I hope that those Invernessians who read the book will acquire a strong sense of pride in their City's history, as there is much to be proud of, whilst others will hopefully gain an understanding of why it is that Invernessians possess such passion and respect for their own metropolis, no matter where they wander to in the world.

At times in the book, I may appear to be overly hard on the architects of the 1960s and beyond (up to the turn of the century) for the buildings which they were responsible for erecting around the town. I fully realise that they had to work within the constraints of their paymasters and town planners, but when one looks at the legacy they have left for us, and compares it to what it has replaced, then I would say that, in most cases, it is not to their credit. The responsibility for this loss of heritage, and the erection of buildings which neither harmonise with their surroundings nor look in the least way attractive, must lie firmly at the door of those planners, town officials and architects, who made the decisions at that time. Unfortunately, we all now have to live with it. Fortunately, however, lessons seem to have been learnt from the mistakes of the past, and the new buildings of the last few decades show that some effort is being made to blend in and harmonise the new with the old – if not to retain the façade of the old and incorporate the new behind it, a strategy which surely must be applauded. Let us hope and pray that future generations will value their architectural heritage more than my generation did, and be insistent when it comes to the preservation of the remaining buildings of note and interest in the city.

It is interesting to note that, as I write, the newspapers are full of stories of City centre shop closures and the demise of the Old Town, principally as a result of the developments on Eastgate and the attraction of 'park-and-shop' at the "Golden Mile" on the east side of the City. There is no doubt that some parts of the City centre are sorely in need of refurbishment to attract new shops and business, and there is no denying that the 'centre' of the city has drifted eastwards since the work on Eastgate was completed. This should not be viewed as a problem, however, but rather as an opportunity to move the City forward in the 21st century. Optimism is a wonderful tool in overcoming difficulties – one should see a solution to every problem, rather than a problem in every solution. The City planners and officials have an excellent opportunity here to produce an exciting plan for future development, within the City centre, to ensure that the older parts of the City are refurbished and restored. If they can do that well, as I have no doubt they can, then future generations will look back and praise the vision and insight of their work. If they do it poorly, however, they will be damned by all who view it and criticise their lack of discernment and farsightedness. I pray that they have the courage to move forward with bold, decisive plans for renovation, which will enliven the City centre whilst retaining the character and history of its architecture.

Personally, I would pedestrianise the centre during the working day (9.00am 'till 5.00pm) with collect and deliver access only for traffic, then open it up again to traffic in the evening to allow parking for restaurants, hotels, etc. Refurbish areas like Lombard Street and Baron Taylor's Street (in the old style) and have attractively fronted shops which retail individualised products and crafts – witness "The Shambles" in York and "The Lanes" in Carlisle, both of which are huge attractions for these cities. Give a facelift to areas like Grant Street and Clachnaharry and give them "Village" status as many other cities have done with similar areas. Provide numbered plaques in all the historic buildings in Inverness so that tourists can hire listening stations from the tourist office and learn of the city's history as they wander about. Turn the Castle into the tourist office with a quality tourist shop and have an historic video show about the city (similar to that of Urquhart Castle and Culloden Battlefield). Change Farraline Park back into an actual park once again, a haven of respite in the city centre; allow the building of restaurants and cafes around the periphery of the park where people can sit and enjoy a cup of coffee, relax during their lunch break and enjoy a meal or go out in the evening for dinner. Although I welcome the addition of the new marina east of the harbour area, I personally think that it should have been in the area east of the Kessock Bridge, with additional plans for associated hotels and restaurants to attract international yachts and the tall ships which cannot sail under the Kessock Bridge.

Other cities within the European Community seem to be able to access funding for similar city centre development projects – so why should we not do the same. Within the space of a few decades the city could be among the most attractive in Europe – historically, culturally and socially – with all the associated tourist income. Is it not so that one has to speculate to accumulate?

The city centre is relatively small and compact, yet the periphery of the city grows at an alarming rate with new houses –

practically all of which will have at least one car. Because the river divides the city in two, and there are swing bridges over the canal crossings, there are additional transport difficulties to that of other cities – but still (at the time of writing) the traffic is all channelled through the centre of the city and at busy times, and especially in the summer, there are huge tailbacks and traffic chaos. Let's have a clear long-term transport plan for the city which has a proper road network and yet encourages car users to make use of good rail and bus services into and out of the city.

My greatest fear is that Inverness will be left in the 20th century whilst other, more enterprising, cities will forge ahead with innovative solutions to transport and city development. What a great pity that would be – another lost opportunity one might say, although it need not be that way at all.

Chapter 1

Early History

It is probably true to say that geological movement within this area and the Great Glen Fault, which has been in existence from Pre-Cambrian times, have both had, over the last few hundred million years, a considerable impact on the geographical history of the Inverness area. When one adds to that the continued effects of water erosion and glacial action within the last 100 million years, you will arrive at the geography of the Inverness area, as we know it today. The Great Glen rift valley, which splits Scotland in half in a diagonal, east/west direction, is relatively inactive although there is no doubt that slight tremors are felt in Inverness and the surrounding area from time to time. This Glen, which is narrow at the north-east end of Loch Ness, begins to widen as it approaches the Moray and Beauly Firths and then forms a plain, only slightly above sea level, upon which Inverness is situated and dissected by the River Ness. Almost surrounded by Devonian Old Red Sandstone rocks which have been carved into their present form by successive ice sheets of up to 1,500 metres thick, Inverness sits comfortably on the shore of the Moray Firth on a raised sea bed which is floored with glacial deposits. One need look no further for proof of glacial meltwater deposits (eskers) than Torvean and Tomnahurich, whilst Culloden Forest, and the Slochd Mor, which carries the A9 south towards Tomatin, are examples of dried-up glacial meltwater channels.

The post-glacial period was closely followed by well-defined climate change which saw a marked increase in dense vegetation cover; this was inevitably followed, eventually, by the formation of peat deposition. As the centuries rolled by the river deposited its alluvium on top of previous glacial sediment in a slow methodical manner and thus the landscape around Inverness was slowly formed.

The flora and fauna of the area was, and still is, extremely diverse. The river valley initially had a very affable climate, and was comparatively mild in winter, but climb a couple of hundred metres into the hills and there was a marked difference in both temperature and rainfall. These factors controlled the type of vegetation which existed within the Inverness area as well as the fauna which seemed to survive on it. Over the last 25,000 years, as the glaciers repeatedly advanced and retreated over this part of Scotland, the area around Inverness would have changed from a barren, frozen waste, into arctic tundra with permafrost and low shrubs and mosses, and eventually into thick, dense woodland. The various animals best suited to these changing conditions would have been plentiful at various times and included, in colder climes, woolly rhinoceros, mammoth, wolf, bison and arctic bear. As the climate improved, extinction, probably aggravated by hunting, would have taken place, and these animals, in turn, would have been replaced by reindeer, horse, elk and red deer. By around 8,000 B.C. much of what is present-day Scotland was covered in woodland supporting ox, wild pig, red and roe deer, which would have formed much of the diet of the Mesolithic hunters who were present in the region. With the passage of time, however, the people would have relied less on hunting and more on fishing and gathering nuts and fruits, and would have used seasonal camps rather than tracking the migrating herds of wild animals. As domesticated plants and animals were adopted by the locals, hunting would have slowly died out and people would have settled permanently in the Inverness area.

And what of these people? Who were they? Who are we descended from? One would suppose that Invernessians, like any other populace, are the descendants of every other people who ever lived here, or indeed, passed through here. We are, like all Scots, descended from immigrants, even though our immigrant ancestors came here many centuries ago. Humans first visited Scotland following the retreating ice some 8,000 years ago, and probably came from the European mainland driven by curiosity, hope and chance. In due course, some of these visitors were content with their new surroundings and saw a future in remaining in their new-found land, so they settled here. At first, not in a permanent way but rather living a nomadic existence fishing and hunting along the shores, sometimes boldly entering the forests in search of food. Our knowledge of how and when this sequence of events took place will never be known precisely, because all of this took place before oral or written records. One source of evidence is, of course, archaeological, but even this area of investigation has limits as to what it can tell us, and the identification of sites of historic interest is often largely a matter of luck rather than good judgement. Precision, therefore, must give way to probability, at least in this period of time. From this we can begin to see a parade of the earliest primitive hunters, followed by more skilled agriculturalists, then metal-working Beaker people, who buried their dead in individual tombs, the Bronze Age people, the Iron Age people, the Romans, and finally the Norsemen. These then are our ancestors. They came from far and wide and each succession of invaders left its legacy upon the people, enriching their skills as well as their genes. The dominant ones would impose their

14

kind of society and customs upon the local people, until they were superseded by the next group, and so on.

It is not possible, therefore, to precisely date when man first inhabited the Highlands, but we do know that around 6,500 B.C. small kinship groups of Mesolithic nomads, who would have hunted, fished and gathered food as they moved from camp to camp, reached Oban and the Islands beyond. This is not to say that they were necessarily the first inhabitants but simply that their refuse heaps, left along the coast, are the earliest evidence of human presence in the area. They used flint, antler and bone to fashion tools for hunting, some of which resembled those found in Ireland and also those as far away as France and Spain. Unfortunately, they did not appear to possess the artistic cave drawing skills of their contemporaries in France and Spain and so left no such record of their existence in this part of the world. It was probably not until the 4th millennium B.C. that the area around Inverness became attractive enough for Neolithic people to settle permanently there, thus marking the beginning of a new Stone Age in the Highlands. As time passed, new waves of visitors arrived in this area, bringing with them new customs and skills and, perhaps more importantly, new genes.

The sheltered position, fertile soil, low rainfall and access to fishing would have made this area ideal for a settlement, which would most probably have been on the fringes of the flood plain of the River Ness and on the slopes and higher ground of the surrounding hills. Some time around the 3rd millennium B.C., although there is debate about this date, the people began to build chambered tombs constructed of large stones, many of these megalithic tombs can still be seen around the Inverness area and throughout the Highlands and Islands, through which the people would display their sense of community, identity and religious beliefs. The cairns at Clava are a typical example of this, and they so resemble similar ones at Iberian sites that it has been suggested that the Neolithic people who settled the Clava area journeyed not, as others did, by the main west coast route and via the Great Glen to arrive here, but more directly from south-west France and Spain through Brittany and across the North Sea although, again, this has had some doubt cast over it. Another Clava type cairn once stood at Stoneyfield (Achnaclach) before being moved 3km south because of road re-alignment. The cremated burials, in urns and pits, and shards of Neolithic pottery found inside the cairn dated from around 2,000 B.C., whilst the underlying structure was dated much earlier at around 3,000 B.C. There are surprisingly few other notable prehistoric sites from this time in the history of the Inverness area, possibly due to their destruction during building operations throughout the centuries.

Around 2000 B.C. the Bronze Age hit the Highlands and, although little is known of the domestic life of early Bronze Age people, various bronze artefacts have been found throughout the Highlands and Islands to suggest that, even then, women had a liking for earrings, necklaces and bracelets. Stone cists which were dug up at the Bught Park were found to contain bronze daggers whilst other finds in the local area include bronze axes, halberds and even bronze-smith's moulds from the 2nd Millennium B.C. Whilst there is little evidence of large-scale occupation around Inverness at this time its geographical situation would suggest that it was a busy crossroads then, as it is now. The presence of the hill fort on Craig Phadrig and a large Iron Age hill fort on the Ord Hill, suggest the possibility of there being important and large population centres in this area.

Severe climatic changes in the 7th century B.C. saw a rise in inland water levels with a subsequent decline in tree growth in high areas all over Europe. It is highly likely, therefore, that the Highlands were particularly hard hit with cooler and wetter weather conditions probably playing havoc with agriculture, although it is difficult to assess the effects precisely. The late Bronze Age, around 600 B.C., saw an influx of European traders, craftsmen and smiths into Britain so it is likely that they arrived in this area in small numbers shortly after that. They brought with them iron tools and weapons and used the Celtic dialect, thus introducing the Iron Age to the Highlands. A great deal is known of these European Celts, not just through archaeology but also through Roman and Greek writers. It is reported that they were a warrior people reliant on agriculture and willing to barter a slave for a jar of wine, although whether that knowledge is applicable to life around Inverness at that time is somewhat debatable.

The influence of the Romans in Britain varied greatly from north to south. Agricola never really consolidated his victory at Mons Graupius and eventually withdrew to Hadrian's Wall leaving security to some of the Celtic tribes under Roman patronage. Records show that in the year 140 A.D. Lollius Urbicus, an Imperial Lieutenant, placed a Roman station at Ptoroton, which was the chief town of the Vacomagi Tribe and was situated in north Britain near the mouth of the River Vararis. It is unclear where the town was actually situated and which river they are referring to although Forres, Burghead and Inverness are strong contenders, with the River Farrar as the Vararis. This claim is supported by the existence of a small Roman Fort known to have been at Bona, six miles west of Inverness, where Columba encountered the Loch Ness monster.

By the 3rd century A.D. Roman writers were describing the inhabitants in the 'north' of Britain as the 'Picts' and thus it was in 563, when Columba sailed up the Great Glen on his famous journey from Iona to visit King Bridei (Brude) at his headquarters in Inverness, that he caught sight of the Loch Ness monster on the way here. Columba was actually seeking permission to build a church on St. Michael's Mount in Inverness as well as attempting to convert the Pictish King to Christianity. Columba (or Columcille, as he was known in his own language), was actually a prince of the royal house in Irish Dalriada who had been forced to leave home after a dispute over the copying of a Christian psalter. He left Ireland, in 563 AD, for exile in Scottish Dalriada, landing on Iona and setting up a mission which eventually became a centre for Christendom. The story of Columba's visit is told in Adomnan's "*Life of St. Columba*" which states that he saw the victim of the monster being buried on the banks of the River Ness, and in defiance of the monster he ordered one of his disciples to swim across the river to fetch a boat from the other side. The monster made for the swimmer with open jaws but Columba made the sign of the cross and commanded it to withdraw. The monster fled, and both the brethren and the "barbarous heathens" were impressed by the greatness of the miracle.

Despite this, Brude did not give Columba a very cordial welcome because he closed the door of his fort against him when he arrived. Columba, on discovering this, first made the sign of the cross then, having knocked on the door, he laid his hand upon it. It is said that the bolts of the door were forced back with great force and the door instantly flew open. When Brude heard what had happened he was filled with alarm and immediately went to meet Columba "with conciliatory and respectful language". Brude was subsequently converted to Christianity and offered Columba safe passage to the Pictish court in Orkney. Although no trace now remains of Brude's fortress, it was more than likely built on high ground, for security reasons, and also because the area where Inverness now stands would have been liable to frequent flooding. Since the City is surrounded by high ground, there is no shortage of suggested sites for King Brude's fortress, although three areas can be singled out. These possible sites are the hill on which Victoria Terrace now stands, Torvean and Craig Phadrig. Victoria Terrace is the least likely through lack of any evidence, although there are those who think that that was the site of

MacBeth's Castle and hence the name Auldcastle Road. Torvean is a possibility coupled with the fact that in 1807 during the construction of the Caledonian Canal a massive silver chain, the probable badge of office of a very high ranking official such as a '*mormaer*' or perhaps even Bridei himself, was found close to Torvean during the excavations. Craig Phadrig, a strong contender because of the impressive hill fort, also has the Gaelic name "*Larach an Tigh Mhor*" (the site of the great house).

Whatever the appearance of Brude's fort may have looked like there is little doubt that the 'common' people would have lived in huts which would have been clustered nearby for protection and these would have represented the earliest buildings of the town. Later, other areas of high ground would have supported better buildings as the town grew in size. There can be little doubt that even after it ceased to be the capital of Pictland, the place still remained important and prominent.

The Inverness area is particularly well endowed with a large variety of Iron Age monuments – hill forts, brochs, duns, hut circles and crannogs – the best of these being the vitrified fort on Craig Phadrig which was excavated in 1971. It was probably built around 350 B.C. and had walls 6 metres thick and 8 metres high. With the exception of a few minor skirmishes history records little about the Inverness area between the time of Bridei and the 11th century, perhaps suggesting that it had ceased to be a Pictish capital before the union of the Pictish and Scottish crowns in 843 A.D. by Kenneth MacAlpin. The Viking invasion of the Highlands took place between 800 and 1150 A.D., although much of it was confined to the north and west coasts of Scotland, and Norse settlers closely followed on their heels. The dividing line between the Norsemen and the Celts was the Cromarty Firth with Dingwall being an important administrative town. Although the Vikings raided along the Moray coast from time to time there is little evidence to suggest that they had more than a passing interest in the Inverness area, which they seem largely to have left alone. Sometimes the Vikings came as raiders, sometimes as settlers, as the number of surnames ending in '-son' would suggest. In these times of frequent insurrection the Scottish kings occasionally visited the town in order to quell turbulence and disorder and to restore their authority.

Chapter 2

The Middle Years

With the historic background of the previous chapter, it would be true to say that from earliest times Inverness had some presumption to be a 'Capital'. Already recognised as having a geographical position of some importance by the Picts, and at the centre of a natural east-west and north-south passageway, its citizens would have begun to build a town the layout of which was determined not only by the River Ness and its estuary but also by the hills which surround it. Settlers would have been wary of the fast flowing river and its flood plain and initially, at least, according to excavations, built dwellings on the slopes of the east bank, rather than on the west side of the river. The focal point for much of the early growth of Inverness appears, not surprisingly, to have taken place around Castle Street, near the protection of the Castle, and Church Street, en route to where St. Columba built his church on St. Michael's Mount.

Provincial rulers in Scotland were called '*mormaers*', a Pictish term meaning "high steward", and it distinguished these royal ministers from the lesser '*maers*', later called "thanes", who were hereditary tenants and administrators of portions of the royal demesne. One such '*mormaer*' was MacBeth, by birth the mormaer of Ross and by marriage the mormaer of Moray; he later became King of Scotland. Unlike Shakespeare's character, the real MacBeth was a great king whose father had been the ruler of Moray and whose mother was of royal descent. At the age of 35 years he killed King Duncan I and succeeded to the throne of Scotland with his wife, Queen Gruoch (Shakespeare's Lady MacBeth). He was defeated at Dunsinane 14 years later, in 1054, by the Earl of Northumbria, who had invaded Scotland with an English army on behalf of Malcolm Canmore. Fleeing from a second invasion 3 years later MacBeth was cornered at Lumphanan and killed. His stepson Lulach, nicknamed "The Simpleton", succeeded him, but only for a few months, before he too was killed and Malcolm III (Canmore) took the throne. Although MacBeth had strongholds in Moray it is thought that when he became king in 1040 he took control of the castle in Inverness.

Very little is known about the Medieval period in Inverness principally because little archaeological excavation has been carried out, but also because it is likely that building work over the centuries has destroyed a great number of the earlier sites which existed. Some archaeological work carried out in the 1970s points towards the medieval town being relatively small in size and enclosed by a ditch or 'fosse'. This evidence was reviewed in the early 1980s and today, more than 30 years later, little new has been added to it. The town ditch roughly followed the line of what is now Academy Street, along to meet the junction of High Street and Eastgate, on the eastern side of the town, and somewhere around Friars' Street on the North side. The River Ness would have formed a natural barrier on the western side and the high ground to the south and east of the Castle Hill would have formed another barrier. In 1229 a powerful chief named Gillespick M'Scourlane burned the town in an attempt to assume royal authority and slew all who would not acknowledge him. He was later defeated, captured and beheaded. The first bridge over the River Ness is recorded in the 13th century so it is unlikely that there would have been much, if any, development to the west of the river before the bridge was built. There was also no development in the Hill area of the town until at least the middle of the 13th century. Excavations in Castle Street in the late 1970s uncovered evidence of a middle 13th century house containing Yorkshire pottery, known as Scarborough-ware, and substantial timber buildings of the 14th century. These properties stood for some 50 – 80 years before being burnt to the ground in the early 15th century. This is not surprising since the area was burned on more than one occasion around that time, as we shall see later. Small hearths and ovens to the rear of the properties indicate that they were probably used as workshops as well as dwelling houses, a practice which was quite common in those days. One landmark building of the 13th century was the Blackfriars' Friary, built around 1233, in Friars Street; it must have been a commanding structure and housed many Royal visitors to the town, despite its apparent lack of residential friars.

Post 12th century, Inverness grew in importance both as a key centre for trade and also as a town in its own right with official charters from the Kings and Queens of Scotland. The First Statistical Account of Scotland states that a Charter was granted to Inverness by Malcolm Canmore (1057 – 1093) but there is no actual evidence to support this claim. The earliest known charter, issued during the reign of William the Lion (1165 – 1214), was not restricted to the Burgh but was granted to all Burgesses in Moray. Since most of them lived in Inverness it was considered to be the first Burgh Charter. King William the Lion issued another three charters to Inverness conferring on the Burgesses freedom from tolls, the right to hold a weekly market, the exclusive right of trading within the shire (a very valuable privilege at that time) and a number of other rights. In one charter, granted in 1180, the King undertakes to make a ditch around the town, which the Burgesses were to protect with a palisade. Inverness flourished at this time. Its maritime position enabled a thriving shipbuilding industry as well as a bustling port. The fishing industry, and particularly herring fishing, was highly developed with Inverness being the principal port on the Moray Firth. The town's merchants were exporting wool, cloth, fur, fish, cattle and hides as well as importing all sorts of things from foreign parts. The fur may well have included beaver skins, for, according to Boece, beavers were at one time found on the banks of Loch Ness and an Act of Parliament in the time of David I recorded beaver skins among Scottish exports.

The Burgh met its financial obligations by renting out lands granted to it by charter and it is from monies raised in this way, along with petty customs, which founded the Inverness Common Good Fund. In 1180 the lands of the Haugh area, and in 1236 the lands of the Merkinch area, were granted to the Burgh. This was added to in 1369 by the lands of Drakies along with the fishings, mills, tolls and petty customs of the Burgh, and it was this charter which made Inverness a Royal Burgh. The Great Charter of 1591 reaffirmed all previous charters and defined the properties and privileges of the Burgh. More importantly it confirmed Inverness as the most important Burgh in northern Scotland and made it clear that Inverness had trading rights over all northern Burghs, such as Dingwall, Cromarty and Tain. Sadly the charter allowed for only one tavern in the town which is perhaps a good reason for not pressing for the charter to be reintroduced – or is it?

Malcolm Canmore's sons were strongly influenced by his English wife and when in power they tried to anglicise Scotland. Inverness was no exception to this process and saw its share of lowland people settling in the town most of whom had influence in trade or commerce, many of whom became Burgesses. The first Burgess of whom there is a record was called Geoffrey Blund – hardly a local name one would imagine. Early records show that Inverness was largely a town of lowland people, customs and manners, with the 'local' Celtic folk having little sway in the business world. It was perceived by many as a peaceful English-speaking market town, supportive of the Crown in the midst of a Celtic and Gaelic speaking population – but more of that later. Expansion of the town would probably have tended to cluster round important areas such as the harbour, where fishing boats would land their catch and boats would come and go from the continent with imports and exports, the Dominican Friary, in Friar's Street, and the area around the Castle. The hostility of the clans, in particular the MacDonalds, Lords of the Isles, and also the lack of suitable roads saw little communication and trade between Inverness and the neighbouring districts. It is interesting to note that Town Council records show that in 1733 a deputation was sent to Dingwall to ascertain what sort of place it was. They reported back to say that there was little trade to speak of and the little there was had no harbour to operate from, there was no prison, the loch nearby the town kept people from Kirk and market, for lack of a bridge to cross it, and that the buildings of the town were in a ruinous state.

Following the accession of Bruce, and probably for the next century, Inverness was constantly exposed to predatory visits from islesmen and northern clans. There is a long record of skirmishes between the town's inhabitants and their assailants and of the price paid to buy off the aggressors. On one occasion, a large body of clansmen approached the Kessock Ferry and sent a message to the town of its impending destruction if a large sum of money was not forthcoming. The Provost pretended to agree to the demand and sent a large quantity of spirits to the chief for his entertainment whilst the ransom was obtained. The islesmen, rushing headlong into the trap, became helplessly drunk at which point the townspeople rushed at them and routed them, killing a large number. Despite the thin veneer of culture and respectability surrounding the town and its inhabitants in the 15th century, the perspective of 'Highlanders' in general, by Lowland Scots and those south of the border in particular, was one of a wild people who were uncouth and barbaric. Not helped by the fact that in 1410 Donald, Lord of the Isles, had sacked the town and burned the Castle on his way to the Battle of Harlaw because he received no support from Lord Lovat, and was frightened that unless he asserted himself he might lose other support as well. This was a violent and lawless age during which time Inverness suffered several disasters, but always seemed to recover and continue to prosper.

In 1426 James I restored the Castle and the following year held parliament there, inviting a number of local dignitaries and clan chiefs including Alexander MacDonald, Lord of the Isles, and his mother the Countess of Ross. When he got them into the castle he imprisoned them all in the newly restored tower and many of them were put to death whilst others were imprisoned in different castles throughout Scotland. It must have been no surprise, therefore, when two years later the MacDonalds returned to Inverness and burned the Castle to the ground yet again. The King's army eventually met with the MacDonalds in Lochaber and, following desertion by the Clan Chattan and Clan Cameron men, MacDonald was beaten. The MacDonalds were Earls of Ross as well as Lords of the Isles and took the responsibility seriously, issuing charters from Tain, Dingwall and Fortrose as well as Inverness. Around 1475 the MacDonalds fell on hard times and John, the last Lord of the Isles, was forced to relinquish large tracts of land as well as to renounce the earldom of Ross and the office of Sheriff of Inverness and Nairn. Boldly appearing before the Scottish parliament six months later John had the forfeiture rescinded but lost the Earldom of Ross. Because he continued to cause trouble by himself and also with his son Angus, in 1493 he lost his remaining lands and titles, with the title of "Lord of the Isles" going to the Crown, hence the reason why Prince Charles, the Prince of Wales, wears the Lord of the Isles tartan when he visits northern Scotland.

Anarchic times indeed, yet, despite the periodic fears of raids from the wilder parts to the west of Inverness, the town's people seemed to prosper well enough. The residences of 'ordinary' people often lay next to the town homes of the landed gentry and the wealthy town merchants, some of whom would have resided above their shops. Sanitation in the home would not have been a high priority in those days and, since the river was nearby, the sewers would probably have been open drains which eventually found their way to the river. Under such conditions a heavy shower of rain, to wash away the filth lying on the streets, would surely have been welcomed by all the town residents. Few people would have washed on a daily basis and where houses were two storeyed the equivalent cry of "Gardyloo" would undoubtedly have been heard in the street below. The harbour area would have witnessed the export of wool, pelts and hides as well as timber, cattle, salmon and herring. Ship-building had flourished since the 13th century and some Burgesses owned their own ships for the purposes of trade. The townspeople would not, however, have been without distractions to their work, one of which would have been the not infrequent public executions, which took place on the town's gallows, situated at Muirfield. In 1925, during excavation of a site for houses, opposite the back entrance to Hedgefield, a row of skeletons was discovered. Further digging uncovered many more, all in a row, but unfortunately they were reburied without investigation. Could this have been the site of the hangman's gibbet? The Magistrates of the time dispensed a range of punishments on the local miscreants, one of which was "banishment from the town", a sentence passed on those who persistently disturbed the peace, although it was not always strictly enforced. Those concerned often slipping quietly back into the town some time afterwards and keeping a low profile until their sentence was forgotten. In 1739 the town hangman cut off the ear of a man convicted of thieving, and in 1759 a woman was sentenced to be transported to America for child murder. Even as late as 1842 it is reported that the jailhouse contained, and used, many implements of torture – including a cocksteel, a thumbkin, a bootkin and a brangus. Criminality was seen as a weakness of the 'lower classes' and punishments were often cruel as well as severe.

In the 16th century Inverness continued to prosper as a busy port and a market town. The Reformation seems to have passed relatively peacefully in Inverness as it is barely documented. Which was not the case, however, of the first Protestant minister, David Rag, appointed in 1560. He seems to have been a 'ladies man' and, whilst greatly admired by the women of the town, he was clearly disliked by their husbands, apparently with good reason. A year after his appointment, in 1561, he took court action against one Arthur Byrnaye who had accused him of adultery with his wife. Rag won his action and poor Brynaye had to appear before the Church congregation, apologise for his 'offence' and ask forgiveness from the minister – a task which could not have been easy for him. Rag's position was greatly undermined by the case, however, and he was replaced in 1565 by a Thomas Howieson. Rag left the town in 1567 and was never heard of again.

The following century was dominated by the wars of religion which, from the middle to the latter part of the century, tore the country apart and ended in James II being removed from the throne. In 1638 Charles I, King of England, tried to force his prayer book on the Scots, who clearly did not want it. The Reformation had followed a different path in Scotland from that which it followed in England. The National Covenant, drawn up in Greyfriars Churchyard in Edinburgh was immensely popular, protesting Scotland's right to its own Church and parliament. James Graham, Marquis of Montrose, led the Covenanters against the Royalists at Bridge of Dee in 1639, and defeated them. When the second Covenant was drawn up in 1643, however, Montrose opposed the set up and, this time, joined forces with the King. He was given the office of Lieutenant-General in Scotland and charged to win Scotland to the King's cause. Many

Highland clans rallied to his banner and, through his brilliant leadership, he won many startling victories before his much depleted army was defeated at Philiphaugh towards the end of 1645. Three years later Charles was beheaded. The Frasers of Lovat had fought against Montrose at Auldearn and when Montrose laid siege to Inverness early in 1645 he allowed his army to take revenge against the Frasers with devastating results. A few weeks after laying siege to the town, however, Montrose began to run short of supplies and, leaving the Inverness garrison intact, he withdrew at the approach of the Royalist army. Shortly afterwards, Charles surrendered and commanded Montrose to disperse his forces and go abroad for his own safety. Montrose did as he was asked and fled to the French court in 1646. In 1649 the Covenanters of Inverness mutinied but were overwhelmed by a force of 700 in the service of the King. The following year, 1650, Charles II asked Montrose to return to Scotland and raise an army to retake the country before going on to defeat Cromwell and establish him (Charles II) on the throne of England. Montrose did so, but on his return was betrayed by Charles and was defeated and captured at Carbisdale in 1650. He was first taken to Inverness before going on to spend the night at Castle Stuart, then onward to Edinburgh where he was executed on Charles' instructions a few weeks later. On his entry to Inverness he stopped at the "Well of the Washing", which was situated opposite the Muirtown Toll House, to quench his thirst before being taken to the Town House.

Although there are few accounts of the history of Inverness in the 17th century one rather splendid example is the "Wardlaw Manuscript" of the Rev James Fraser, minister of the parish of Wardlaw (Kirkhill), which gives clear eyewitness accounts of many happenings in and around Inverness at that time in history. Inverness at this time was, as one would expect, firmly supporting the King against 'the wicked tyrant' Cromwell. In 1650 the Council ordered that a company of able-bodied men be raised and sent to assist the cause. By September of that year, however, Cromwell was in Edinburgh and the following September he was in control of the whole country. He was clearly fully aware of the importance of Inverness as the key to the Highlands, and it accordingly became the locality for one of the two forts which he constructed to control the Highlanders, the other being at Fort William. Work on the Inverness Citadel began in 1652 but, since the German engineer in charge of construction spent little time here in Inverness, work progressed very slowly, unlike the cost which more than doubled before its completion in 1655. After the

Restoration, an Act of Parliament, in 1662, ordered the demolition of all the citadels built by Cromwell, so some 7 years after its completion it was abandoned by the garrison of soldiers, prior to its demolition. In 1685 some of the stones from the Citadel were put to good use in the construction of a new bridge across the Ness to replace a previous wooden construction.

The 17th century may have begun peacefully enough but it finished on a very different note altogether. All Highland chiefs were required to swear an oath of loyalty to William before New Year 1692 with any refusals facing the traditional 'fire and sword' repercussions. All complied, much to the surprise, if not annoyance, of Sir John Dalrymple of Stair, the king's Secretary of State in Edinburgh, who had hoped to take revenge on the Clan MacDonald. The only flaw being that MacIan, chief of the MacDonalds of Glencoe, had gone to Fort William instead of Inveraray. Having been redirected, MacIan was late in swearing the oath, and this presented Dalrymple with the opportunity he needed. He ordered the appropriate army officials with instructions to proceed against MacIan and his clan " ..… to burn their houses, seize or destroy their goods or cattle, plenishing or clothes, and to cut off the men." His opinion was that, "It will be a proper vindication of the public justice to extirpate that sect of thieves." The story of the massacre is sadly familiar. Whilst parties of soldiers guarded each end of the glen, another was sent in to seek hospitality from the MacDonalds on the pretence that they were passing through the glen. On 13th February 1692 the Campbells, led by Robert Campbell of Glenlyon, betrayed highland hospitality and, obeying their government masters, treacherously and ruthlessly slaughtered their hosts, the MacDonalds of Glencoe. Most of the clansfolk were either shot or stabbed, although MacIan's son managed to lead a small party of survivors over the mountains and through the snowdrifts to seek refuge with the Stewarts of Appin. When, months later, news of the massacre reached Edinburgh it barely ruffled a few feathers amongst the lowland politicians. Dalrymple was removed from office but only for a short time before being reinstated, and that was an end to the matter. It was, however, a bloody incident which had deep repercussions for clansmen throughout the country, and was the beginning of the destruction of the Highlanders, a people who once formed a significant part of the Scottish population and who, through their military skill, had largely helped to maintain the Scottish monarchy. Unfortunately, their tribal and feudal society was ill led, in many cases, and did not change to meet the demands of a changing world. They also proudly refused to bow to the ways of the lowland Scots and their English masters, and eventually came to be regarded as an obstacle to the political union of Scotland and England. Thus their downfall was plotted. One of the principal characters involved in the massacre said afterwards:

"It is not that anybody thinks that the thieving tribe did not deserve to be destroyed ..."

Which was a measure of the contempt which Highlanders were held in, by some factions at that time, and which showed itself again after the battle of Culloden in 1746. It is indeed regrettable that men, women and children should have been murdered in such a dishonourable and deceitful way by their own countrymen.

It is ironic, however, to note that when Bonnie Prince Charlie's army was retreating back to Scotland in 1746, they camped overnight near Stair Castle, home of the Dalrymple's. There were those in the army, not surprisingly, who thought of taking revenge upon the Campbells for their evil deed. They were prevented from doing so by a guard, mounted by the MacDonalds of Glencoe, who thus saved from destruction the home of the man responsible for the massacre of 1692. Would that they had been shown the same degree of respect and honour in Glencoe some 50 odd years before.

Chapter 3

The Growth of a Town

By the time 1715 had arrived, Mackintosh of Borlum would have been gathering up Frasers and Chisholms to combat the Earl of Sutherland's army at Alness and the town of Inverness would have been occupied by the MacKintoshes for the Jacobites; soon to be recovered by the Lairds of Culloden and Kilravock, aided by Lord Lovat. Four years later the Inverness garrison would have marched out of the Castle en route down the lochside to Glenshiel to meet the rebels and their Spanish allies. But if the 18th century, in this area at least, is remembered for any individual happening, then it must surely be for the Battle of Culloden which took place on Drumossie Moor on 16th April 1746. The consequences and aftermath of Culloden reverberated throughout the Highlands for many years afterwards. It is difficult to exaggerate the importance this affair had on the Highlands, and it is perhaps worthy of note that the battle is still commemorated annually at the battlefield, with propriety and dignity, some 260 years after the event. It was not the first defeat the Highlanders ever suffered in battle but it is the one which is remembered with fervour and distaste every year.

A lost cause will always triumph in men's imaginations but it is interesting to ponder on why it is that no British regiment has Culloden among its battle honours. Perhaps, and more than likely, because there was no honour accrued from the aftermath of the battle. Much of the rancour of the defeat at Culloden, however, emanates from the after events of the battle rather than what took place on the field itself, where it was not unusual to be shown 'no quarter' from the victorious side. In this case, however, the Jacobites, and those suspected of being Jacobites or even sympathisers, were relentlessly hunted and slaughtered for several days after the battle, not to mention the men who were found and bayoneted, for weeks afterwards, in the hinterland of Inverness. Although Prince Charlie was eventually able to secure rescue in a French ship, which carried him into exile for the remainder of his life, for the Highlanders who had followed him their suffering did not end on the battlefield, or at the hands of the punishment squads of Cumberland the Butcher. His draconian purge of Scottish Gaeldom, nowadays called ethnic cleansing, was nothing short of a disgrace and one of the major troughs for British Imperialism. Not that the clan chiefs themselves come out of the situation without fault – eventually putting their own rights as landowners above the welfare of their clansmen. The whole Highland way of life was soon to perish, as Parliament in London devised laws to ensure that another uprising would never occur again. The Disarming Act removed all weapons from the clans whilst the playing of the bagpipes, as well as the wearing of Highland dress, were banned. Another Act destroyed the bond of military service between chief and clansman whilst yet another removed the chief's sovereign powers over his tenants. The estates of all the Jacobite chiefs were forfeited to the Crown and placed under the control of Commissioners.

The Jacobites had returned north from Derby, after a number of victories both north and south of the border, and arrived in Inverness around the middle of February 1746 when the town was rife with measles and smallpox. They blew up the Castle, the original Fort George, two days later and remained in command of the town until the day of the battle. Following their defeat, many of the Jacobite army, who had fought at Culloden, fled towards Inverness and were hotly pursued by Cumberland's soldiers on horseback. One such group of Highlanders, on arriving in the town, rushed down Bridge Street only to find that the Campbells and the Argyllshire militia had closed the gate at the western end of the Ness Bridge in order to prevent their escape. The Highlanders, tired and outnumbered, turned and fought as best they could whilst some of them managed to ford the river and escape. Many of those who were captured after fleeing from the battlefield were housed in the Old High Church, and one can still find two stones nine paces apart, one of which has a v-shaped groove and the other has two curved hollows. It is thought that Jacobite prisoners were taken for execution and made to either kneel or sit on one stone whilst their Redcoat executioners rested their muskets in the groove of the other stone. The morning after the battle, the Duke of Cumberland gave orders for the wounded and the dying Jacobite soldiers to be piled into two heaps, whereupon a six-pound cannon was fired into each heap to dispatch the unfortunate men. There can be no doubt, from the eyewitness accounts which exist, and the many articles which have been written about the aftermath of the battle, that Cumberland had no love for Highlanders and proved it by carrying out many barbarous and atrocious acts against the town and its people, whilst his soldiers murdered, raped and pillaged, often without restraint. The Tolbooth and jail, churchyards and houses, which had been commandeered by the Provost Marshall, and the transport ships in the harbour, were filled daily with prisoners brought in by patrols of

Redcoats. Many of the prisoners died, or starved, in these jails and eventually the wailing of the wounded and the stench of death and excrement became so bad that the Town Provost, John Fraser, was asked to complain to Cumberland about the treatment of the men. He and a companion, former Provost Hossack, went to the Town House, which was Cumberland's headquarters, along with the neighbouring Horn's Hotel, and made a plea for mercy for the Jacobites. General Hawley looked up from his papers and yelled, "Damn you puppy, do you pretend to dictate here?", and ordered them kicked out.

Poor Hossack was seized and kicked down the stairs and out on to the street in full view of the townspeople. Provost Fraser made a quick exit before he received the same treatment. Hawley, however, had not forgotten him and later that evening sent some Grenadiers to make Fraser clean the General's stable as a punishment. Fraser, a proud Highland man, said that since he did not clean his own stable he certainly was not going to clean the General's. His stout attestation found favour with the officer in charge and he was allowed to hire a couple of "common fellows" to carry out the task whilst he stood and watched. Despite the dent to its civic pride by this insult to its dignitaries, the town saw humour in the situation and from then on Fraser and Hossack were known as Provost Kick and Provost Muck.

Deserters from the government army were also treated harshly with the trial of each man being miserably brief to say the least, taking place in a tent in the Crown area of the town, with the usual outcome being, "......sentenced to hang by the neck until dead". The hangings usually took place at eight o'clock in the morning with the men walking the mile or so from the town to the gallows and the whole affair being watched by the comrades of the condemned as their only source of entertainment. By the end of May there had been so many hangings that the men had "become bored" with them and rarely turned up to watch. The last man hanged for desertion remained on the gallows, as an example to the other soldiers, until the army left Inverness. Cumberland ordered that no man should go more than a quarter of a mile from camp, in an attempt to contain looting and stealing, but every morning the sound of the lash was heard in the Crown as the perpetrators who had been caught were flogged. Although no man seems to have died from a flogging while the army was stationed in Inverness, one poor fellow was sentenced to one thousand two hundred lashes for "morauding and steeling". He received two hundred and forty lashes a day for five days. It is a miracle that he ever survived such a punishment, but it is also a measure of the brutality of Cumberland and the way he treated his soldiers.

Many of Cumberland's officers thought the town small and insignificant and, comparing it to London, thought the three principal streets (High Street, Castle Street and Church Street), which met at the Merkat Cross, were dirty and unkempt. Nevertheless the town must have had a certain crude charm which they failed to pick up on. The red sandstone houses, with their stepped gables and turnpike stairs, must have possessed a certain quaintness. Some had upper galleries that hung over the narrow streets, such that the Dragoons of the Duke's Grand Guard had to bend on their horses as they rode by. Bridge Street was as narrow as 6 feet in places and until the 1790s riders had to dismount and walk their horse along the street. Many houses were marked on the outside with the owner's initials or had the words of the prophets and the psalms painted on the walls. Some houses retained the old fortress character of the town with few windows of any size on the ground floor. Outside the town, on the west side of the river and at the Crown were groups of dirty hovels, windowless and roofed with turf, with a hole in the roof for a chimney and livestock roaming the narrow and unkempt streets. These buildings mostly housed clansmen and their families who had split from the wider clan family and chose to live in the town. It is highly unlikely that any of them spoke English at all. Many of the men would have worn Highland dress – a plaid gathered round the waist (a kilt) with the end thrown over the shoulder and fastened over the chest, and a blue bonnet – or else in tartan trews. Some would have been barefoot whilst others would have worn rough leather shoes slashed to let the rain and water drain through – perhaps the forerunner of today's sandals. The women had their plaids draped over their heads with one end at their feet and the other hanging over their arm. They went without shoes or stockings and washed their clothes in the river watched by the soldiers who threw stones and shouted invitations at them. Of course the more anglicised amongst the townsfolk would have dressed in the English fashion. All this came to an abrupt end with the Hanoverian banning of Highland dress which lasted until 1782.

When, following the battle, the expected wholesale sacking of the town did not take place, life slowly returned to normal with business being conducted daily at the Merkat Cross. Until Admiral Byng's fleet filled the firth, more ships had called regularly from Boulogne and Bordeaux than from London. Despite the fact that there were probably no more that 500 houses within the town and around three thousand inhabitants, Inverness was a thriving port. There were regular sailings to Rotterdam each week and ships regularly brought the merchants of the town, and those of means in the hinterland, their claret, books, lace, Spanish silver, velvet, silk, gun powder, broadsword steel, shot and spices, often returning to their home ports with malt, meal, beef and wool. Many of the Highland chiefs, like the MacKintosh, had winter homes in the town and to the ordinary Highlander, coming only occasionally to the town from their glens, it must have been a wondrous place full of the hustle and bustle of everyday life.

Cumberland had deployed only 9,000 troops at Culloden, but within four days he was reinforced by a further four regiments. Chains of military posts were strung out throughout the Highlands, with troops quartered in almost every important town, and by 1st September 1746 there were over 15,000 troops in Scotland. An army of this size needed good lines of communication and good transport links to maintain supplies and materials. But for a memorial sent by Lord Lovat to George I in 1724 concerning the state of the Highlands, and the volatility of the clansmen who lived there, it is unlikely that General Wade would ever have set foot in Scotland. The substance of Lovat's claims prompted the English parliament to send Wade to investigate the situation and his report did nothing to allay their fear of a future upsurge in support of the Jacobite cause. He suggested, amongst other things, that a fort be built at Killichuimen (Fort Augustus) with another at Inverness (Fort George) and that roads and bridges be built between many of the garrisons and barracks for the better communication of troops in the event of any future emergency. The government were impressed by his report and empowered him, as Commander-in-Chief, North Britain, to implement it. The lack of stonemasons in the Highlands prevented the forts at Killichuimen and Inverness being built, but Wade's troops pressed on relentlessly with road building and between 1725 and 1727 he had completed the road from Fort William to Inverness. In the ensuing years many roads were completed, by Wade, connecting Inverness with the south of Scotland and garrisons throughout the Highlands. Fort Augustus was started in 1728 (though still not fully completed in 1740 when Wade relinquished his command) and Ruthven barracks was built in 1734 at a cost of £360. Promoted to general in 1739 he returned to London in 1740 and was later made a Field Marshall. Wade's departure from the scene did not mean the end of road building, however. Major William

Caulfield took up where Wade had left off and between 1740 and 1767 he planned about 900 miles of military roads. He settled in Cradlehall, outside Inverness, and continued his road making from there until his death in 1767. Despite the fact that he built about three times as many roads as Wade did, and had a greater impact on the Scottish communication system than anyone bar Telford, Caulfield still 'lives' in Wades shadow. Caulfeild had been Wade's principal assistant at one time and his admiration for Wade inspired him to write the following couplet,

"If you'd seen those roads before they were made,
You'd lift up your hands and bless General Wade."

Improved communication, by road, with other parts of the country, not only aided the military but also had a positive effect in encouraging visitors to venture north to Inverness. Daniel Defoe, author of Robinson Crusoe, Welshman Thomas Pennant, Boswell and Dr Johnson all visited Inverness, mostly as part of a wider tour of the Highlands, and wrote accounts of their visits. It is from these accounts, and those of others like Captain Edmund Burt, an English Officer stationed here during the 1730s on road-survey duty with General Wade, that information on the town, its people and their way of life is obtained. Defoe's often patronizing remarks, written in the 1720s, on the influence the English soldiers had on this "savage outpost" of Inverness is often in sharp contrast to Pennant's 1760s complimentary and appealing account of the town and its inhabitants. Perhaps it is the different viewpoints of an Englishman and a fellow Celt, or maybe just the passage of 40 years. Defoe did, however, say that the people of Inverness were "more polite" than those in most towns in Scotland. By the time Boswell (a Scotsman) and Johnson (an Englishman) passed through Inverness in 1773 they would, no doubt, have read Pennant's account. Johnson, too, is scathing in his remarks about the people of Inverness (and indeed of Highlanders in general) and the positive influence the presence of English soldiers had on the town, although it is interesting to note that Boswell wrote to a friend:

"Dr Johnson expatiated rather too strongly upon the benefits derived to Scotland from the Union, and the bad state of our people before it. I am entertained with his copious exaggeration upon that subject; but I am uneasy when people are who do not know him as well as I do, and may be apt to think him narrow-minded."

Burt's letters to a friend in England are not exactly flattering of conditions in Inverness, but do supply an interesting and honest insight into the life of the town and its people. One must bear in mind also that although these reports seem very uncomplimentary to us today, the conditions they report were probably no worse than those in any other town in Scotland, or England for that matter, at that time in history.

Of course, one must not forget when speaking about improved communications that the Caledonian Canal played a very important role in this area. Thomas Telford was the engineer in charge of its construction and the Redcastle stone houses built on Telford Street, to house some of the contractors who worked on the canal, are still there today. John Mitchell, Telford's Superintendent of Roads, lived in one of them and his son, Joseph, who succeeded him, built and lived in "Viewhill" at the top of Castle Street (at one time it was the Youth Hostel) now, sadly, burnt and in ruin. He died in London in 1883 but was brought back to Inverness and buried in Tomnahurich cemetery. In his will he left funds for a Library to be built in Inverness, though it wasn't until 1877, when the Free Libraries Act was passed, that the town had an official Library. The Canal was started in 1803, during the Napoleonic Wars, to open up a safe communication between the Atlantic and the North Sea, particularly for the Royal Navy, but also for trade vessels. It was completed in 1822, taking much longer to finish than was first envisaged, although ships sailed from Inverness to Fort Augustus long before the official opening. After the opening regular sailings took place to Glasgow and Liverpool, amongst other places, with passengers and goods, and this made a huge difference to communications in the Highlands.

As a consequence of these, and other, accounts a broad picture is painted of a town which, through the first half of the century, had gone into decline due to the loss of the 'hide' trade to Glasgow and the levy on the export of corn, both of which had been extremely important industries in the town. Empty and ruinous houses, and other buildings, including a huge number of kilns, malting houses and granaries, did nothing to improve the appearance of Inverness to the casual visitor, and economic hardship would have been reflected in the situation of the poorer classes in particular. Perhaps it would explain why Burt commented on the "miserable condition" of the poorer women and children and the "wretched food" that they ate. Housing conditions and overcrowding, in areas like the Merkinch and Muirtown, would have been particularly poor, as indeed would have been the sanitary situation, the water supply and drainage. The river would have provided much of the water required by these people, but bear in mind that it was also used for washing their clothes, cleaning the skins for the hide factory and for sewage disposal. Into the river also ran the street drains which contained manure and general muck dumped by the residents. No wonder people complained about finding hair, wool and all sorts of other things in the drinking water. Public health issues such as these were always a concern and often linked with disease and epidemic – although this was in no way confined to Inverness. In September 1832 a dreadful cholera epidemic swept the Highlands and Inverness did not escape its ravages. By the end of October there had been 553 cases with 175 fatalities, the vast majority, not surprisingly, from the poorer areas of the town.

Most of the 'poor' women and children would have been barefoot, even in winter, and the women would have had a plaid, or shawl, over their head and shoulders. That said, the people of Inverness were far from being uncultured or uncouth, as one may think from these accounts. The town had a Grammar School, later the Academy, which had an excellent reputation and which had been in existence since the late 16th century, although it is true to say that a school had been in existence in the town, at the Friary, since the 12th century. Bustling markets took place in the town and on these days the High Street, in particular, would have thronged with people along its length. The town also boasted a library of over 1,400 books as well as a hospital and a poorhouse.

The townswomen and maidservants from the larger houses would have carried their washing in a wooden tub to the river, where they would have trampled on the washing, in the tub, to clean it before laying it out to dry on the river bank. Those without tubs would tread their washing on the stones of the river with their bare legs as red as their hair in the cold winter weather. The women often stopped en route to, or from, the river at the Clach-na-cuddain Stone (Stone of Tubs), now spelled Clachnacuddin, outside the Town House, to rest their weary load and enjoy a 'wee blether' with their friends and neighbours. Defoe noted that the women, many of whom had red hair, were remarkably handsome and when they tied up their skirts to tread the washing they often received admiring comments from the men watching.

Life for a woman, right up to the early 19th century, was extremely hard. She either served her husband at home or served a master in some other house – there being no trades or guilds for women unless they were tavern keepers. Other than that she was condemned to prostitution. If her husband died or she was thrown out of service then there was little prospect of employment – and if there were mouths to feed she had no other choice. If accused of prostitution a woman had to plead her innocence before the Kirk Session and prove her accusers wrong - not an easy task. When found guilty, prostitutes would be jailed and banished from the town with the threat that if they returned they would be either hanged or transported to the colonies. Banishment usually took the form of being whipped through the town by the hangman – usually on a Fair or market day for all to see and jeer at. Women who were banished had little choice but to turn to crime or continue prostitution in order to feed themselves and their children. Most of them congregated in the Haugh area which would not be visited by any respectable women – unlike their husbands who frequently paid secretive visits. Women who behaved in a lewd and disorderly fashion were also treated harshly by the magistrates – either being fined, jailed or publicly flogged. One such harsh flogging was reported in the Inverness Courier in 1817, and the matter raised in Parliament, resulting in a Bill being passed to end the public flogging of women. Floggings were carried out by the town hangman, or Dempster, who was generally hated because he was more than likely a criminal himself. The job of hangman seldom ever brought any applicants for the post so any criminal awaiting sentence would be offered the job which, if accepted, would save him an often severe sentence. The job was not to be sniffed at because it was well paid, £5 per year, and came with a free house, clothes, food and heating. In addition he would be paid extra for floggings and executions. Notwithstanding, the hangman frequently disappeared before an execution never to be seen again, often leaving the Council with a replacement problem.

After Culloden the revenue circulated by the military helped the establishment of new industry, which in turn engendered an influx of money from the East and West Indies and gave rise to a demand for goods and luxuries to be imported. The price of land improved and the state of the agriculture industry showed great improvement. The general standard of living of the townspeople improved, especially (and not surprisingly) that of the landowners and other businessmen who benefited greatly by the revival in industry. Despite this, however, the population of the town continued to fall, almost halving in size in the latter half of the century to just over 5,100 in 1791. The woollen mill at Holm was built in 1798 and was part of a huge upsurge in thread and cloth manufacture throughout Scotland at that time. A wave of depression in the early 1800s saw the mill close down for a few years but was reopened by Messrs. Mackenzie, Gordon & Co. in 1808. This business failed, however, in 1815, and was bought in 1817 by Dr John Nicol, later Provost of Inverness. The mill, now only a factory shop, was at one time the oldest woollen factory in Scotland and was known far and wide for its tweed and tartan. It was worked by both water and steam and employed around 100 people in various trades, making tweeds, mauds, plaiding, and blanketing. A weir built some distance away directed water into the lade for Holm mills. The sluice gate for the mill is still there. Water flowed from the lade through a pipe to the wheel house where there was a 12 ft high wheel. It is in one of the mill worker's houses that I was born, (at number 7) my grandfather having been a mill foreman. The house no longer exists but my memories of it, and the other families who lived in the 'street', are still as strong as ever they were.

The last decade of the 18th century saw riots taking place in Inverness, as well as in other parts of the country. The price of grain, and hence meal, the staple diet of the poorer classes, soared in price causing general unrest. In 1793, in Dingwall, the local militia fired on protesters, injuring some, and the following day, in Inverness, a large crowd tried to prevent a ship full of grain from leaving the harbour to sell its cargo at an inflated price elsewhere. Ignoring the local militia they stormed the ship and began to unload the grain, claiming that it should be ground into meal in Inverness and sold to the people instead of being transported away for profit. In 1796 there were further riots for the same reason in many towns throughout Scotland. These rioters would have had the 1714 "Riot Act" read to them – which is where the modern day expression "to read the riot act" comes from.

By the turn of the century, Inverness had developed and expanded into a good-sized town with generous and forward thinking men on the Council. The Royal Northern Infirmary, one of the first of its kind in Scotland, was under construction, opening in 1804 with two basement rooms for the "housing of lunaticks". These poor unfortunates were incarcerated there and seldom, if ever, allowed outside their cells. This sad situation remained like that until the Inverness District Asylum was built at Craig Dunain in 1864. On a different note the Northern Meeting Rooms, built in 1790 on Church Street, probably saw more glamour during their existence than any other building in Inverness. It was here that members of the Northern Meeting Society held their Annual Ball in October to which all members of "society" came, including members of the Royal Family on several occasions. For nearly two centuries it was the highlight of "the season". In 1801 it was seriously damaged by fire because a candle-maker, who owned premises nearby, left his tallow-kettle to boil whilst he popped out for a dram, but apparently stayed in the pub too long and his premises caught fire. Unfortunately the Council had a gunpowder store situated above his workshop which also caught fire and exploded killing several people and injuring over 40 more. It is reported that there was hardly a glass window left undamaged in the town. Robin Goodwin, the candle-maker, fled town and his death was reported in the Courier several years later, in 1818, saying that he had been found dead in the River Clyde.

Fire had long been a serious concern for the Council who had made many rules for the townspeople regarding fire prevention. All fires had to be damped down and lights put out by 10.00 pm and townspeople were obliged to provide long handled rakes for pulling down burning thatch as well as leather buckets for water. Those who had an upper floor to their house were also supposed to have long ladders for rescuing anyone who may become trapped. It would appear most unlikely that such rules were adhered to by the townspeople, so in 1778 the Council ordered two fire engines from Holland and shortly afterwards employed a firemaster at the princely salary of £2 a year. He was clearly not the most reliable character, however, because he could not be found during the first fire after his appointment, which had to be doused with buckets of water. The new engines remained in their fire station on Castle Wynd because he had the key, and people were reluctant to break down the doors. He later appeared from some hostelry but was not, apparently, dismissed from his post.

The Highlands had long been an area where recruitment for the army, whether it be for or against the government, had been a happy hunting ground for those in need of good soldiers. If one looks at the record of the Highland Regiments and their battle honours then one can understand why they were so highly thought of, albeit not often publicly. Often the first sent into battle because of their fierce fighting spirit and unwillingness to retreat, they were all too often considered 'expendable'. Inverness was no exception to the recruiting scene and several "regiments" of men were raised from the town and its surrounding area. In 1802 Sir James Grant raised the Inverness Militia (designated the 10th Militia), which was stationed in Portsmouth for five years during the Napoleonic Wars, returning to

Inverness in 1814, at the end of the war, to be disbanded. The Militia was resurrected again in 1855 during the Crimean War as the 76th Highland Light Infantry, and a barracks was built in Telford Street for stores. In the 19th century the military saw no shortage of recruits to swell the ranks of the Volunteer Regiments and the late 1850s and early 1860s saw seven companies raised in Inverness-shire. In 1880 they were consolidated as the 1st Inverness-shire Rifle Volunteers, and in 1883 became the 1st Volunteer Battalion, Queen's Own Cameron Highlanders. Since then there have been many amalgamations of Highland Regiments but although the name may disappear, their exemplary history on the field of battle never will. The government resolved to make Inverness a garrison town and in 1883 the Cameron Barracks were built, in the Scottish Baronial style, to the east of the town at a cost of £60,000. They were occupied by the 79th Highlanders or the Queen's Own Cameron Highlanders.

On the 4th December 1817, the *Inverness Courier and Advertiser* published its first issue and is still going strong today. The Castle lay in ruins, having been demolished by the Jacobites in 1745, until 1834 when the courts were started, and then in 1846 the prison was added. A new stone bridge replaced the one washed away in the flood of 1849 thus ending the practice of dangling morsels of food in front of the grating of the prison cell in the bridge to tempt the poor unfortunates who were confined there. Union Street and Queensgate were built in the second half of the 19th century and formed an impressive group of Victorian shops, hotels and other buildings. Although Queen Victoria made only three flying visits to Inverness during her reign, in 1847, when she and Prince Albert were staying at Ardverikie Lodge, Albert was given an invitation by Baillie of Dochfour to visit the town. He accepted and the town was decked out accordingly, even to the extent of having guns brought from Fort George to the Castle hill from which a Royal salute was fired in his honour. Prince Albert received the freedom of the town and addressed the assembled crowd on the Exchange in front of the Town Hall.

Progress was made, indeed, when the railway arrived in 1855 linking the town to Nairn. Rapid development and expansion of the rail system, east and south of Inverness, followed soon after, with the addition of the north line in the early 1860s. From then until the turn of the century the rail network slowly expanded, with lines heading out of the town in all directions and the railway station being extended to cope. This era heralded the chance for businesses to grow and expand and local businessmen were not slow in recognising the opportunity. If the building and improving of the road structure, to and from Inverness, had served the town well in terms of increased tourism, then the rail network had done so ten-fold. The tartan shops, hotels, shooting and fishing lodges and their associated industries all gained from the increase in tourists to the town and the surrounding areas. It is reported that some tourists, imagining Inverness to be at the "outskirts of civilisation", were astonished to find that it was far more "agreeable" than they had imagined, and surprised that they could actually purchase most things which were "to be had" in London. The Free Libraries Act had prompted the council to build one, and in 1888 a Library of 5,440 books, a Museum, and School of Art were opened in the Castle Wynd at a cost of £3,482. In 1893, in the square outside the railway station, a white Portland stone statue was unveiled, by Cameron of Lochiel, in memory of the officers and men of the Queen's Own Cameron Highlanders who died in Egypt and the Nile campaigns between 1882 and 1887. The statue was originally to be erected in the esplanade of Edinburgh Castle but was switched to Inverness in compliance with the wishes of the Provost and the Town Council.

Throughout the Victorian era the town continued to grow in size, and between 1830 and 1900 its population more than doubled from 9,633 to almost 21,000, a far greater increase than during the following 60 years. Much has been written about Victorian Inverness, its architecture, people and way of life, and I am sure that the reader will have read at least some of it. No better insight into the people of this time, and their manners and customs, can be found than to read "Reminiscences of Inverness" by John Fraser and "Inverness Before Railways" by Isobel Anderson. With that in mind it is time to move on, from a general look at the way Inverness was, and how it came to be that way, and look specifically at what remains of its heritage. The architecture, and the history of it, is as exciting and surprising as that of any City.

Chapter 4

Buildings Past and Present

It would be fitting and appropriate, I think, to include in this section, buildings which once existed in the town but of which there is either very little still remaining, or nothing at all – the buildings of the past - as well as those which either remain intact or at least in part. Unfortunately, town planners in the past have not always been prudent in managing the changing face and development of Inverness, resulting in our present City having lost a great number of historical, as well as classically beautiful, buildings. In retrospect, a substantial amount of post 1960's town centre development was particularly poor both in style and robustness, compared to what it replaced. One must remember, however, that hindsight is a most wonderful thing.

As has already been stated in an earlier chapter, there is little archaeological evidence of building in the town's early existence, most likely because the wooden structures were, from time to time, burned either accidentally or deliberately in acts of retribution. If one discounts the forts which were built by the Picts and the Romans, then we must jump in time to the "Middle Years" to find our first contender for the earliest known building of some importance.

Inverness Castle

I have already expounded that great debate surrounds the actual situation of the first castle in Inverness. Such debate is usually  settled by real archaeological evidence in favour of one site or another. To date, no such evidence is available to aid the positioning of the original castle and we must rely, therefore, on historical evidence – real and legendary, though hopefully not chimerical.

The Pictish Kingdom once covered most of Scotland from an area north of the Forth-Clyde line and included the Islands, with its stronghold in the eastern part of the country. By the time Columba visited King Brudei in Inverness, in the 6th century, the Kingdom had been divided in two, with Brudei ruling the area north of the

41

Grampians. The province of Moray formed a major part of Brudei's Kingdom, and seems to have stretched from the Hebrides to the eastern Moray Firth. Irish historic sources and the Norse sagas both refer to Moray as a Scottish province, the historic centre of which seems to have been in the vicinity of Inverness with important secondary focal points at Elgin, Forres and the Auldearn/Nairn area. The "Chronicle of the Kings of Scotland" reports that Malcolm I (1005 – 1034) "went to Moray with his army and slew Cellach", the implication being that Cellach was the *mormaer* (provincial ruler) of the province. Malcolm's son, Duncan I (1034 – 1040), was killed by MacBeth (1040 – 1057) at "Bothnagoune", according to the Chronicle of Melrose, which has been identified as Pitgaveny, three miles northeast of Elgin. It is most likely that there was a castle of some sort in Inverness at this time and even more likely that MacBeth took control of it after defeating Duncan. MacBeth, however, seems to have spent the greater part of his time in Fife and Angus rather than in the northern part of his realm. In 1057, Malcolm III (Canmore) invaded Scotland and his troops chased MacBeth north to the safety of his "strongholds in Moray". MacBeth was caught at Lumphanan in Aberdeenshire and killed and it is interesting to speculate that he may have been heading for the safety of Inverness Castle at the time. It is highly likely that when Malcolm III vanquished his father's murderer, he naturally would have seized his strongholds and in all probability razed the castle at Inverness, replacing it with another fortress of some kind, even perhaps in a new location.

With all these historical facts in mind we still cannot be certain when the first castle was built in Inverness or, indeed, where that castle was actually situated. Local tradition points towards the east side of the City, in the Crown area around Auldcastle Road, where it would have been able to command the sea approach to the town and also the road to the east along the Moray coast. There is no doubt that this would appear to be an excellent site for a castle, it has all the attributes one would look for and also has strong legendary connections. This claim would be further substantiated by the presence of 'King Duncan's Well', not far away at Culcabock, but there is no evidence whatsoever to support the assertion that the well has any connection with royalty. It is true to say, however, that at Maryfield, on Midmills Road, a town cross once stood, suggesting that this was in some way the 'centre' of development at one time, and at that time in history, life would certainly have centred round a castle if there had been one. A castle on that site, at that time, would most probably have had a mound, or motte, surrounded by a timber palisade – unfortunately there is no archaeological evidence to substantiate this claim, other than local tradition. One must conclude, therefore, that it is possible that some kind of structure may have existed there at some time in history, but, if so, it is unlikely that it was a substantial 'castle' as we know it.

The present castle site is the other option, where the mound is partly artificial and hence built for the purpose, and where a castle would be in a commanding position to guard the original ford across the River Ness and also the gateway to the Great Glen and the North. Is it possible, or even likely, that great military minds would always pick the same spot for a castle? Or perhaps the perception of the direction where one imagines the danger to approach from is seen differently by distinct individuals. Perhaps we will never know the answer to these questions – or perhaps there have been castles on both sites at one time or another. We do know, however, that Malcolm Canmore is attributed with having destroyed the castle at Inverness and having a new one built in its place, although there is persuasive evidence to suggest that it was actually built by his son, David I (1124 – 1153). There is also a strong possibility that this new castle would have been built in stone – at least in part – since reference is made to the use of lime in expenditure accounts.

In 1163, David's son, Malcolm IV (1153 – 1165), came north and successfully suppressed a rebellion in Moray. He was accompanied by one the Earl of Fife's sons, Shaw MacDuff, who, for services rendered to his King, was made hereditary Constable of Inverness Castle. He changed his name to MacIntosh (Son of the Leader) and apart from short periods when the castle passed into English hands, the honour of governing the castle remained in his family for over two hundred years. It became the prison of Sir John Bisset of Lovat, in 1245, for ascribed crimes in connection with the murder of the Earl of Athol and for paying homage to the Lord of the Isles. Soon after this it was captured by the Comyns of Badenoch and it remained in their possession for a considerable time. In 1291, during the Interregnum (1290 – 1292) when the Norman King of England, Edward I, arbitrated in the disputed succession to the Scottish throne, Inverness Castle was given into the control of Sir William de Braytoft. At which time all the Church dignitaries, nobility, landowners and burgesses north of the Spey were forced to swear fealty to Edward at Inverness Castle. The following year the castle was handed over to John Balliol, but the outbreak of war four years later saw it recaptured by Edward's troops. William Wallace commenced his fight for independence in 1297 and, ably assisted by Andrew de Moray, eventually captured Inverness Castle as well as Urquhart Castle. Six years later the English had retaken the castle and it remained within their control until 1307 when Robert Bruce captured it and, true to fashion, demolished it. It was from the town of Inverness that Bruce gained his staunchest support and, with the town as his base, and an army drawn from the town and its neighbourhood, he rallied the Highlands to his cause. It was also Inverness that he looked to when his campaign went into crisis in 1307. One of the town burgesses, Alexander Pilche, served Bruce so well that he appointed him Sheriff of Inverness; later two of his sons became Provosts of the town.

When the castle was rebuilt, and by whom, is not recorded, but in 1383 the town castle was again occupied, this time by the troops of King Robert II, and from there the castle seems to drift undisturbed into the 15th century. We are now at a time when the MacDonalds, Lords of the Isles, were flexing their muscles. In 1410, when Donald MacDonald was claiming the Earldom of Ross and making his way to Aberdeen, he passed through Dingwall and camped at Muir of Ord. On hearing that he would gain no support for his cause from Lord Lovat or in the town of Inverness, he marched on the town, burned the bridge and other buildings before destroying the castle. His march was halted at Harlaw, in Aberdeen-shire, by the Earl of Mar, where a fierce battle took place. Neither side could count it a victory on the day and Donald returned to the Western Isles not best pleased since a victory would have secured him the title he claimed was rightly his.

A year later the Earl of Mar, a cousin of the Lord of the Isles, rebuilt the castle for £640 at the King's request, for protection against rebellious Highlanders. But trouble with the MacDonalds continued and in 1427, James I (1406 – 1437), visited the castle and held parliament there summoning a number of local dignitaries and all the clan chiefs, including Alexander MacDonald, Lord of the Isles, and his mother the Countess of Ross, to attend him there. He imprisoned them all in the newly restored tower of the Castle, before putting some to death whilst others were thereafter imprisoned in different castles throughout Scotland. Soon after his release two years later, MacDonald returned with an army at his heels, to take revenge on the castle. He pillaged the town and set fire to it although his bold attempt to seize the castle was successfully resisted. In 1455 Alexander's successor, John, or possibly Donald Balloch, John's lieutenant, rushed the town, took the castle by surprise, and again plundered and burned the town. Trouble wasn't over yet, however, because in 1463 at the behest of the English King, Edward IV, the Lord of the Isles, another Donald, returned to Inverness with his men, seized the castle and proclaimed himself King of Scotland. His adventure was short-lived, however, and he decamped back to the Islands quite happily with all the plunder he could carry. This misdemeanour could not have been taken seriously by King James III because the following year he was in Inverness to grant a Charter to the town and The Lord of the Isles was present as a witness. As if that was not enough, again in 1491, another MacDonald, this time Alexander of Lochalsh, took the castle in a vain attempt to become head of the MacDonald Clan despite the fact that the Lord of the Isles still lived. His futile attempt was more of a gesture of defiance than anything else and he gave up his fruitless quest very quickly and retired to his home.

The beginning of the 16th century, 1508 to be exact, saw a large extension built on to the castle by order of the King. The Earl of Huntly, who had been appointed Heritable Sheriff of Inverness and Governor of the Castle, was charged to build a large hall, kitchen and chapel. He was clearly not in any hurry to do so, however, because it took forty years to complete the work. In 1555 the castle played host to the Queen Regent, Mary of Guise, and was the scene of a Convention of Estates and of extraordinary courts, summoned by her to punish caterans. The Earl of Caithness being one of those imprisoned in the dungeons for harbouring freebooters. This was a period of relative stability, compared to the 15th century, and the next point of note was in 1562 when Mary, Queen of Scots, visited Inverness attended by the Earl of Moray. On arrival at the castle, Mary was refused entry by Alexander Gordon, the Earl of Huntly's Deputy, probably because the Earl was in rebellion at the time. She was consequently forced to take up residence and hold her court in a private house in Bridge Street, thereafter known as Queen Mary's House. Furious at being refused entry to her own castle, Mary ordered her supporters, strengthened by the addition of the MacKintoshes, the Frasers and the Munroes, to capture it and teach Gordon a lesson. This they did, and Alexander Gordon was hanged for his insult to the Scottish Queen. This incident must have had a lasting effect because little else appears to have happened at the castle until 1639, during the time of the Covenanters, when a group of marauding clansmen stormed the castle and wreaked havoc inside. They broke the windows and doors, tore up the furnishings and generally destroyed the décor of the castle. Repairs must have been carried out fairly swiftly because it was only six years later that the Duke of Montrose besieged it before retreating from General Middleton's army. Four short years later saw the Parliamentary soldiers overthrown by the Royalists, under MacKenzie of Pluscarden and Sir Thomas Urquhart of Cromarty, who captured the castle before demolishing it. It lay in ruins from then until 1715 when it was repaired and used as a stronghold for the Jacobites who had the favour, at that time, of the town magistrates. By 1718 it was back in government hands again and rebuilt by the Hanoverian King George I who named it Fort George. He converted the older part into barracks for his troops and added a new part as a governor's house. According to Burt's Letters from the Highlands, written in 1725, it was an imposing structure of six stories with pointed roofs and corner turrets. Occupied by Sir John Cope and the Earl of Loudon in 1745, on behalf of the government, the castle yet again came under fire the following year when Prince Charles ordered its destruction in order to prevent it falling back into English hands on his army's return from England. This particular destruction of the castle has a very interesting tale attached to it. Apparently, the officer who was instructed to light the fuse to blow up the castle was a Frenchman called L'Epine. On thinking that the fuse had gone out he slowly approached it to relight it and was followed by a dog. As he drew near, the explosion took place and he was blown up, along with the dog and the castle. He was found dead on the green at the far side of the river, some 300 yards away, whilst the dog, also found there, got up and walked away minus his tail.

This was the end of Inverness Castle as a stronghold and the castle lay in ruins, once again, until 1834 when the Duke of Gordon, a descendant of the Earl of Huntly, sold the Castlehill to the town for the construction of a courthouse and jail. The building of the courthouse took two years and was completed in 1836 at a cost of £7,000, whilst construction of the jail was not completed until 1849. The statue of Flora MacDonald, still keeping a look out for her prince as she peers down the Great Glen, was erected in front of the castle in 1899 by Captain J. Henderson MacDonald, having been sculpted by Andrew Davidson of Inverness. The Gaelic inscription on the statue reads, "As long as a flower grows in the field, the fame of this gentle lady shall endure". Although the castle has not changed much since then, the jail was transferred to Porterfield in 1901 when that part of the building became the Inverness-shire Police headquarters, whilst the main chamber became the Chamber of the County Council. At the demise of the Inverness County Council in 1975, the room was turned into the District Courtroom.

But for the intervention of the townspeople following the Battle of Culloden, the Castle would probably look quite different to its present construction. It was the Duke of Cumberland's intention to build a new Fort George where the Castle stands, but a deputation of town dignitaries met Cumberland to complain about the behaviour of his soldiers towards the young ladies of the town and persuaded him to rethink its position. Initially, Cumberland considered reconstructing the Citadel as his new fort but the Council held firm, claiming that compensation would be asked for because of the loss of harbour facilities and refused to release the land to him for building. The Government then purchased land at Blackness at Ardersier, well away from the town, where Fort George stands to this day.

Blackfriars' Friary

Gothic Pillar

Although nothing remains of this building today, with the exception of the castle it was the oldest known structure of any stature in Inverness and, as we shall see, contributed to the construction of several other buildings throughout the history of the town. When it was first constructed is not precisely dated in any document still in existence, but it is thought to be around 1233 when Alexander II (1214 – 1249) granted the Dominican Friars a piece of land stretching from the Kirkgate (now Chapel Street) to the River Ness; its existence is recorded, however, in documentation dated 1240. It is on this land, on the north side of Friars' Lane, that the Friary was built and the only remnant remaining today is in the Greyfriars' Cemetery in Friars Street, which contains a two-metre high Gothic octagonal pillar, once part of an arch in the Friary. Anyone taking the time to explore this cemetery will find the memorials of many old Inverness families, including the Mackintosh Chiefs until 1606, the MacLeans of Dochgarroch, the Mackintoshes of Borlum, the Baillies of Dunain and the mausoleum of the Clan Chisholm. There is also an early 15th century stone effigy of a knight in armour, damaged and set into the wall.

Stone Effigy

It is thought to be Alexander Stewart, Earl of Mar, who fought the MacDonalds at the Battle of Harlaw. He was an illegitimate son of the notorious Wolf of Badenoch and was Sheriff of Inverness and Justiciar of the North before his death in Inverness in 1435. Why the cemetery is called Greyfriars is not known because the Friars were of the Dominican (Black or Teaching) Order and had no connection whatsoever with the Franciscan Order or Greyfriars. In 1795, however, Provost Inglis claimed that the monastery at Inverness was called the "Grey Friars", possibly in error. The Dominican Friars, however, founded by St Dominic in Toulouse, would have worn a white robe and hood when in the Friary but donning a black cloak when outside so maybe there was some confusion in his mind. The Dominican Friars were a teaching and preaching Order which was given a universal mission in 1216 by Pope Honorious III. The Order spread fairly swiftly throughout Europe and reached England in the early 1220s. When they arrived in Inverness is uncertain because all their papers and Charters were lost in a fire at the Friary in 1372.

Although the Friary was quite extensive there never seems to have been more than a few Friars here at any one time. It is recorded that in 1523 the Friary contained a prior, a sub-prior and three brothers and that had not changed much by 1560. That is not to say, however, that other Friars from the Friary were not involved in teaching and preaching journeys much further afield. Since their Order was a teaching one, every Friary had to have a school and a Doctor of Divinity as its Rector. Inverness was no exception to that rule and the school stood outside the Friary walls on the corner of Friars' Lane and Chapel Street. It is from this small beginning that the Inverness Royal Academy owes its *fons et origo* (its origin).

In addition to land for the Friary, Alexander also granted the Order extensive lands to the north-west of the site between Glebe Street and Waterloo Place, bordering the River Ness. This area includes the "Maggot", thought to be a corruption of the name Margaret, and is described as an island – possibly because the river estuary was larger at that time, and water surrounded some of the land.

In addition, they were given the Shiplands, the Mill of Kessock and the fishing rights of the Friars' Shott on the River Ness. The Monastery of Arbroath also granted lands to the Friary, these being to the east of it around what is called Chapel Yard, which was used by the Friars for growing food for their own use. Several other tracts of land were owned by the Friary including an acre north of Chapel Yard, a plot on the corner of Bridge Street and Castle Wynd, and two plots of land on the west side of the river roughly between Ardross Terrace and Alexander Place. Beyond the town they had land in the Black Isle and the Island of Cava in Orkney. One could not describe them, therefore, as being poor – at least in terms of the land they owned. Quite apart from this, Robert Bruce granted them an annual payment of £10 Scots, although after the Reformation Queen Mary diverted this to be payable to the town hospital for the benefit of the poor of the town. This payment was in existence until the Burgh dissolved in 1975 – although there is no trace of any payment having been made to the poor.

In 1263, Alexander III defeated Haco of Norway at the Battle of Largs, in a dispute over the ownership of the Western Isles. Haco died shortly afterwards and Alexander, seizing his chance, sent an embassy, in 1264, to negotiate the abnegation of the Islands. They were finally handed over to Scotland in 1266 although the treaty was not signed until 1312, during Bruce's reign. The treaty was signed in Inverness and Bruce was accompanied by four Bishops and three Earls whilst Magnus, the Norwegian King, had one Archbishop, two Bishops, one Earl and two Barons. Such distinguished company, including Royalty, would undoubtedly have stayed at the Friary since the castle at that time would neither have been large enough nor suitable for such dignitaries. One wonders if it was because of their hospitality that Bruce bequeathed them the £10 the following year?

The Friary and part of the town were badly burned in 1372 by an armed band sent by the Abbot of Arbroath, as the result of a quarrel between himself and the Bishop of Moray. It was during this fire that the Friary's early papers and Charters were lost, including those which were given to them for safekeeping by town dignitaries and noblemen – a practice not uncommon in those times. It must have been fairly quickly restored again, however, because the Bishops of Moray and Ross, arbitrating in a dispute between the Wolf of Badenoch and his wife in 1389, read out their decision "… in the church of the Preaching Friars, Inverness." The Friary buildings were in an almost ruinous state by 1436 and the arrival of the Reformation in the 16th century saw the end of its existence. In 1559 the Prior, Robert Riche, was forced to surrender all the Friary's properties, valuables, tenements and rents over to the Town Council for safekeeping. The then Provost, George Cuthbert, personally took them into his care, but after his death his widow denied all knowledge of their existence and they were never found. What became of the silver chalices, and other valuables which were handed over, will never be known. The Friary closed in 1567, just over 300 years after it opened, and Queen Mary issued a Charter transferring its possessions to the Burgh for the poor and the hospital. Provost Cuthbert fared very well by acquiring the feu to the Friary itself and all the land within its walls, which remained in his family until 1640 when the Presbytery started proceedings against the Cuthberts for the recovery of it. This was finally completed in 1653 when the stones from the ruined buildings were sold to the Cromwellian army commander, Colonel Lilburn, for the construction of the Citadel and the Friary finally passed into history.

In 1834, in an area now built over between what was Friary Yard and North Church Place, a 14th century earthenware jar was discovered 300mm below the ground containing 3,000 coins. These dated from the early 13th to the late 14th centuries and were from the reigns of the Scottish Kings Alexander III, Robert I and David II, as well as English Kings Henry III and Edwards I and II. One wonders was the jar part of hidden treasure from the Friary, since it is unlikely that any citizen of Inverness living in that area would have owned such riches. If so, is there more hidden somewhere?

Cromwell's Citadel

The town's support for the King in 1650, when the Council tried to raise a company of able-bodied men against 'the wicked tyrant' Cromwell, is not surprising since the majority of the town's influential citizens were Royalist. By September of that year, however, Cromwell was in Edinburgh and the following September he was in control of the whole country. Although Cromwell never ventured further north than Perth, he decreed that two forts should be built in order to control the Highlanders. One was at Inverlochy (Fort William) the other at Inverness. Work commenced in Inverness in May 1652 under a German engineer called Hanes, but when General Monck arrived here in 1655 to inspect progress he reported that progress was slow and the fort would need £500 per month for the next two years to complete it. Perhaps things had not gone too well because Hanes had spent a good deal of time in England and France instead of in Inverness supervising the work. The final cost is reckoned to have been in the region of £80,000, a great deal of money considering that it was demolished in 1662, some five years after its completion.

The fort (or Citadel) was built in the area known as the "Citadel" bounded by Cromwell Road and Lotland Street, where the petrol storage tanks stand, and where one can still see earthen mounds which formed part of the perimeter of the Citadel – it is interesting to note that these mounds were used as air raid shelters during the Second World War. It is extremely unlikely that even Hanes would have dreamed that some of his construction would be in use almost 300 years later. Construction of the Citadel started with the building of barracks for the soldiers, consisting of a long row of buildings made of bricks and planks along the side of the river; this was surrounded by earthworks for protection. The Citadel itself had a pentagonal shape and was surrounded by a large trench filled with water, one channel of which led to the sea and allowed access for small ships to sail up to the Citadel at high tide. The walls of the Citadel were three stories high, built of hewn blocks of stone and lined with brick inside, and each corner of the pentagon had a guard house of stone with a bastion. The main entrance to the north had a large gate with a strong drawbridge of oak called the blue bridge, and a stately structure over the gate had "TOGAM TVENTVR ARMA" carved in stone. From this bridge the fort was reached by a vault 22 metres long, with seats on each side. On the south side, facing the town, there was a "sally port" which would allow the troops to exit the fort quickly if there was trouble in the town.

In the centre of the Citadel stood a huge square stone building which housed a magazine and granary with a church on the 3rd storey. The church was well equipped with a stately pulpit and pews, topped with a tower containing four clock faces and four bells. The southeast side had a large four-storey building called the English building because English masons had built it, while the southwest side had the Scots building of the same dimensions but built by Scottish masons. No doubt there had been a great deal of rivalry between the two sets of masons during the construction of these buildings. The English masons were there because too few Scots masons could be found in the area. The north-east and north-west sides had lower buildings housing ammunition, timber, stables, provision stores, brewing houses and a large tavern selling beer, wine, ale, cider and viands so that the whole regiment could be contained within the Citadel. A tunnel ran under the Citadel with iron gratings at either end, thus allowing the ebb and flow of the tide to carry away all the waste from within the fort, which had accommodation for 1,000 men. The oak planks used in the construction were transported to Inverness from England and landed at the harbour whilst all the softwood used was purchased from Hugh Fraser of Struy and came from the forest in that area. The stone blocks came from far and wide, including Greyfriars' Church, the Bishop's Castle at Chanonry, the Church and Abbey of Kinross and Beauly, Blackfriars Friary and St Mary's Chapel in Inverness, amongst other places.

Apart from the stone masons and other trades associated with building works, large numbers of labourers would have been needed to work on the Citadel. It is reported that for digging the trenches every man received a shilling (sterling) per day, which would have been a very good wage in those days, perhaps that is why so many soldiers also worked in its construction. People flocked in from the countryside to work on the building, so much so that "yow could hardly get one to serve yow", a situation which no doubt affected the landed gentry more so than the 'ordinary' man in the street.

An act of Parliament in 1662 ordered the destruction of the forts in Inverness and elsewhere and, ten years after the laying of the foundations, the Inverness Citadel was destroyed. Demolition work started on the guard houses and the outer walls, eventually bringing down the magazine and other internal buildings. It is reported that the work was carried out "with demonstrations of joy and gladness" because the people were glad to be rid of the "yock and slavery of usurpation" which had hung around the town for so long. On 11th April, 400 of the 1,000 strong garrison left for Leith with their wives and children, with another 400 leaving the following day. Although crowds had flocked to the town to see the destruction of the Citadel, and much is made, on record, of the joy of that happening, it is also recorded that the soldiers, some of whom had married Inverness girls, were reluctant to leave the town and were in "great griefe" at having to do so. Midst sighs, tears and embraces they marched out of the town where they had had peace and contentment for ten years. *Sic transit gloria mundi* (so passes away earthly glory). The building stones from the Citadel, once used to construct the Blackfriars Friary, were in turn reused in the building of Dunbar's Hospital and the Ness Bridge in 1681. Indeed the Citadel became a quarry for the burghers of the town and its materials were freely used in the construction of many of the stone houses of the day.

I finish the story of the Citadel with a note on an edifice, known as "Cromwell's Clock Tower", which still stands in the area nearby where Cromwell's Citadel once stood. This tower was once thought to be part of the original Citadel but an archaeological investigation in 2002 proved it to be a fake; it is probably a reconstruction of part of a rope factory and hemp works which once also stood in the area. Built in 1765 it employed upwards of 800 people and was one of the largest industrial concerns in the north, another being built some 7 years later in Cromarty. They produced bags for the London – West Indies trade which accounted for about 20% of the British import export trade.

Dunbar's Hospital

The Royal Charter of 1567 makes reference to a hospital in Inverness, but there are no records to show where it was actually sited in the town. Several other references to a hospital appear in various

documents but only one, in 1664, pertaining to the building of a Grammar School, states that a school is to be built "beside the house used as a hospital". Other evidence shows that a school was situated on the corner of Bank Street and Bank Lane at that time and it is presumed that "the house used for a hospital" was also in that locality. Any hospital existing at this time, however, would not have been a hospital as we know it today, but rather a 'Poorhouse' maintained by voluntary subscription. The hospital had a treasurer who administered all the accounts, and when Baillie John Hepburn handed over his accounts to the incoming treasurer, Alexander Dunbar, in 1663, the sum of £5,994 was to hand.

It is also recorded at that time that he spent £1,091 on a "hospital house" for repair and building work, proving that a hospital was in existence at the time.

Dunbar was a rather dynamic character and inspired those around him with his effort and enthusiasm. Within five years of taking office he had built a new hospital, Dunbar's Hospital, at his own expense and on his own land. Built in 1668 with stones from the Citadel, which lay in ruins by this time, and situated where it still stands today on the corner of Church Street and School Lane. He also coaxed a large number of prominent citizens into subscribing to the maintenance of the hospital and bequeathing funds to it. It was a well-constructed three-storey stone building with three-foot thick walls, the entrance to which had a Norman arch above it. On the wall above the entrance is a tablet inscribed with the date 1668, the arms of Provost Dunbar and the motto "Suum cuique tribue" (to each his own). It is, in fact, a replica tablet, the original one being held in the Inverness Museum. The entrance hall led to a stone staircase giving access to the upper floors and the high-pitched roof had a belfry in the centre. The ground floor had six windows, the upper eight, and the attic floor had seven dormer windows. Each of the attic windows had an inscription on the pediment above it, which reads from left to right as one looks at the building:

First: "This poor man cryed" and includes the figure of a bedesman and the date 1668.
Second: "And the Lord heard him, and saved him out of his tryel".
Third: "A little that a righteous man hath is better nor the".
Fourth: "Richis of manye vikid men" and includes the date 1668.
Fifth: "Hie that giveth to the poor leneth to the".
Sixth: "Lord and Hie vil paye them seavens tyms mor" and the date 1668.

The first, second and fourth pediments have fleur de lis at the top whilst the third and fifth have what appear to be thistles, although the carvings are worn and difficult to make out. The sixth has an angel. Some, in addition, have griffins or scrolls on the upper part. The rear of the building has four dormer windows, two of which are inscribed "Invernes" and two have the date "1668". There were originally another two but alterations to the building have removed them, one was turned into a chimney stack and has the pediment, containing the date, built into it.

When Dunbar retired from the treasurer's post in 1683 he handed £11,164 over to his successor, which was a handsome sum indeed, and thereafter he was generous in gifting monies to the hospital on more than one occasion. He served as Town Provost on three separate occasions between 1666 and 1683 and as was customary he was given the courtesy title of "Provost" for the rest of his life. He also donated substantial sums of money to other good causes, among them the fund for rebuilding the main bridge which had been destroyed in a flood, for which his coat of arms was placed on the eastern archway. When he died is not known. but in 1701 he is referred to as the late Provost, so presumably it was some time around then.

The hospital has been used for many different purposes although seldom for the one for which it was originally intended. Half the lower floor, nearest to Bow Court, was used as a school while the other half was a weigh-house, the rent from which was to be used to maintain the rooms above for the use of the poor. Unfortunately, Dunbar's bequests and the rent from the lower floor rooms were never used for the purpose he intended, for a Baillie James Dunbar, probably a relative, appears to have used all the funds for his own business without paying any interest to the Kirk Session. The Session, which administered the funds, had to take drastic action to try to recover the money, and eventually James Dunbar had to give some of his land as security. Litigation continued long after Dunbar's death and his lands remained in the hands of the hospital until they were redeemed in 1762. James Dunbar was not the only one at fault, however. It is clear that it was Alexander Dunbar's intention that the upper floors be used by the poor people of the town, chosen by trustees, with preference given to those with the name Dunbar. The poor may have been maintained, but they never resided in the hospital – rather the rooms were let by the Magistrates, with or without the knowledge of the Session, and without any regard to the wishes of the donor. It is unlikely that any poor people actually lived in the hospital except for a short period after 1845.

Another James Dunbar, who became Treasurer in 1712, appears to have been one of the few people who showed any concern for the fact that Alexander's wishes were not being followed. He pursued the matter to the extent of consulting an advocate in Edinburgh as to how he might obtain possession of the upper floors of the hospital from the Magistrates and Council, but despite several attempts he appears to have been unsuccessful. It is probably a measure of the power wielded, in those days, by those in office, that they could blatantly ignore the wishes of the former Provost, who had been clearly held in high esteem, and use the money to suit their own ends rather than for the good of the community at large. Perhaps it is also a gauge of the regard with which they viewed the less fortunate citizens of the town. On one occasion, during James Dunbar's absence from the Council meeting, they agreed to let the chamber above the school to the Master of the school, so that he could attend upon his school and library, because the room was vacant at that time. Had James Dunbar been present at the meeting he would no doubt have reminded them that the room was only vacant because they would not allow the poor to occupy it.

The school left the hospital building in 1792 and at that time the Magistrates suggested to the Session that the lower floor be used as a Poorhouse, which was very much needed in the town. The sudden change of heart on their part is surprising, as is the Session's approval shortly afterwards. Unfortunately it never came to fruition and the hospital continued to be used for a variety of purposes, other than for what it was intended. In 1845, however, it finally became a Poorhouse, but only for 16 years, and for some of those it was an isolation hospital for cholera victims. In 1857, the ground floor had a female dormitory and a matron's sitting room, bedroom and kitchen. The first floor had a male and female dormitory and a toilet in each, only boarded off in the room. Between these was a bath, but there was not enough room to use it, so they washed in a tub. The second floor had one male and one female dormitory with a washroom, and the mortuary. Since room was scarce meals were eaten in the dormitory, and it was difficult to clean people and their clothes when they arrived, thus dirt and disease spread quickly. The hospital held between 60 – 70 people of all kinds, old, young and lunatics. It ceased to be a Poorhouse when the one at Muirfield opened in 1862.

Throughout its existence Dunbar's Hospital has had many uses including a school and a weigh-house (for which the lower floors were intended), hospital for the Regiment of Fusiliers, English school, female school, storage rooms, library, female work society, flats for residence, fire station, soup kitchen, cholera hospital, poorhouse and Boy Scout Headquarters, gift shop and senior citizens social centre. The interior is now greatly changed with the exterior undergoing renovation in the early 1960's.

Abertarff House

This house was built in 1593 and used by the Frasers of Lovat as a town house, although some other families did use it at various times throughout its history. It is the oldest secular building still standing in Inverness and is an excellent example of Scots domestic architecture. It is situated in the middle of the west side of Church Street and for years it was hidden from sight by houses facing on to Church Street and had to be approached through Abertarff Close. The

house was in a dilapidated state when the ground it stood on was purchased, as part of a larger area, by the Commercial Bank who built their property on the corner of Church Street and Fraser Street, next to Abertarff House. The Bank kindly gave Abertarff House to the National Trust in 1963 together with funds to restore the building. When completed, it was let to An Comunn Gaidhealach, the society for the preservation and extension of the Gaelic language and culture, who remained there for several years. Once home to an exhibition it more recently has an art gallery and a coffee house. Built on two floors the interior boasts a rather splendid stone spiral staircase and is tastefully restored.

There is another house in the Crown area which is sometimes referred to as Abertarff House, but its correct name is Crown House. The confusion arises because Archie Fraser of Lovat, who died in 1816, left the Abertarff estate to a grandson, his own five sons having predeceased him. This grandson spent most of his time living in Crown House which was often referred to as "Abertarff". The older house, in Church Street, has always retained the estate name.

Bow Court

This building was originally built some time around 1729 by Katherine Duff, Lady Drummuir, as a tablet on the wall in School Lane bears witness to. It stands in Church Street on the corner of

School Lane, directly across the Lane from Dunbar's Hospital. The building originally had one large central archway and four windows on the ground floor, but when it was reconstructed in 1968 by James Campbell, a local builder, the central arch was retained and other arches were formed to provide arcades for shops. The adjoining building was incorporated into the reconstruction and given an arch to match those in Bow Court, as well as the addition of a bow-fronted shop window. Above these new shops there are modern flats, one of which has reproduction panelling similar to that of the original rooms. The wrought iron lamps which now hang in the courtyard and also along School Lane, with the addition of new brackets, were formerly on the Raining Stairs.

The original building was U-shaped with a court at the rear, which was accessed through the central archway. This courtyard led to two separate houses, the kitchens of which backed on to Church Street, making that the rear of the house. A rear door led from the kitchen on to Church Street but at some time these doors were changed into windows and remained that way until the reconstruction. A wing on the north-east side at the rear of the house was occupied by the six Incorporated Trades of Inverness whose armorial bearings are portrayed in six of the windows of the Town Hall. This part of the house was, at one time, also used as a Masonic Lodge. During the reconstruction this part of the building was reduced in size, and, indeed, the south-east wing of the building had been demolished prior to the reconstruction. The courtyard was also reduced in the reconstruction and now has a rock garden and an archway as a rear exit. The National Trust has stipulated that the public should still have access to this court.

A tablet built into the wall of the building facing onto School Lane depicted the date 1729. When this stonework was being cleaned it was realised that a larger inscription existed but had been puttied over, probably when that wing of the building was rebuilt in the early 19th century. It has been suggested that the tablet had originally been in the wall of the north-east wing but had been moved to its present position during the 19th century rebuilding. The tablet contains the arms of the Duffs of Drummuir and the inscription,

58

"Katherine Duff Lady Drummuir gifted the six Incorp Trades and Masons of Inverness the ground on which this building stands 1729".

The two houses of the original Bow Court had been occupied separately, with the north-east wing, at one time, being the residence of the Rector of the Academy and the other wing a hostel for boys. As time passed both wings were gradually occupied by tenants each of whom had a room or two, but eventually the house fell into disrepair.

The Steeple, Courthouse and Jail

Situated on the west corner of Church Street at its junction with High Street the steeple occupies a strategic position in the centre of the city, close to the Town House. When the first steeple was erected is not known, but in 1436 a Cristina Makferry feued the town, in a "Charter of the Tolbooth", the land on which the steeple now stands, and records show that in 1569 the Council ordered that the "town charters and public records" should be put into the steeple for safekeeping. In 1593 Lachlan MacKintosh of Dunachton demanded that the Provost surrender the "house and fortalice called the Steeple of Inverness" to him, and was politely but firmly told to mind his own business. The story in "Dunacton Past and Present" says that:

"A curious engagement 'twixt Lachlan Mor and the Town of Inverness is thus recorded : — " On the 10th September 1593, the Provost, Bailies, and Council of Inverness, did engage themselves by bond to the Laird of Mackintosh as Joint Commissioner with the Earl of Athol, then Lieutenant of the North, and Andrew Lord Ochiltree, for prosecuting Huntly and his accomplices for the slaughter of the Earl of Moray; that they would keep the steeple of Inverness from Huntly for the King's service, and the penalty to be incurred by them for not performance was, that they would willingly incur and accept the deadly feud of Mackintosh, his kin, friends, assisters, and partakers in them in case of failure, as the said bond extant among Mackintosh's evidents more fully bears. The subscribers of this bond, granted to Mackintosh by the Council of inverness, were — Alexander Paterson, one of the Bailies; Gilbert Paterson, one of the Bailies; John Cutbbertof Auld Castlehill; John Ross; Jasper Dempster; William Cuthbert; William Cumming."

The earliest known picture of Inverness, by Slezer, is about 1680 and the steeple can be seen in it, and another in 1725 shows it as having a square tower with a slim spire carrying a weather vane shaped as a cock. It is also recorded as having a bell and a clock. In 1691 the steeple was taken down and rebuilt with a stone spire being added, the cost being raised by public subscription, and some of the funds used were taken from money collected by the townspeople to buy off Coll MacDonald of Keppoch. The town clock at that time was a 12-hour one and the Council employed a "Keeper of the Knock" at 30 shillings a week to wind it twice a day. This enterprising chap managed to convert the clock to a 24-hour version and was rewarded for his work by a reduction in salary – since his workload had been reduced. The battlements of the spire had spikes for fixing the heads of criminals who had been imprisoned in the steeple – hence the expression "in prison "Neath the cock". In 1758 the bell was removed and transported to London for repair, being returned the following

year and re-hung on the steeple. When the bell was rung to celebrate the victory at Waterloo in 1815, however, it was again discovered to be cracked but was not repaired until 1844. The belfry once held three bells known as the "Skellas" which is Scots for tin-pan, presumably because of the sound they made. One was inscribed "London", another "I Hossack, Leicester, Inverness 1759" and the third, the oldest was dated "1658". During the rebuilding of the jail in 1788 it was realised that the steeple was in a dangerous condition and the Council immediately set about raising funds to erect a new one.

The foundation stone of the present steeple was laid in 1789 with a great ceremony, having been designed by William Sibbald an Edinburgh architect although the Inverness Courier records it as being by Alexander Laing. The construction rises from the ground with three square towers reducing in size, then with two octagonal ones, likewise reducing, and topped with a slender spire pierced with a rod supporting two balls and a weather vane. The top square tower contains a clock, donated by Sir Hector Munro of Novar, with a face on each side of the square, which was converted to an electrical drive mechanism in 1979. From top to bottom it stands 150 feet high with the walls at the base being several feet thick. It is said that the larger of the balls beneath the weathercock contains coins, newspapers, photographs and a pint of whisky from Millburn Distillery. The town was shaken by an earthquake in 1816 which threw down a large number of chimney pots and also succeeded in knocking the spire on the steeple out of alignment, much to the amusement of the locals who likened it to the leaning tower of Pisa; the straightening of it in 1828 did not, therefore, meet with universal approval in the town.

Shortly after the jail and courthouse were demolished controversy again surrounded the steeple when, in 1853, plans were produced to build shops and offices to replace it. The value of having a steeple in the middle of new buildings was debated and it was suggested that the steeple be demolished, but fortunately this was never acted upon. At that time an arched doorway to the stair of the steeple was blocked up and a shop incorporated into its base. Almost a century later, in the 1960s, when Bridge Street was being redeveloped, a fierce argument raged in the Council as to whether it should remain or not, and again it survived. During repairs, carried out in 1948, the eight topmost urns were removed and, sadly, never replaced.

A jail and courthouse were built next to the steeple in 1732. In the courthouse the Provost and Baillies sat as the Burgh Court and passed judgement on all who appeared before them. Justice seems to have been dispensed fairly enough but at times was extremely hard, unless you were an erring Burgess, in which case you appeaed to be dealt with somewhat more leniently. Curiously enough one poor soul who poached six salmon was sentenced to have his ear nailed to the Tron and had to remain there for nine hours. On a sadder note three young boys who had taken a few coppers from the collection plate of the Seceders' Church were sentenced to be transported to Botany Bay. The prison is reputed to have contained all the instruments of torture, which were regularly used. The jail consisted of two small cells for criminals, each about 13 feet square, and one "miserable" room for debtors. There were often up to 30 people confined in each cell and conditions were deplorable, but not as bad as the cell which was built into the footing of the Ness Bridge. In 1819 it was recorded that the jail was in "a very bad state" and much in need of repair, principally because it was too small and had no open area for prisoners to exercise or obtain fresh air. In addition the sanitary conditions were very primitive and peats had to be burned in a fire by the jailor to remove the smell from the jail. Not all criminals were imprisoned, or worse, however, as some managed to evade punishment by 'volunteering' to join the army or the navy. One such incident, which is recorded in 1755, states that twenty four men were handed over to a ship's Captain by the name of James Kidd who paraded around the town with a drummer "proclaiming for sailors".

One escapee from the jail, of which there were many, was Roderick MacKay, who had been imprisoned for trying to rescue illicitly distilled whisky. He enticed his warder into his cell, locked him up and then walked out of the prison with the key. He fled to the west coast of Scotland and in 1773 sailed from Loch Broom to Halifax, Nova Scotia, where he and his brothers worked in the dockyards. The key to his prison cell which he took with him when he escaped is still to be found in the public archives of that city. Another was a merchant of the town who was convicted of stealing handkerchiefs and was sentenced to death. Several townsfolk, feeling that the sentence was overly severe, put together an escape plan for the merchant. He feigned illness when confined in the "thieves' chamber" and was allowed to hang sheets on the bare stone walls to prevent draughts. Some tools were smuggled in to him and he proceeded to loosen a few stones in the wall, his endeavours being hidden by the sheets. On the eve of his execution he escaped through a hole in the wall and fled to Strathglass, eventually emigrating to America with his family. Curiously, he prospered well in America and rose to affluence and distinction – although he never actually attained the post of President.

Relief for the prisoners from the dreadful conditions inside the jail arrived in 1788 when a new jail and courthouse were built on the same site – although it did not appear to stem the flow of escapees. One report states that five men accused of stealing sheep from Sir Hector Munro MP were found guilty and sentenced by the court. The first was given transportation, two others sent to jail and the remaining two banished from Scotland for life. Before the sentences were carried out, however, all five escaped and were never heard of again. Perhaps that would explain why Munro was less than enthusiastic to contribute to the erection of the new jail. All was not sweetness and light, however, because a report in 1818 states:

"The outer door of the prison opens into the main street, and immediately on entering you perceive a flight of steps on either hand; that on the left leads to the court-room where prisoners are tried; the deal boards with which the court is fitted up have never been painted, and the dirt on them and on the walls gave to both a rather miserable appearance. At the top of the opposite flight of steps a door opened into a stone gallery facing the cells. This gallery was the appointed place for airing and recreation and as often as the prisoners avail themselves of it they are exposed like wild beasts in a cage to every passenger below."

The report goes on to say that at that time there was only one criminal prisoner, who had been tried for an attempt to assassinate, and sentenced to confinement on account of derangement. This poor man's cell is described as horribly loathsome. He had been in it for six years. This report was refuted in the *Courier*, which claimed that it was better than most other prisons in Scotland and the gallery which extended along the front of the prison afforded prisoners some amusement as it overlooked the busiest part of town, thus allowing them to see and hear all that was going on.

Whichever report is nearer the truth there can be no doubt that conditions were poor and that the rooms were small and inadequate. The courthouse was used in General Elections for voters to cast their votes and despite the fact that only 59 votes were cast in 1826 it is reported that the polling had to move to the High Church because the room in the courthouse was too small. In 1831 the Castlehill was purchased from the Duke of Gordon with a view to building a new courthouse and jail, the former paid for by the County and the latter by the Town. Work started on the courthouse in 1834 and took two years to complete, whilst the work on the jail was not completed until 1848 and the old one on Bridge Street demolished five years later. The jail remained on that site until 1901 when a new one, still in existence, was constructed at Porterfield.

It was not until the late 17th century that a Police force of any kind was initiated in Inverness. At first, in 1692, some tradesmen were coerced into serving as police for a six-month period, but eventually a Police force was created and an office built alongside the jail. It was outside this office that the last man to be hanged in Inverness, John Adam, was buried. When the Police Office was moved to Castle Wynd his skeleton was also moved to lie beneath the steps at the entrance to it. He was, however, left in peace when the Police moved to Culcabock in 1975. Adam was the last person to be hanged publicly in the Longman and his execution was watched by over 7,000 people. Four years earlier the hanging of the Assynt murderer, Hugh MacLeod, was similarly watched by a large crowd of nearly 8,000 people. This was a particularly tragic, yet brutal murder, and the case was regularly commented on in both the Inverness Courier and Inverness Journal. MacLeod was a native of Assynt and had come from a decent, hard working family. In 1819, at the age of ten, he had gone into service and started to pick up bad habits from some of the characters he worked with. His fortunes took a turn for the better, however, because it is recorded that six years later he became a schoolmaster in Lochbroom but left after a year with a strong liking for 'ardent spirits'. Before long he was in debt to every Inn in the district and had also developed a taste for fine clothes and young ladies. He took to petty theft to defray his expenses but it all went badly wrong in March 1830 when he encountered a travelling peddler called Murdoch Grant. MacLeod murdered him with an axe, or other sharp instrument, and stole his money and some of the goods Grant was peddling.

The much-publicised trial was scheduled to take place in Edinburgh but was eventually held in Inverness on 27th and 28th of September 1831. The court sat for 24 hours without a break under Lords Moncrieff and Medwyn and called 76 witnesses, of whom only half a dozen spoke English – further witness to the fact that the town still had a large Gaelic contingent. Although there were no witnesses to the murder, which MacLeod denied carrying out, it took the jury only 10 minutes to find him guilty. MacLeod was transported back to the Tolbooth of Inverness and fed only bread and water until 24th of October, the day of his execution, at which stage he confessed his crime. When the fateful day arrived MacLeod, who had risen at 7am, had his leg irons struck off by the blacksmith. Later, the executioner arrived and pinioned his arms behind his back, after which, at 1.30pm he left the prison, having elected to walk to the execution spot rather than be transported by cart. He wore a long black gown, a white nightcap and had the halter round his neck as he stepped out of the prison to survey the assembled crowd. Accompanied by two ministers, the Town Magistrates, the Constables of the Town, the Inverness-shire Militia and Donald Ross, the hangman, (who had also been imprisoned, following MacLeod's conviction, to prevent him from absconding – a not uncommon problem in those days since the hangman was often a criminal who elected to do the job (if it was vacant) rather than receive his punishment). On arrival at the execution site at the Longman, MacLeod ascended the gallows unaided and, following a short service in Gaelic he addressed the crowd (almost 90% of the population of Inverness) for more than 15 minutes, in Gaelic, on the dangers of whisky, women, Sabbath-breaking and playing cards. After shaking the hand of everyone on the gallows he knelt and said a short prayer and then mounted the 'drop'. He called out twice, "Lord Jesus receive my spirit" before being delivered into eternity, at the age of twenty-two. He hung on the gibbet for three quarters of an hour before being cut down, placed in a black coffin and conveyed back to the jail, where his body was put into a small box. Thereafter, he was delivered to the Professor of Anatomy in the University of Edinburgh, to be publicly dissected and anatomised.

The Town House

Originally, the Town Council met in the Chapel on the Green (situated near Glebe Street) before moving, around the middle of the 16th century, to the Parish Church, the Old High, to deliberate their business which often overlapped with that of the Kirk Session. This is perhaps not too surprising since the Council and the Session largely consisted of the same group of people. The Council met there until around the middle of the 17th century at which point they moved to the Laigh Council House on Bridge Street, where they met until the late 17th century. Their next move was to purchase the town house of Lord Lovat, which was on the site of the present Town House but had been built about 65 years earlier and was in a somewhat dilapidated state at the time of purchase. They continued to meet there until 1708 when, because of the state of the building, it was decided to demolish it and build a new, larger, one at a cost of £600. The councillors were certainly not liberal with the town's funds in the construction of this building because Edmund Burt writes that it was:

"A plain building of rubble, and there is one room in it where Magistrates meet upon the Town's business, which would be really handsome, but the walls are rough, not white-washed or so much as plastered, and no furniture in it but a table and some rough chairs, and altogether immoderately dirty."

It was a three-storied building which housed a public reading room on the ground floor, the Council Chamber on the middle floor and on the top level a sewing and spinning room which was later to become the Guildry room, possibly because they had contributed to the building costs. At street level, on the outside, there was an arcade of seven arches which mirrored those of the old bridge which was demolished by a flood in 1849; otherwise it was a rather plain building. The Council continued to meet in these meagre premises for the next 170 years when, yet again due to the dilapidated state of the Town House, it was decided to build a new one.

The new Town House, the one we presently have, was begun in 1878 and built in Victorian Gothic style; it was completed four years later in 1882, at a cost of around £15,000, and opened by the then Duke of Edinburgh. In the centre at the front is a splendid gable with round towers at the sides, and an oak spirelet. A large, rather impressive, panel over the centre window has the town's arms sculptured on it. The Town House originally sported a large turret in the centre of the roof but that was later removed leaving only the base, which can be seen today. On the outside of the building one can see the old "Merkat Cross" and Clachnacuddin Stone which both stood outside the former Town House and were combined and incorporated into the new one when it was built. On the north gable of the building, facing Castle Wynd, can be seen the Burgh Arms which once decorated the Ness Bridge, until it was demolished in 1849. When the Town House was built it was decided to incorporate them into the side of the building.

One enters the building by passing through a striking arched doorway into a large and dignified entrance hall from which a grand and spacious staircase leads in both directions from the landing to the first floor. On the staircase, and again in the first floor Council Chamber, one sees magnificent crystal candelabra which once hung in the Northern Meeting Rooms. The windows on the staircase are stained glass and show the royal arms, the town's arms and the Scottish arms. The main hall, which is approximately 20 metres long by 11 wide and 10 high, has a pitch pine panelled ceiling decorated with heraldic emblems. The windows in the hall portray the arms of the Scottish clans, the trades of the burgh, the royal arms, the Scottish arms and emblematic illustrations of Art, Science, Law, Education, Literature and Agriculture. Hanging on the walls of the building there are many fine paintings and portraits which are well worth seeing.

The Prime Minister, Lloyd George, was holidaying in the Highlands in September 1921, as were several other Cabinet members, when he received news of a mounting crisis in Ireland following De Valera's rejection of Dominion status within the Empire. Lloyd George immediately summoned his parliament to meet in Inverness on 7th September, until recently the only meeting of Parliament ever held outside of London, and it was convened in the Town House. A huge crowd gathered at the Exchange to see them all arrive and there were cheers for Lloyd George and Winston Churchill because they were known, but the other members of the Cabinet were largely unrecognised in an age before television.

Ness Bridges

From the time of Inverness' earliest inhabitants, if one can call them that, some 5,000 years ago, movement has probably taken place back and forth across the River Ness. There was most likely more than one crossing place, but as time progressed and buildings began to spring up, some of these crossings would have been favoured more than others. Since High Street and Church Street were two of the first main streets of the 'town' it is likely that the crossing places led off these streets, probably accessed by vennels. Originally, these crossings would simply have been in the form of a ford across the river, but at some time the one at the bottom of Bridge Street was replaced with a man-made edifice, probably wooden, which we would class as a bridge. When such a structure was first erected is not recorded but is believed to have been in the reign of Alexander II (1214-49). We do know, however, that Donald, Lord of the Isles, destroyed a fine wooden one in 1410 when he sacked the town and burned the Castle on his way to the Battle of Harlaw. He met with little resistance, save one brave burgher, who donned his armour and, broadsword in hand, defended one side of the bridge with valour. It is recorded that had there been ten more like him neither the town nor the bridge would have been burned.

Surprisingly, very little is recorded about any bridge crossing the Ness at this time although it must have formed an important part of transportation link into, and out of, the town to the north and west. The next we hear is in 1561 when the Council decreed that the carrying of "muck" over the bridge was an offence. The following year the Council appointed a master of works for the bridge and introduced more offences for which they could fine people in order to boost their bridge repair fund. Half a century later, 1613, the Provost and Baillies personally undertook to pay one third of the sum required to repair the bridge, the remainder being raised in land taxes. The bridge was built of oak and probably did not have raised sides to protect those crossing from falling off because it is reported that one woman was blown off the bridge into the river and drowned. Much though the kind financial gesture of the Provost and Bailies would have been appreciated by the townsfolk the end result was short lived because seven years later, in 1620, a flood washed the bridge away and it was four years before a new one was built, again a wooden structure, arched with a house on it. Timber from Glenmoriston was used in the new bridge which could not have had the appearance of a great design because one of Cromwell's officers described it as being too weak for the strength of the flow in the river. His judgement was not altogether correct, however, because it stood for 40 years until 1664 when it too fell into the river, although this time it had a helping hand. A carpenter was carrying out repair work on the bridge at 10 o'clock in the morning and, on cutting one of the beams to replace it with a new one, he clearly made a drastic error of judgement because the bridge collapsed throwing 200 people into the river. It does rather raise the question, however, as to why so many people were standing on the bridge at that time in the morning and one wonders whether, or not, their weight contributed to its collapse.

Although I could find no mention of another bridge being built, there must have been one because in 1677 a tourist remarked "Over the river is a rotten wooden bridge on about ten or twelve pillars. Below this bridge are abundance of nasty women possing clothes with their feet, their clothes tucked up to the middle". It is recorded, however, that people had to rely on a "great cobble" to transport them, and their goods, back and forth across the river. This would, perhaps, not have been as great an imposition as one might suspect since there would, at that time, have been few if any wheeled vehicles in Inverness, with most heavy loads being transported by horse. It is more than likely that the poorer members of society would have simply waded across the river since it is unlikely that they could have afforded to pay for the "cobble". It was the Earl of Seaforth who introduced the first carriage to the area in 1715 and the locals were so dumbfounded by the "contraption" that they bowed in deference to the driver. The first post-chaise appeared in 1760 and was the only four-wheeled carriage here for a long time thereafter. Even as late as 1822 only about 40 private carriages and post-chaises existed in and around the town. So in 1685, the new bridge was built at a cost of £1,300, this time in stone taken from the destroyed Cromwell's Citadel. Some of this stone had originally come from part of the Cathedral in Fortrose and other church buildings and so the bridge displayed some ecclesiatical decoration. Money was raised by public subscription, but MacLeod of MacLeod contributed substantially to the amount and as a reward his Arms were placed on the centre arch – later transferred to the gable of Queen Mary's House.

As a result of his contribution the MacLeod clansmen were allowed to cross the bridge toll free. The Royal Arms were put on the east port of the bridge and later transferred to the gable of the Town House – only to disappear during stone cleaning work in the 1960's. Provost Dunbar's Arms and the Burgh Arms were also put on the bridge with the Burgh Arms later transferred to the west gable of the Town House, where they can still be seen. The other end of the bridge had a gate, supported by two pillars, which you may recall were closed by the Campbells, some 60 years later, sealing the fate of some Jacobites fleeing Cumberland's forces after Culloden. The reason for having a gate on the bridge was so that the collection of the toll for crossing (a "bodle" which was one sixth of a penny) could be more easily collected, something some people avoided by simply wading across the river. Inability to pay the toll charge was the reason some of the residents on the west side of the river gave to the Parish minister for not attending Church. He overcame the difficulty by having the bridge toll-free on Sundays – whether it increased his congregation or not is unknown.

The new bridge, built in 1685, had seven arches and between the second and third arches was a vault which acted as a small prison cell, about 12 feet long by 9 feet wide and 6 feet high, with a stone bench running three quarters of the way round the edge. The poor souls who found themselves incarcerated in this cell had no heating whatsoever and very little light. Access was through a trap door on the bridge and they obtained drinking water by lowering a pitcher, through a hole in the floor, to the river below. In cold weather the conditions must have been almost unbearable, and although some prisoners did die in this cell the cause of their demise is not recorded, but in 1735 the town hangman was paid 12 shillings for burying a man who died in the bridge vault. When the river rose high enough the cell would flood so that the occupants were waist deep in water. The cell was also so infested with rats that the prisoners were often said to be

weary of trying to stay alive. One prisoner, in 1715, was said to have been half eaten by rats. The saddest tale of a prisoner who was incarcerated here is that of Eavan Mackvee, or Cameron, who was captured by the Hanoverians after Culloden and questioned by General Blakeney regarding letters he was carrying. Mackvee refused to tell Blakeney who gave him the letters and who they were for and he was thrown into the Bridge cell as punishment, with the townsfolk being warned not to speak to him or feed him. Eventually he was taken to the Mercat Cross on the Exchange to be stripped naked and whipped. It is reported that he was lashed 500 times on two separate occasions, but still refused to answer Blakeney's questions. In a fit of temper Blakeney had him returned to the Bridge cell without food or water. When eventually he was allowed food he was so far through that he could not eat it and was taken to the Tollbooth where he died. The town stopped using the cell for prisoners around 1770, although it had been used as a "mad-house" for a time prior to its closure. On a happier note, the artist Turner thought that the bridge had great charm and sketched it along with some of the surrounding area. The resulting picture can be seen in an early edition of Scott's "Tales of a Grandfather".

In January 1849 the Caledonian Canal burst its banks and raised the level of the river to such an extent that the bridge was destroyed and large areas around the river were flooded. The people of Inverness were yet again without a main bridge across the Ness and the river had to be crossed by boat at a charge of one halfpenny. This time, however, the authorities moved more swiftly and a temporary footbridge was erected. The building of a replacement bridge was to

take far longer than first envisaged, for a number of reasons. Initially, the Council debated not only what type of bridge they would have but also where it would be sited, as a number of alternative locations were looked at. In the end Bridge Street prevailed and in June 1852 work started on a new stone bridge. By October the company was bankrupt and work ceased for several months, commencing in the New Year with a new firm and much anticipation by the public. A year later, it too was bankrupt. The Council complained to the Commissioner of Roads and Bridges, who was responsible for the rebuilding work, that after five years the bridge was still at an early stage, without one pier being completed. A third company was appointed and commenced work in March 1854, the bridge being completed and opened in August the following year at a cost of £30,000 (about £1,755,000 today). While the foundations were being dug in 1853, a hoard of bronze and silver rings and pins was discovered.

The new bridge was a suspension one with a span of 225 feet. At the eastern end was a large stone archway, somewhat narrow in breadth, whilst at the western end stood two smaller towers. Some say the design was adapted from another much longer bridge, which was scaled down for Inverness, and that is why it looked truncated and out of balance. Whether this is true or not the bridge remained in use for over 100 years before being replaced. By the late 1930s, the narrow archway at the eastern end was causing problems with traffic flow, and the ever-increasing weight of traffic was taking its toll on the structure of the bridge. A report was commissioned from Sir Hector MacDonald, engineer and MP for Inverness, in which he stated that repairs to the bridge were urgently required and that sooner, rather than later, a new bridge would have to be built. In order to ensure that the bridge was not overloaded a traffic control system was put in place – this took the form of a man with a red flag whose job it was to manage the volume of traffic on the bridge at any one time. A temporary bridge was built slightly upstream to enable repair work to be carried out, but the outbreak of war in 1939 put an end to traffic control and also delayed the start of construction on the new bridge for 20 years. In 1959 another temporary bridge was built and the old one closed following a midnight ceremony with Council Officials and a pipe band. The new bridge was opened on 28th September 1961, exactly 297 years, to the day, after the wooden one collapsed into the river in 1664.

Of course, more than one bridge spans the River Ness, and has done for some considerable time. In 1808, the Waterloo Bridge was built as the second crossing of the river, to connect the village of Merkinch which was incorporated into the burgh of Inverness the same year, and until 1836 a toll of one halfpenny was charged for crossing it. It was originally called the "Black Bridge" because of the dark colour of the wood it was constructed of and, although it was replaced in 1896 with a metal bridge made in the Rose Street Foundry, the name still persists. In 1829 a third bridge, for foot passengers, was erected connecting Ness Bank to the Ness Islands, and five years later another footbridge from the Islands to the Bught, thus completing a link across the river through the Islands. Both these bridges were washed away, along with the main bridge, in the flood of 1849, with one causing some damage to the Black Bridge as it was washed downstream. Both Ness Islands bridges were fairly quickly replaced four years later where they stood until 1987 when they were replaced with the present bridges.. With the expansion of the railway in the 1860's, the new north line required to cross the Ness, and so a railway bridge was built in 1863, just downstream from the Waterloo Bridge, - it collapsed in 1989 when extremely high water washed away some of the footings and was replaced in 1990. Two further footbridges were built in the late 19th century, both of which were made in the Rose

Street Foundry in Inverness. First the Infirmary Bridge, which was opened in 1879 at a cost of £2,000, about £220,000 today, having been made by W. Smith and Son at Ness Iron works on Rose street, later to be the Rose Street Foundry, and this was followed by the Greig Street Bridge in 1881, very similar in style to the Infirmary Bridge but larger. This bridge was also constructed by the Rose Street Foundry. The last one to be built was the Friar's Bridge, which appeared in 1987 to ease the volume of traffic crossing the main bridge. It is not that difficult to imagine what traffic chaos there would be today had it not been built.

The railway bridge, about 80 yards downstream from the Waterloo Bridge, is the newest bridge spanning the Ness opening in April 1990. The original railway bridge was swept away by the river on the morning of 7th February 1989 after heavy rainfall on the 5th and 6th. There were no trains on the bridge at the time although the train to Kyle of Lochalsh was due to leave Inverness station at 8:30 a.m. Fortunately warning was received in time. The original bridge had stood since 1862 and consisted of five arches each spanning 73 feet. There were additional arches on each bank and two girder bridges to span Anderson Street on the Merkinch side and Shore Street on the town side. These latter sections survived the collapse, but the bridge over Shore street was damaged on 5th October 2003 when it was hit by a low loader carrying a JCB.

One does not have to be a good mathematician to know that with the addition of the Friars' Bridge, and counting the Islands' crossing as two bridges, 8 bridges now span the River Ness. If the reader has ever taken the time to examine the predictions of Kenneth MacKenzie, also known as Coinneach Odhar, the Brahan Seer (see Chapter 9), then you will know that the building of one more bridge will bring disaster to the City. The prediction states that:

"The day is coming when two false teachers shall come from across the seas. At that time there will be nine bridges in Inverness. The streets will be full of ministers without grace and women without shame."

If, however, the Kessock Bridge is included as being "in Inverness" then either the prediction is wrong, or we have all failed to notice something!! Of course, as I write, a new bridge is planned to cross the river from Tomnahurich to Holm Mills. Now that could be interesting.

Friar's Bridge

Greig Street Bridge

Infirmary Bridge

Infirmary Bridge 2

Black Bridge

Main Bridge

Railway Bridge

Post Office

Prior to the middle of the 17th century a postal service was not available in Inverness, or indeed many other parts of Scotland. Any letters which one required delivered had to be either transported by boat, or horse, and thereafter privately delivered by hand. In 1669, the Privy Council granted a warrant for a "constant foot post between Edinburgh and Inverness" to go and return once weekly, weather permitting. This must have been a huge godsend to communication at that time, there being no other way to contact business or individuals, other than to go personally and hand deliver the mail. Although the postage rates were quite expensive, around 2 shillings per letter, the service seems to have been successful. At the same time as the postal service was introduced to the town, Inverness also had its first Postmaster appointed, a William Trent by name. In 1715 there was a horse post between Edinburgh and Inverness, which went via Badenoch, but after three years it ceased to operate. A year later a plea was made to have it reinstated and, in addition, to have two post horses each week go by the coastal route. Some years afterwards this mode of delivery was replaced by post coach which left the Grassmarket, in Edinburgh, and made a return journey to Inverness twice weekly. Not until 1855 was this service upgraded to three times weekly.

In 1737 Archibald Douglas, Postmaster General for Scotland, appointed Helen McCulloch to be Postmistress in Inverness. It is recorded that she was responsible for all letters posted north of the Firth of Forth, which seems to be a huge area to have responsibility for and hence doubt has been cast on the authenticity of the report. She later married a Robert Warrand who was subsequently appointed Postmaster, jointly with Helen. It was the practice, in those days, for people to attend the Post Office to collect their own mail, having first given the Postmaster sufficient time, following its delivery, to sort it out and bag mail for onward transfer to places further north and west of Inverness. When the mail was ready for collection a horn was blown, by the Postmaster, to inform the public that their mail was ready for collection. Warrand, however, is reported as having used one Margaret Robertson, an elderly lady of around seventy-seven, to deliver mail in and around the town of Inverness. It was not unusual for Margaret to overcharge for delivery, nor was she averse to allowing the Excise man to explore the contents of some letters to aid him in his 'enquiries'. Around this time there were several accusations made about the Warrands, who were accused of opening mail to observe the contents, and also one where Mrs Warrand was accused of retaining £10 posted to a Nairn man. The sender of this letter finally confronted Mrs Warrand and she produced the letter from a drawer in her desk along with the £10. Warrand himself also fell out with a Hugh Falconer over a dispute regarding a boundary on adjacent plots of land at the Longman, which they owned separately. Relations between them deteriorated to such an extent that Falconer wrote to the Postmaster-General complaining about Warrand's malpractices in the Post Office. Warrand, who by this time was a Town councillor and Burgh Treasurer, sued Falconer at the Court of Session for £500 in 1770. Although I can find no record of the eventual verdict on the case it is interesting to note that a new Postmaster, Robert Sharp, was appointed in Inverness that same year.

The first recorded site of a Post Office in Inverness, in 1790, is at 32 Castle Street, in a building long demolished on the west side of the street, and in 1794 it is reported that a daily post to Aberdeen left from there. One presumes that prior to that there must either have been an unrecorded Post Office, or the Postmaster must have used his home. Only one postman and a Postmaster are recorded to be in position in the early 19th century. The postman received 6 shillings a week plus one halfpenny for each letter delivered to outlying areas. To that end it was his custom to stand at the Merkat Cross on a Friday and read out the addresses of these letters to see if anyone who was in town for the day from these areas, would deliver them for him and save him the journey. 1803 saw the addition of an Edinburgh coach with onward transmission to London for letters and packets, but it failed through lack of support and stopped operating for some time before it was re-established in 1810. The Post Office remained in the shadow of the Castle until that same year when it moved to another building beside the Exchange. Coach travel was becoming popular and, as the Highlands opened up to tourists, as well as business travellers, new coach routes were added to existing ones, with a coach to Aberdeen starting in 1811 and one to Wick in 1819. Early in 1820 the Post Office was on the move again, this time to the north corner of Bank Lane and Church Street where the letter box mouth was 4 inches by ¼ inch, principally because letters were generally one sheet of paper. A letter to London cost 3½d, Edinburgh 0½d, Aberdeen 10½d and Fort Augustus 9d. But by 1840 all mail cost 1d and was called the "penny post".

Another new route, started in 1836, was the daily mail coach travelling between Inverness and Perth. Around that time a traveller could leave Inverness early on Monday morning and, travelling by coach, first to Edinburgh and then to Liverpool, both overnight stops, catch a train from Liverpool to arrive in London on Wednesday evening. It was a long tiresome journey but was also a giant step forward from having to travel the journey on horseback. In 1847, the Royal Mail Coach from Edinburgh via Perth and Badenoch arrived at 12.30 am and left for the return journey at 1.45 am. These coaches had two staging posts in Inverness one was the Caledonian Hotel on Church Street and the other was the Union Hotel on High Street, allowing passengers to join the coach from either stop. Onward passengers for Tain left at 1.15 am whilst the one coming from Tain arrived in Inverness at 1.26 am in order to allow passengers for Edinburgh and Aberdeen to catch their connecting coaches. Aberdeen passengers had the choice of two coaches.

Customs House

The "Mail" left at 2.00 am and went to Aberdeen via Ardersier and Nairn, whilst the "Defiance" left at 6.00 am and went direct to Nairn before going on to Aberdeen. The fare was £2 inside, if you preferred to be dry, or one guinea outside where you had to brave the cold and the weather. The "Duke of Wellington" left daily for Perth at 6.00 am, the return coach arriving back in Inverness at 8.00 pm and a similarly named coach journeyed to Strathpeffer and back during the summer months, leaving Inverness at 3.00 pm daily.

The introduction of the "Penny Post" in 1840 saw an increase in letters being posted and the Post Office required larger premises. Its next move was in 1844 when it shifted to High Street into what later became the Customs House and was probably designed by Archibald Simpson of Aberdeen. Situated at the east end of High Street it was a good early 19th century classical building with Greek details and it is comforting to note that the front of the building still stands, despite recent renovation to the interior. It was a three storey building and the postmaster lived on the top floor. At that time sixty three people worked for the Post Office. Slightly further east on High Street, a set of steps, called Market Brae Steps, runs up to Ardconnel Terrace. This footpath is also known as the Post Office Steps because of the close proximity of the Post Office at this time. In   1883 parcels were

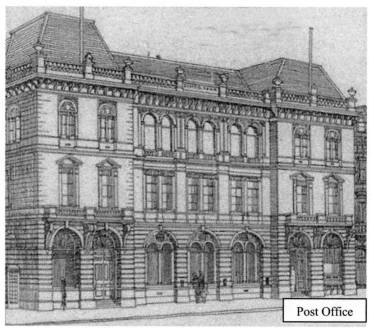

Post Office

accepted as post and they had to commandeer the top floor to accommodate the additional postage. In 1888, a new building was erected in Queensgate taking two years to complete with 100 people working there by 1897, later increasing to 150. It too was a beautiful classical building, built in Italian renaissance style, all in sandstone and well detailed. Oh that it stood there now instead of what replaced it in the 1960s. Despite the fact that it was damaged by an earthquake very shortly after its construction the building remained in use until 1966 when it was demolished. The post office was temporarily housed next door until the present one was opened in 1969. There can be no doubt in anyone's mind that the former building was architecturally vastly superior in design and construction to the present one and was a perfect match to the other buildings in Queensgate.

Ardkeen Tower

This building stands at the top of the Castle Street hill on the junction of Old Edinburgh Road and Culduthel Road. It was built in 1834 with the foundation stone being laid the same day as work started on the Courts at the castle. The original scheme was apparently of a more ornate design, but, as carried out, it is a good classical building. One report states that the children walked up from Dunbar's Hospital to attend the ceremony, although it is not clear whether it is the laying of the foundation stone for the Courts or Ardkeen Tower which was the purpose of the journey. It is also known as the Observatory Building and the United Charities Building. Originally occupied by the Infants School, the Female Work Society and the Juvenile Female School, these were all formerly situated in Dunbar's Hospital and later combined as the United Charities. The dome of the building was reputedly used as an observatory by a separate body, but there is some doubt as to whether this is actually true and I could find no records to

prove it.

The building was enlarged in the late 19th century to become the private residence for the Canon of St Andrew's Cathedral. At this time a second storey was added on the Old Edinburgh Road side and the rear angle filled in with several new rooms. The second storey unfortunately is at variance with the dome, but the construction suited the conversion of the building into a private home. The house was originally approached by a massive flight of steps right on the junction of the two streets, but was shifted when the volume of passing traffic increased. The former hall is now the drawing room, it is elliptical and has a fine view from the windows, and the entrance hall was under the dome which has now lost its weather vane. A tablet in the gable end has the words "United Charities 1830" painted on top of the half obliterated words "Observatory Buildings".

Balnain House

This elegant Georgian mansion was built in 1726 and is situated on Huntly Street, slightly north of Greig Street. It is a well-proportioned classical building with dressed angle quoins which once had a portico at the front with wooden columns painted to resemble marble. Called "Fairfield House" in 1821 it was originally the home of a Mr Munro, a retired indigo planter, and was the first house in Inverness to be roofed with Ballachulish slates. Whether it was the blue tinge of the slates or the owner's former employment that gave  rise to it being known as the "Blue House" is not recorded. A large garden once stretched as far back as King Street and included all the north side of Greig Street and the site of the Queen Street Church, in addition to reaching down to the river. It was used as a hospital for Royalist troops after the Battle of Culloden, and also used by Royal Engineers when they were engaged in survey work for the Ordnance Map of 1868. Later owned by a Captain Fraser of Balnain, hence Balnain House, it was eventually developed into flats, the occupants of which used the grass at the front of the house as a drying green, and which, apparently, was the cause of frequent disputes between the neighbours. In the 1960's the building fell into disrepair and, following the re-housing of the tenants, the building was taken over by a Trust, sponsored by the Inverness Civic Trust, which fully restored it. The trustees set about raising money from public and private sources, eventually opening to the public in 1993 as the 'Home of Highland Music'. Unfortunately the venture failed to be self-supporting and closed in 2001 with the house being taken over by the National Trust when they moved out of Abertarff House on Church Street.

Queen Mary's House

    This house, demolished in 1968 when Bridge Street was developed, stood on the north side at the bottom of the street. It became famous because Queen Mary was forced to lodge there in 1562 when she visited Inverness and was refused entry to her Castle. It was in a ruinous state on more than one occasion and had been altered and rebuilt several times from the 18th century onwards. In 1787, when William Inglis of Kingsmills extensively altered the upper floors and removed the turnpike stairs and outside forestairs, there remained only the barrel-vaulted ground floor, the close leading to a rear courtyard and the four walls of the original 16th century house. When it was finally demolished in the 1960s it still contained the medieval vaulted cellars, some of which were retained and built into the Highlands and Islands Development Board building which was erected in its place. Although a somewhat plain and unremarkable house, when standing, its demolition saw the city lose yet another piece of its history. One wonders why developers could not retain the façade of such buildings and redevelop the remainder along with their interiors.

Workmen's Club

Once situated on Bridge Street, opposite Queen Mary's House, this beautiful building was a casualty of street widening works in the 1960s. It was a good classical building with imposing double columns and arcaded windows at the first level. The building was designed by John Rhind, a former Provost of the Burgh. The Highland League was founded at a meeting on Friday 4 August 1893 in the Workmen's Club. Six Inverness clubs had representatives at that first meeting - Caledonian, Citadel, Clachnacuddin, Cameron Highlanders (based at Fort George), Thistle and Union. These teams, and others, had for five years competed for the North of Scotland Cup but now wanted regular competitive matches like those of the Football League. J Allison (Caledonian), as Chairman, and H Dallas (Union), as interim secretary, conducted the business and it was noted that clubs from Elgin, Forres and Dingwall had been invited to attend but had not been in touch. A motion to form 'The Highland Football League' was proposed by Colour Sergeant J Macpherson of the Camerons, seconded by Colin MacRae of Union, and agreed unanimously. A Mr Johnstone was elected Secretary with H Dallas as Treasurer. The post of President was left open in the hope that J F Finlayson would accept, which he did in time to chair the General Meeting two weeks later.

The YMCA

Built in 1867 it stood on the corner of Castle Street and High Street opposite the Town House and was well suited to stand across the High Street from the Caledonian Bank building. On the ground floor there were shops and on top of that there were a series of magnificent Roman composite columns stretching over the next two floors and supporting the roof. The top was decorated with a balustrade and three large statues, the work of an Inverness sculptor, Andrew Davidson. The statues were known as Faith, Hope and Charity and they had kept watch over all that happened in the Exchange for many generations. At the foot of the columns and above the ground floor windows were placed a number of carved heads of various religious leaders, one of which was John Wesley. The building functioned as the Mackays Clan Tartan warehouse and then the YMCA until it was demolished in 1955 when the statues found their way into a Council yard before going to a private owner in Orkney, where they remained for several decades, and the carved head of Wesley was removed to the Methodist Church in Union Street before eventually going to the Church on Huntly Street. The statues were recently bought back from the Orkney owner and they now 'grace' the small garden next to the Ness Bank Church – they still look out over the River Ness. At the time of writing the building hosts an electronics store and a fast-food restaurant.

Castle Tolmie

Originally, Bridge Street was a narrow wynd leading to a dead-end at the river's edge, and even after the first bridge was built the street was still not of major importance in the town – although it undoubtedly led to a ford across the river Ness. At right angles to Bridge Street only a narrow pathway followed the river in either direction. To the north, the path led to a building called Castle Tolmie which blocked most of the access along the river side, whilst to the south the lands of the castle stretched right down to the river. Behind Castle Tolmie stood Queen Mary's House. In 1794 the riverbank was widened and strengthened and a road was made to run parallel to the river forming what is now Bank Street.

Castle Tolmie had been erected in 1678, presumably for a Fraser since it had elaborately carved "fraises" or strawberry flowers, from the Fraser family coat of arms, in the stonework to the attic windows. The dormer heads from these windows were later used in an extension to Redcastle in the Black Isle. During the 17th century Castle Tolmie was occupied as the town residence of Forbes of Culloden before being owned in the late 18th century by one William Tolmie, hence the name Castle Tolmie. Later it was developed into several flats belonging to a grocer, a vintner and a saddler, but by the 1840s the building had deteriorated badly and was used as a third-class hostelry. Sadly, it was badly undermined during the flood in 1849 and finally demolished when the new bridge was being built in 1852. The name was not lost, however, as it was transferred to the opposite corner of Bridge Street where a pleasant row of small houses on Gordon Place was replaced by a new building. The second Castle Tolmie was designed by Robert Carruthers and built about 1900 comprising of three houses of a rather interesting design. The building fitted in well with views of the Castle and the bridge, from the opposite side of the river, and among its occupants was Mr Gossip, the dentist. Although still in reasonably good condition this building, too, was demolished in 1961 when the road was widened for the new bridge.

Royal Northern Infirmary

Towards the end of the 18th century it was realised that Inverness badly needed an Infirmary to treat the sick and the poor. At that time the Provost was William Inglis who had long been involved in development in the town, and was one of the most able Provosts and Magistrates the town has known. He was given the task of chairing a committee to raise the required sum for the Infirmary by private donation and public subscription, ably assisted by Thomas Gilzean, a future Provost, who was to act as treasurer. Most of the private donations came from the same people who had built the Academy some thirty years earlier. Within two years a contract had been agreed and land feued, at Ballifeary, from Fraser of Torbreck. Sadly Provost Inglis died in 1801, three years before the Infirmary opened, but was always regarded as the driving force behind the project. The committee had its feet firmly on the ground on this project, stating that it wanted a decent building which would,

".... do credit to the liberality of the subscribers but by no means forget that it is to be inhabited by the sick poor for whom to provide anything beyond comfortable accommodation would be absurd."

This statement was reinforced when the committee turned down one design as being "too gaudy for use". Clearly, since the Infirmary was to be built by subscription, the committee felt that its aspirations were to be limited by public generosity. It is interesting to note that a metal subscription box with a lock mechanism was once built into the gate pillar on the riverside entrance for the receiving of donations from the public. It remained there until the Infirmary was redeveloped at the turn of this century.

The Infirmary opened its door in 1804, celebrated with much local pomp and circumstance, and the first patient, Elspet Munro, was a resident in the Parish of Urquhart. The ground floor had staff accommodation as well as a kitchen, medicine shop and a clerk's room. In addition, there were two bathing rooms, one for hot and one cold baths. On the first floor there was a directors' room, surgeons' room and two wards (30 feet by 16 feet) and the second floor contained an operation room and another two wards. As previously stated, the Infirmary also had accommodation for the mentally insane. At each end of the building there was a two-storey wing, the ground

84

floor of each having four small cells (8 foot square) for "lunatics" and each also containing a slightly larger room for a warder. Prior to this accommodation being made available, the mentally disturbed were frequently treated as common criminals, very often being imprisoned for stealing or disturbing the peace. In addition their relatives were often summoned before the magistrates and charged with failing to keep them under proper 'control'. If the "maniac" was violent in any way then the relatives could ask the magistrate to have the person imprisoned until cured. Since there was no treatment whatsoever administered to these unfortunates, it meant that they would spend the rest of their lives locked up in prison.

If one thinks that the accommodation in the Infirmary was inadequate then consideration of the treatment was often just as unsatisfactory – at least by today's standards. One must bear in mind that before the middle of the 18th century there were no medical schools in Scotland at all, and the 'surgeon' of those days was often the barber, who had a young man apprenticed to him to learn his 'trade'. Most women had a little knowledge of the use of herbs and medicines as remedies, although they had to be careful not to be seen to be 'dispensing' cures in case they were accused of witchcraft.

The first patient of the Infirmary died ten days after the hospital opened and one recovering patient was given 'garden labour' as the cure for his complaint. Infectious diseases were often a problem with cases of typhus, cholera and smallpox being recorded in the town. By far the greatest danger of infectious diseases came from the ships which landed at the harbour, and in 1720 a dreadful outbreak of plague on the continent saw all foreign ships being quarantined in Munlochy Bay for 3 weeks before being allowed to enter Inverness harbour.

Notwithstanding, the Infirmary had some excellent and devoted staff, one of whom, Dr John Nicol, was noted for his humanitarian approach to his work and, in keeping with his character, fell victim to cholera whilst treating his patients during the outbreak of 1849. Prior to that, and as a mark of respect for his work, he was co-opted onto the Town Council and elected Provost. Salaries at the Infirmary were not large and paid half-yearly, with the Matron receiving £5 and a nurse £2, the same as the cook and the chambermaid. Curiously enough the gardener's wage was £7 10 shillings for the same period – changed days indeed. Visitors were not always as welcome as they are nowadays in a hospital, and their presence in the Infirmary was strictly restricted to only one hour in the morning and three in the afternoon.

From time to time throughout its history the Infirmary was extended with most of the wards being built in the 1920s. The Tweedmouth Memorial Chapel, gifted by Lady Tweedmouth, in 1898, in memory of her husband, and designed by Dr Ross's firm, had the nave used for Presbyterian worship and the transepts for Episcopalian and Roman Catholic services. In 1929 the Duke and Duchess of York visited the Infirmary and opened another extension which included the York Ward for children. They again visited in 1948, this time as King George VI and his Queen, to mark the passing of the Infirmary into State control.

The Infirmary finally closed its doors as a hospital in 1990s and was converted into flats. A new modern RNI Community Hospital was built in the grounds (to left of main building) and ancillary buildings to the right were demolished and the site used for housing. The main building is now the Headquarters of the UHI (University of the Highlands & Islands) Millennium Institute.

Other Buildings

There are a number of other old buildings of interest which stand, or once stood, around the City of Inverness and are worthy of note. The first of these is the **Mausoleum of the Robertsons of Inshes**. Dating from 1660 this elaborate and imaginative piece of Jacobean work is situated behind the Gaelic Church, in the grounds of the Old High Church on Church Street.

Eden Court is a well-known name nowadays, but once it was the name of the very stately home of the Bishops of St Andrew's Cathedral. Built just after the Cathedral itself, it was incorporated into the building of Eden Court Theatre in the early 1970s, and has recently undergone a new phase of renovation along with the theatre. The first dedicated theatre in Inverness was built in 1805 in Castle Raat (later called Theatre Lane before becoming Hamilton Street) and may have extended into Inglis Street. There is an earlier mention of a theatre in 1791 but no location is mentioned. The 1822 Valuation Roll shows that the Inverness Theatre and Opera House Co. had a theatre, the Theatre Royal, on Bank Street, which was destroyed by fire in 1931.

Will Fyffe was performing in the theatre at the time and the performance had to be transferred to the Central Hall Picture House, built in 1912 in Academy Street, for the rest of that week. At that time there were three other cinemas in Inverness – the La Scala in Academy Street, the Picture House in Huntly Street and the Playhouse in Hamilton Street. The Central Hall Picture House was utilised to fill the gap, and in 1934 it changed its name to the Empire Theatre, which finally closed its doors in 1970 and was demolished a year later, to be replaced by a ghastly building with no character which has now been converted into a hotel, after lying unoccupied for many years. After a short gap Eden Court Theatre was proposed and designed, taking three years to build. When it was finally opened in 1976, the town, once again, had a theatre.

The **Northern Meeting Rooms**, mentioned in Chapter 3, were once the meeting place of "those and such as those" for social events. Situated in Church Street, they were built in 1790 and had a somewhat severe exterior, much different to its splendid and ornate interior. There was a ballroom and a dining room each about 18 metres long by 9 wide. The ballroom contained a full length portrait of the Duke of Gordon, one of his wife by Hayter, and a kit-cat of the Duchess of Gordon. The Northern Meeting, instituted in 1788, was held annually in September and was the great gathering in the North for the gentry and the nobility. The forenoons were devoted to exhibitions of highland games and the evenings given over to grand balls. The building was yet another casualty of the 1960's development.

Lady Drummuir, of Bow Court fame, also had a house which stood in Church Street on the site of number 43. She had the dubious honour of playing host to royalty on two occasions in the middle of the 18th century, once to Bonnie Prince Charlie and then to the Duke of Cumberland. At that time, 1746, Lady Drummuir was aged seventy-six and her daughter remarked about the visits "I have had twa King's bairns living with me in my time and I wish I may never have another". The house was demolished in 1843.

The last standing mill was that at **King's Mill** on the road to Culcabock, just below where the Kingsmills Hotel now stands. Once sporting a good overshot water wheel the large stone built mill was destroyed when the road was altered in the late 1970s. Another casualty to "progress". When the town was created a Royal Burgh in 1150 the burgesses were obliged to use one of the town's three mills situated in this area, which were owned by the King, hence the name. Nearby is the area referred to as Diriebught and an apocryphal tale, associated with the King's Mill, explains how it got its name. One day the miller was tippling on the product of his grain as the Mill ground away. He lay down to rest and eventually fell asleep near the millstone, thus allowing the Mill to run empty. The millstone eventually broke and shattered in all directions, one piece striking and killing the unfortunate miller. When he was eventually discovered, his wife was distraught and cried out, "It's a dear-bought mill to me" – hence the name. A more likely explanation, however, is that in 1362 the land known as Doire nam Bochd (grove of the poor) – or Tir nam Bochd (land of the poor) – was conveyed to The Altar of the Holy Rood of the Church of Inverness. At the time of the Reformation this land was taken over by the Town Council and the name eventually corrupted to Diriebught.

The last thatched cottage in Inverness, **Mile End Cottage**, once stood on a side road leading from the A82 Fort William road to Craig Dunain. After being vacated in the late 1950s it quickly fell into disrepair and vandals stole and broke up much of its interior. This pretty cottage once had a small windmill at its front and a pump behind.

The **Highland Orphanage** stood on Culduthel Road and was

partly bounded by Daviot Drive. It was opened in 1887 at the Golden Jubilee and an extension was added in 1897 at the time of the Diamond Jubilee. In 1959 the Highland Orphanage was closed and the 18 remaining children moved to Carrol House Orphanage which was officially opened at 3.00pm on Wednesday 26th August by Lady Maud Baillie CBE. Robert Gilbert, chairman of the Board of Governors presided at the well-attended ceremony, which was also addressed by Provost Robert Wotherspoon. The matron was Mrs M. Maclean and the two house-mothers were Miss I. Ross and Miss N. Donaldson. A bouquet was presented to Lady Baillie by Heather la Freniere, one of the children in the home.

The **Poorhouse,** known as Muirfield Institution from 1921, was situated on Old Edinburgh Road (also known as General Wade's Military road) opposite its junction with Damfield Road, and was built in 1859 - 61 at a cost of about £6,000, having been designed by James

Matthews and William Lawrie. It was used to rehouse 'inmates' from the overcrowded Dunbar's Hospital in Inverness, with accommodation for around 170 people, and was a handsome building with large grounds extending to about 8 acres. The main building was a typical H-shaped layout similar to many other Poorhouses built in Scotland at that time. The larger building at the front, facing the road, had a central portion which would have contained the Master's quarters, committee rooms and clerk's office. The poorhouse dining-hall and chapel were located in the central block at the rear, while the two wings of the front block contained male and female accommodation, probably with the aged at the front side and able-bodied or "dissolute" inmates at the rear. Children's quarters were usually placed at the far end of each wing. In the rear range of single-storey buildings were found various work and utility rooms including a bakehouse on the men's side and laundry on the female side. Children born in the Poorhouse had their birthplace registered as a house number in Old Edinburgh Road, to avoid the stigma of being born in a Poorhouse (few other Poorhouses in Britain were as considerate back then). It became known as Hilton Hospital when the Poorhouse closed in 1961. Hilton Hospital finally closed its doors in 1987 and was turned into some flats years later. It is now known as Old Edinburgh Court. The old entrance to the Poorhouse has been bricked over and now forms a bus shelter at the front of the flats.

An interesting insight into conditions in the Poorhouse comes from an article by Jennifer Howie, an Invernessian who worked there at one time. She says, *"My father would have left school about 1948 and he went to work for the local ironmonger, Fraser & McColl. As was the way in those days one shop covered many lines and this company also sent men to lay Lino. My father was sent with a couple of more senior men to lay Lino at the Poor House at Hilton. He tells me that the hospital was so cold that the men had to use blow torches* to thaw the oils in the Lino each morning so that they could unroll the material in order to cut it. It became obvious to them that although the blow torches worked to unroll the stuff they were not of any use in the laying of the Lino. They, therefore, had to instruct matron to have a fire lit in the room where the Lino was stored so that they could come back the next day and have a material supple enough to lay.

Throughout the duration of the job the room containing the Lino was the only heated room in the Hospital. My father says that he lost quite a bit of weight during the job as he found the conditions so dreadful that he was put off his food. He says that the patients were urinating everywhere and the men doing the job of laying the new floor covering had to crawl about in the mess and try to clean up as they went in order to have a clean surface on which to lay the Lino. Dad says that the conditions there were the worst he ever saw and he longed to forget the experience. However, his mother was wanting a piece of new Lino for the back room and there was some left over from the job at Hilton, so my father's boss told her she could have the left over piece. The Lino was 3/8" thick and made to last, so for the rest of the years during which my family lived in Broadstone Park, some 40 years, Dad had to look at the Lino and remember the awful job of laying the stuff at Hilton. In the late 1970s I went to Inverness to train as a nurse and one of my secondments was to Hilton Hospital. The Lino was still there!"

Chapter 5

Education

From earliest times, in the Highlands, there were strong links between Education and the Church, and indeed one could argue that were it not for the influence of the Church, then Education would not have reached the "ordinary man" in the Highlands, and indeed in the whole of Scotland, quite as soon as it did. In 1560 the reformed church's "First Book of Discipline" called for a school in every parish, but for one reason or another this plea fell on deaf ears. It was not until 1696 that the "Act of Settling Schools" made it statutory for a school to be set up in every parish and even then this was ignored by many, and where schools did exist attendance was often sporadic for a number of reasons. Firstly, whilst a village school served those in the immediate vicinity it did not, generally speaking, attract many children from outlying areas. Secondly, children were often needed to help with the work on the croft and hence school attendance had to be very much a secondary consideration to a crofting family, even though many did value a good education. The Society in Scotland for Propagating Christian Knowledge was set up in 1709 and it was largely responsible for setting up many rural schools throughout the Highlands and for encouraging parishes to set up their own schools.

The story of education in and around Inverness has a two-tier element attached to it, which relates largely to the class system which existed at that time. Generally speaking, as regards the outlying areas, education was slow to develop and took until the beginning of the 19th century for an educational system to take hold and flourish. There were a number of reasons for this, not the least of them being that country people were largely Gaelic speaking and hence the number of suitable books available for teaching were few and far between. Couple this with a total lack of concern by the Lairds, who openly suppressed any development in education for the masses, and the general poverty of the people, and one can understand why it was slow to progress. Lord Lovat is reported to have once said that,

"..... so long as men of family can have their children tutored in what arts belong to their position, either in their homes or furth the country, the setting up of schools for all and sundry of the folk is contrary to the welfare of the State."

It seems that this attitude was a fair reflection of the views of the "gentry" at that time and goes some way to explain why there was a dearth of schools in country areas. The lairds usually made private arrangements for the education of their own children whilst the rest of the population remained largely illiterate. In the town of Inverness, however, the situation was somewhat different. I have already stated that a school existed at the time of the Blackfriars' Friary around 1233. Also the town's position as a centre of trade and commerce called for educated men to take control of its affairs and to manage justice and administration. Such men of substance, whose interests differed from those of their country counterparts, saw to it that the town's children were well served throughout the centuries.

The Blackfriars' School was situated outside the Friary grounds on the corner of Friars' Lane and Chapel Street. The "Head" of the school was probably a Doctor of Divinity, since every Friary of this type had one, although who the pupils were is a mystery. Most likely they would have been the sons of important townspeople and country gentry, though it is likely that the number of pupils would have been relatively small. It seems most probable that the school closed when the Friars dispersed in 1542, after the Reformation, although this was not the end of schooling in the town because there is mention, in 1557, of the Council deliberating on how much to pay the Master of the School. There is also mention, in 1664, of the existence of a Grammar School on a site on the corner of Bank Street and Bank Lane, next to the old Caledonian Hotel site where the Inverness Courier office was once situated. The school would have been called a "Grammar" school because the pupils were taught Latin Grammar and the "top" pupils would have gone on to University to be taught law and divinity in Latin. This practice continued until the end of the 18th century, although the name "Grammar" school continued thereafter for many years.

The Grammar School appears to have been well run by masters with sound discipline, although it did not stay long on that site, moving in 1668 to Dunbar's Hospital in Church Street. The school originally occupied one ground floor room, although at various other times during its stay on this site it had spread to two and then three of the four floors of the building. While the school only ever appears to have had one "Master" at a time he did have "assistants" to help him in his duties. The Council were not good at paying the master's salary, however, and in 1712 there is a record of him resigning over a dispute regarding outstanding payments. Things did not appear to improve with the passage of time because the new master also resigned for the same reason in 1715. Since a Master's salary at that time would not have amounted to more that £16 per annum, and was probably nearer to £10, it would appear that the Council were being rather parsimonious to say the least. His salary may well have been supplemented, however, by fees paid to him by the pupils and also by income from some private tuition. In addition, Masters were often employed as scribes and registrars within their community. By the middle of the 18th century, however, the fall in value of the pound sterling had brought real poverty to many "Dominies" in Scotland. It was not until the Act of 1803 that the salaries were raised to £22 and provision made for the Master's house to have two rooms besides a kitchen. One wonders why men, who were often highly educated, made teaching their career in those days, although many used it as a stepping-stone to the ministry.

The living conditions were usually frugal, often one room which was sometimes also used as the classroom, and the salaries were poor. School started at 7 am and went on until 6 pm although in winter the day was shortened by a couple of hours at each end to catch the best of the daylight. School also took place on Saturday mornings when pupils were tested on their weeks' work and scholars were also expected to attend church, along with the Master, on Sundays at 10am and again at 2pm, often being tested after church service on the content of the sermon. Heaven help any poor soul who could not deliberate on the main points of the minister's sermon when questioned by the Master. Every Sunday one could see the boys of the Grammar School, led by the Master and his staff in top hats and frock coats, marching to the Old High Church for the service. In those days, holidays were limited to a short break in the summer months and the occasional fast day and fair holidays. Two important ones being Candlemas, when the boys were expected to bring a present of money to the Master, and Cockfight Day, when the Master kept all the birds which were beaten in the fighting for himself.

In 1719 one Donald Forbes, a "strange and unauthorised schoolmaster", upset the Master of the Grammar School by setting up a school for 'ordinary boys' on the Muirtown Green. The problem of 'rogue' schoolmasters setting up schools in competition with the Grammar School seems to have been an on-going one which raised its head from time to time. It is unlikely, however, that these schools would have had any serious affect on the numbers attending the

Grammar School since their Masters were not qualified to teach mathematics, book-keeping and navigation – although some did 'dabble' in these subjects. It is likely, therefore, that they concentrated mainly on reading and writing and charged a much lower fee than the Grammar school. I dare say their mere existence helped the sons and daughters of many Invernessians to learn the basics of the three 'R's – something they may well otherwise have had to do without. One famous former pupil of the Grammar School was General Wolfe, of Canada fame, who studied mathematics at the school when stationed in Inverness as a soldier following the Battle of Culloden. The Master at that time was one Robert Barbour who was highly thought of in the town, as well as by Wolfe, and it was he who was commissioned to repair the bridge sundial which was damaged when the Jacobites blew up the Castle in 1746.

Up to about the first half of the 18th century girls had received no 'formal' education whatsoever in Inverness, despite the pleadings of the landed gentry for the town to educate their daughters instead of them having to be sent away to school. There had been 'unofficial' schools run by some 'ladies', much to the displeasure of the Council, but these tended to attract the daughters of merchants rather than the gentry. In 1732, the Council allowed a Mrs Thomson to set up a "Spinning School" for girls in the upper floor of the Town House and it is possible that she also taught her girls the three 'R's. In 1766, however, the Council decided to employ an official headmistress at a salary of £10 a year. Miss Margaret Kerr was appointed to run the boarding school for the daughters of Highland gentlemen. In 1778, the records show that an English and Writing School was also opened in the Grammar School building although very little is known of it. The Grammar School closed in 1792 and transferred to New Street (later called Academy Street after the school) as the Inverness Academy, and even the bell which summoned the boys to school moved with them. The school was situated on the corner of Academy Street and Strother's Lane, where M & Co. and the Exchange is now. When it opened on this site it boasted five masters and several classrooms, a substantial school for those days, and one wonders if size was the reason for its move to the new site. There were three acres of grounds and a large play area behind the building. In addition there was a large hall and library for the 300 fee-paying pupils who were charged 10 shillings a quarter for Latin, 7/6 for arithmetic and 15 shillings for painting. A Royal Charter of incorporation was granted to the school in 1793 by King George III, hence the use of the word

"Royal" in its title. In 1806 the Academy opened its doors to the fairer sex, with the addition of a girl's extension, and one presumes that these girls must, therefore, have had an "elementary" education elsewhere in the town before transferring to the Academy. When Boswell and Johnson arrived at the Inn at Glenmoriston, Dr Johnson was informed that the landowner's daughter, a well-spoken and mannerly girl, had been to Inverness "to gain the common female qualifications". For a long time a girl's education did not extend beyond the skills of housewifery and even thereafter it was often restricted to just the three "R's". Girls also seemed to have enjoyed the privilege of an Academy education throughout the 19th century – but only sporadically for some reason. The school had many bright students, boys and girls, and indeed many fine masters in its time. Many of the "old boys" who left the school and went on to make their fortunes, both at home and abroad, left legacies of money to the school, some of which still exist today.

Sexism, however, was hard at work in those days because the records show that one female student who was a brilliant mathematician, streets ahead of the boys, was refused the Mathematics Medal in 1850 because it was thought inappropriate to award it to a female. The medal was given to one of the male students instead. In the early 1890s, following various inspection reports, it was realised that the existing building in Academy Street was unsuitable for the type of education then required and plans were laid for the construction of a new building.

Royal Academy

The site in the Crown area was selected after several other sites had been considered. Although there had been little urban development there before that time, the site offered easy access from the town, being at the top of Stephen's Brae and Stephen's Street. The local architectural firm of Ross and Macbeth were the architects (Alexander Ross is best known for his design of St. Andrew's Cathedral, Inverness). The foundation stone was laid on 27th June 1893, by the Grand Master Mason of Scotland, the Earl of Haddington. The opening ceremony for the new building was on 25th February 1895. It ceased to be an independent school in 1908 when it was taken over by the Burgh School Board, although it remained a fee-paying school until 1945. Its final move was to a new building in Culduthel, its present site, which it moved to in 1977, although it took until 1979 for the complete move to be made, with the old building latterly being used by Inverness College campus. The original gates for the school were on the two front corners of the site, and it was only shortly before World War II Memorial gates were erected in November 1954 that a single entrance was created in front of the main doors. As I write, work on a new school, which is sited next to the existing Inverness Royal Academy, has begun and the new building is expected to be completed in June 2016 and open for pupils in August 2016.

John Raining, a Scottish merchant living in Norwich, left the Church of Scotland £1,200 to build a school "in any part of Northern Britain where they think it is most wanted." The Church passed the funds on to the Society in Scotland for Propagating Christian Knowledge who chose Inverness as the site for the school. Why Inverness was chosen is not recorded and is a curious choice since the town was already well served at this time and normally the

Raining's School

Society maintained rural schools only. The school originally opened in Dunbar's Hospital in the floor above the Grammar School in 1725.

Although this was supposed to be a temporary measure it stayed there until 1757 when it moved to a purpose built school at the top of Raining Stairs on Arconnel Terrace, where it remained for 37 years. In 1894 it was absorbed into the new High School (later Crown Primary School) in Kingsmills Road.

Inverness High School

Around 1800 there is mention of a Female School being in existence in Dunbar's Hospital but information on it is scant. By the time of the New Statistical Account (1835–41), school provision had been considerably extended throughout the area and every parish had its parochial school. An increasing number of schools were maintained by voluntary bodies like the Society in Scotland for Propagating Christian Knowledge, the Church of Scotland and the Inverness Society for Educating the Poor in the Highlands. It was noted that there was a greater interest in education among ordinary people and that "education was prized very highly". The next school to come on the scene was the High School which was initially built in the late 1840s by the Free Church Institute. It was first sited in Ardconnel Street roughly opposite where the Blind Institute is now, later moving to a new site in Kingsmills Road, in the 1870's, to what is now the Crown Primary School. At this time it also merged with Raining's School. In 1937 it was on the move again, this time to Montague Row, its present site, and was renamed the Technical School. Its name changed yet again in the 1960's (while I was a pupil there) when it became known as Inverness High School.

About the same time as the High School was first built another school appeared on the scene. This one was called Dr Bell's Institution and was built in 1841, in Bell's Park (now called Farraline Park). It is the building presently used as the Library and was built in the Greek revival style for around £10,000 – a great deal of money in those days. The building was regarded by some, and particularly the Governors of the Royal Academy, as being rather grandiose for the purpose. During excavations 9 skeletons were discovered and were

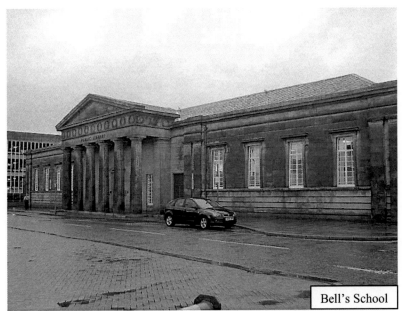

Bell's School

thought to be the remains of men who had fallen in battle. The school opened with two teachers, one to teach English and one to teach Commercial Subjects, and throughout its time it, too, can boast many famous former pupils (including my father – although his 'fame' was limited to the family home). It closed in 1937 and was amalgamated with the High School and Raining's School to form the Technical School. The building has had a number of uses since then including a theatre, police station and courthouse. Interestingly, in 1847 it was suggested that the Academy should take over Bell's Institute and turn it into a Collegiate Institution with power to award B.A. and M.A. degrees, but government finance was not offered so the proposal did not come to fruition. This would have seen a much earlier appearance for the University of the Highlands and Islands had funding been available.

The last school of note has a strange name. It was called the Ragged School and was situated in Tanners Row (now Alexander Place), a lane opposite the Tesco store on Young Street. It opened in 1853 in the teacher's own house and had "a considerable number of bairns". The master advised the Council that he would be teaching children the "elements of education", so one presumes he refers to the three "R's". This establishment should not be confused with the Inverness Reformatory or Ragged School which opened in 1858 behind Dr Bell's Institution in Farraline Park. It was demolished in the 1950s.

Lack of sufficient information forbids the mention of other establishments, of which there were several in existence, including a Music School, a Kindergarten School, which operated in the Old High

Northern Counties Collegiate School

Church Hall in the late 19th century, and a number of private and boarding schools, sometimes called "adventure" schools, throughout the 19th and early 20th centuries. Generally speaking the authorities did not support any establishment which was in competition with the Grammar School and hence they tended to exist for a short time only. Earlier times saw the existence of "dame" schools and occasionally an "adventure" or private school within the Burgh. The Inverness College, or Northern Counties Collegiate School, started out in Ardross Terrace before moving, in 1873, to a building in Ardross Street designed by Alexander Ross. This "English" type Public School was used as a training ground for young gentlemen who aspired to careers in the army and navy and was managed by a council of "thirteen influential gentlemen". This was not surprising, given Mr Ross's close connection with Inverness (Episcopal) Cathedral, which he had designed and was a member of the congregation. That relationship between Cathedral and School seemed to have continued, given that several headmasters were "Reverend". It is particularly interesting to note that the Collegiate School was constructed literally "just over the border" – only a matter of feet out of the Inverness Burgh Boundary. Thus it lay outwith the Burgh and was not subject to the control of the Town Council of Inverness. The establishment being intended to be of the highest quality, it is remarkable that no fancy coat of arms or Latin motto was produced. Instead the plaque has the Burgh motto "Concordia et Fidelitas" on a scroll above a shield - and another scroll below the shield with the words "Onwards and Upwards". Ross subsequently designed an extension to the building a decade later, but this was not by any means an ultimate completion as he presumably envisaged. Although it seemed to have had several Headmasters with excellent degrees from Oxford and Cambridge it was never highly successful as an educational establishment and closed for a while at the turn of the century before reopening briefly. It finally closed its doors in 1914 and was used as a Memorial Hostel for the Royal Academy in 1921; it is now part of the Highland Council buildings in Glenurquhart Road. There was also an Inverness Ladies College which started in 1913 in Glen Mhor on Ness Bank; later changing its name to Heatherley School for Girls and moving to Heatherley House two years later. The period following the First World War was a difficult time for the school and it changed to a day and boarding school in order to exist. Continuing in this way until 1956 it finally closed following the retiral of the owners, Miss Bedale and her sisters.

In addition to the Burgh RC School there was also a convent school, associated with the Roman Catholic Church on Huntly Street. The convent and the school, managed by Nuns of the Order of Notre Dame relocated to Culduthel Road (what is now Mackenzie Kerr Chartered Accountants) under the control of the education authority, and was later superseded by Nuns of the Order of La Sagesse. It was a fee-paying school for girls of Primary age, although a few boys did manage to penetrate this female bastion from time to time. The school closed in 1969. Ecclesiastical equality prevailed at this time because boys were catered for at the Abbey School in Fort Augustus. It was run by the Benedictine Order, which had built a monastery on the site of the old Hanoverian fort. The monastic buildings which were begun in 1876 were completed in 1880, occupying the four sides of a quadrangle about one hundred feet square.

In one wing a school for boys of the upper classes was conducted by the monks with the assistance of lay masters. Girls were admitted in the early 1970's but dwindling numbers of pupils saw the school close in 1993. This left the monks with no form of outreach and a drastic drop in income. Inverness and Nairn Enterprise introduced the monks to entrepreneur Tony Harmsworth who was commissioned to install a small Heritage exhibition to provide an immediate income for the monks while he devised a rescue package. It quickly became clear that a small business could never generate sufficient income to support the monks and the rambling Victorian buildings, so a major project was begun.

The business comprised the largest private heritage exhibition in Scotland, study bedrooms converted into tourist bedrooms, a restaurant, gift shop and a number of franchised businesses. The enterprises initially showed great promise, becoming a major tourism force in the Highlands, but it was discovered that the buildings needed far more spending upon them than had ever been envisaged. A larger project was being considered with finance from Historic Scotland and the Local Enterprise Company, but the business was closed down before this could be put into effect.

The heritage centre was closed in 1998 and when the monks left, the buildings, which had been leased to the monks at £5 per year, reverted to the Lovat Family and were later sold to a consortium. They, in turn, sold the abbey to a group who converted the buildings into apartments known as *The Highland Club.*

In 2013, It was reported that Scottish police were investigating allegations that pupils had been subjected to physical and sexual abuse while at the Abbey School. A BBC programme made allegations that Fort Augustus Abbey was used as a "dumping ground" for clergy previously accused of abuse elsewhere, and the authorities were given inadequate notification. The allegations included physical beating, verbal humiliation and sexual abuse. Since the programme was broadcast further allegations of abuse emerged.

The 1872 Education Act made schooling compulsory between the ages of five and thirteen. At this time Parish and Burgh School Boards took over responsibility for education from church and town councils and elementary education became available to all children. What is nowadays recognised as Secondary education was still only available in Inverness and to a lesser extent Drumnadrochit. In rural areas children had to be content with the extent of the Master's ability.

The Education Act of 1945 heralded major change. The Qualifying Examination at Primary 7 stage was done away with and replaced with a Promotion Examination, the outcome of which determined whether one went to a 6-year senior secondary or a 3-year junior secondary school. In Inverness, traditional academic education was centred on the Royal Academy, with the Technical School offering courses in technical and commercial subjects as well as general courses. The Burgh Roman Catholic School also had a small secondary department but pupils

Millburn Secondary

had to attend the High School for instruction in practical subjects. A practice which ceased in 1969 when the RC school lost its secondary status. Pupils who attended Millburn Junior Secondary had the opportunity of transferring to the Royal Academy after two years if merit permitted, the others remaining in Millburn. Interestingly, some pupils who were given the opportunity to transfer preferred to remain where they were, which is a credit to the level of teaching and the staff who taught there.

The introduction of comprehensive education in the mid 1970's saw further changes to the Secondary School set up. Pupils were no longer segregated according to merit but instead attended their local Secondary School. Those on the east side of the river attended either Millburn Academy (note the change of name) or the Royal Academy according to the catchment area of the school, whilst those on the west side of the river attended the High School. Inverness was steadily growing in size and by the late 1970's the High School could no longer hold all the pupils west of the river and the two schools on the eastern side were full. In 1978 Charleston Academy was built at Kinmylies and shortly afterwards Culloden Academy at Balloch, both these new schools took the pressure off the other three secondary's. When Charleston Academy opened the secondary pupils at Beauly school transferred into it as well as some from the High School.

Culloden Academy   Charleston Academy

instruction has long been a trait of Inverness schools. The Royal Academy had, from its inception, offered a fine standard of instruction including English; French; Classics; Gaelic; History; Geography; Science; Navigation; Architecture; Naval, Civil and Military Practical Gunnery; Fortifications; Perspective and Drawing. One wonders where the practical gunnery was undertaken and with what – and for why! Inverness High School also offered an excellent education, initially in technical, commercial and scientific subjects before eventually branching out into all other academic areas with the introduction of comprehensive education. Many students, from both establishments, went on to University and made names for themselves both at home and abroad. One must not forget the "latter day" schools either; Millburn, Charleston and Culloden are all very good schools and one can say without contradiction that the city has long been well served in educational provision.

The reader will perhaps forgive me for not mentioning any Primary schools in this chapter, but there are too many in number to do them justice. No mention either has been made of hostel provision, so much a part of life for those pupils from the west and the Islands who had to attend the High School and the Royal Academy in the early days. Hedgefield Hostel for girls, and Drummond Park for boys, were part of life in my schooldays – particularly the former which held a strange attraction for me on many an evening! Further Education has also been missed out, although Highland education has long had a strong tradition of encouraging pupils to seek further and higher education. As far back as between the wars evening classes were held in technical and commercial subjects, before eventually the Inverness Technical School offered some day classes for apprentices and others. This school stood on the corner of Church Street and Friars' Lane, next to where Leakey's bookshop now is, and was demolished in the 1970s. It was used for technical and art instruction from the 1890's until 1937 when the Technical School opened in Montague Row. After the Second World War the High School Evening Institute offered a range of subjects leading to awards in the Royal Society of Arts, City and Guilds and other examinations. In 1960 the Inverness Technical College was built and has continued to flourish until the present day, now having linked to the UHI. I consider it a great pity that the UHI did not take over the old Craig Phadraig building and associated grounds as a campus because it would have made a first class site for a University with plenty of room for residential halls for the students.

Merkinch Welfare Hall

From the turn of the 20th century there was widespread revulsion to the problems surrounding the consumption of alcohol and temperance movements and temperance hotels were springing up in many cities throughout Scotland and elsewhere. In 1892 the Rev. R. J. Patterson became the minister of the Mall Presbyterian Church in Armagh, Northern Ireland. A great social reformer, he founded the Protestant Total Abstinence Union, in 1909, which was better known as the "Catch-My-Pal" Movement. This movement had a tremendous influence for good, principally on men, between then and the start of the Second World War, in terms of opposing the "evils of drink". Patterson's approach was to conduct mass meetings at which those present would take a pledge for total abstinence and had great success in Ireland where around 140,000 men and women joined the Union in its first year alone. His two visits to Scotland were less fruitful, however, with 1,500 attending a meeting in Glasgow and around 2,000 in Aberdeen. He also visited Inverness in 1911 although I have no idea how many people attended the meeting.

The Inverness area was no exception to alcohol abuse, indeed it was seen by many as having a reputation for the overconsumption of alcohol and, indeed, this was widespread throughout the Highlands. Women had always played a prominent role in the temperance movement in Inverness to the extent that a "Total Abstinence Movement" had been set up in the town as early as 1840. Whilst overindulgence was not confined to the poor of the town, by any means, there is no doubt that there was a connection between drunkenness and living and working conditions. In 1866 the Young Men's Christian Association was addressed by the High School Rector, Joseph Robertson, who clearly identified idleness, intemperance, improvidence and the sickness or death of the family breadwinner as the causes of poverty. Thus implying that they were also linked to drunkenness.

In 1911, following a visit from Patterson, a Catch-My-Pal café opened up in the Merkinch area of Inverness in a converted public house with around 300 pledges being taken in the first few weeks. Its success led to another two branches opening up in other parts of the town, Huntly Street and Academy Street. In April 1914 property was acquired on the corner of Grant Street and Brown Street for £50 by the Trustees of the Merkinch Branch of the Union. Unfortunately, the property was in a dilapidated state and had to be demolished in order to build a new hall. The Trustees, James Walker (Timber Merchant), Joseph Cook Timber Merchant), John MacGruther (Coal Merchant), William Elliot (Flesher), Norman Smith (Stevedore) and James Sinclair (Signal Fitter) took out a £400 bond with the Inverness Investment and Permanent Building Society with other funding to complete the hall being raised locally. The plot of land they purchased was bought from the trustees of the late Captain William Mackintosh who had commanded the East Indiaman, HMS Hindustan. Mackintosh, by all accounts a fascinating character, had made his fortune in the Navy and, following his death, his trustees had invested in property including the Merkinch area.

Shortly after the new Merkinch hall was completed, in 1915, many of the men it was built to serve went off to war and so its 'function' must have been questioned. After the war, with so few men returning home, the Catch-My-Pal Union in the Merkinch initially saw a decline, being listed in 1919 as a "Hall, Store and Baths" suggesting perhaps that it was serving the community in another way, although this may have had more to do with the fact that it had been requisitioned during the war. The Academy Street Branch fared better, however, under the leadership of William Anderson a prominent Inverness baker whose shop and bakery were also in Academy Street whilst the Huntly Street Branch was presumably also prospering since the Town Council gifted them an organ in 1921. The years following the war (in particular the 1920s) saw an acute rise in unemployment in Inverness which triggered a revival of the Catch-My-Pal union with regular concerts in various venues throughout the town, although this was mainly associated with the Academy Street Branch. By the early 1920s the Union's management of the Hall had lapsed and the responsibility for running the Hall fell to the Merkinch Ward Welfare Association who had agreed to take on the outstanding debts. Interestingly, at this time, a Mrs Davidson who was a midwife in the area and had delivered over 300 children started a welfare project in the Hall. She endeavoured to show local women how to care for their children and ensure that they were fed properly. She weighed them and kept charts of their progress as well as informing the mothers about head lice and how to cure it. It is an interesting aside that the Catch-My-Pal movement actively encouraged sporting activity among men who took the temperance pledge and it was from this beginning that a Catch-My-Pal football team sprung up. They reached their peak in the mid- 1920s when they won the North Caledonian Football League and also took part in the Scottish Junior Cup.

In 1929 one Donald MacLennan stood for the Town Council and held a meeting in the Hall to a packed gathering. He won his seat and two years later he proposed that the redundant Drum Clock, which hung on the steeple and belonged to a watch maker and jeweller whose shop stood at the corner of Bridge Street and Church Street, should be relocated on the Welfare Hall, which it was and remains to this day. In the years between the First and Second World Wars the Hall was in frequent use with meetings and social events taking place on a regular basis including the Merkinch Women's Guild, the Post Office Recreational Club and a Guide Company run by Eveline Barron, former editor of the Inverness Courier.

At the outbreak of the Second World War the hall was again requisitioned, this time by the Royal Air Force, whereupon it was used as a dental surgery for troops in the area. The hall was identified as an air raid shelter and fared badly during this period. The records of the Catch-My-Pal Union and the Welfare Association were either lost or destroyed and much of the interior furnishings were also destroyed. In 1939 two new trustees were appointed, Donald Fraser and James

Shand, although there appears to have been no meetings of the Welfare Association between 1938 and about 1950 at which point Donald Fraser suggested that new trustees should be appointed with a view to ensuring that the Hall continued to serve the local community. The Hall was used, however, during this time for concerts and dances on a regular basis.

In the 1950s George Rodgers became a trustee and between then and the middle 1970s the Hall was used for bingo run by the Clachnacuddin FC. Rodgers was a director of the football club and later became the President of the Merkinch and District Welfare Association. With the death of George Rodgers in 1982, and with the Hall in a poor state of repair, its future and its management were once again in the balance. At this time the main user of the Hall was the Inverness Judo Club who had been there since 1961 and remained (with a break between 1968 and 1978) until the late 1990s when they could no longer afford the upkeep of the building. By the early 1980s the Welfare Association had ceased to exist and the building was "in a dilapidated state" requiring repairs of around £30,000. The Judo Club undertook repairs to the dry rot but ultimately had to vacate the building. At that stage the Merkinch Enterprise Company took over the building and it is through that body that a feasibility study was carried out to try to secure a future for the historic building.

In November 2015 the Merkinch Enterprise Company received a grant from the Heritage Lottery Fund of over £700,000 towards a £1.2 million project to refurbish the Hall to its former glory so that the local community can benefit from a range of opportunities which have been planned for the future. Work started in February 2016 and is due to finish in early 2017 on the C-listed building with additional funding from the Common Good Fund and the Archaeological Heritage Fund. I am pleased to hear that the refurbishment will retain as much of the building's integrity as possible.

Chapter 6

Churches

The history of the Church in the Highlands is often abstruse. In many instances records have failed to survive the passage of time if, indeed, there ever were formal documents in the first place. The Church did hold some records centrally, but the sheer remoteness of the Highland dioceses inevitably made contact infrequent and irregular. It would be wrong to say, however, that this lack of documentation suggests that the Church in the Highlands was any the less mindful of its task than in any other part of Scotland.

The 15th century saw mixed fortunes for many of the churches and monastic buildings in and around the Inverness area, with the Friary in Inverness being described, in 1436, as "almost ruinous in its structure and buildings". The abbey at Fearn, near Tain, was refurbished during this century, but in 1541 James V wrote to Pope Paul III to say that it was ruinous and neglected, although, generally speaking, the 16th century saw a marked revival of religious life. Do not let these comments underestimate the importance of the Church in this part of the world and at that particular time in history. The church of St Duthac in Tain was favoured by James II and was an important place of pilgrimage for James IV who made frequent visits there.

Christianity arrived in Inverness along with Columba in 563 A.D., when he baptised the first Picts and built a church on St Michael's Mount. From that day forward the Church grew and prospered, slowly and steadily, sometimes buffeted this way and that, but always progressing forward in stature and in number. The Scottish Monarchy and their Norman successors, the Reformation, the influence of the English influx, the suppression of Gaelic and even the interference of Bishops and the Council all had an effect on the growth and development of the Church in Inverness. Some of it constructive and some of it not so, but taken collectively, over the passage of many generations, it forged the Church that we know and worship in today. The Church once had a strong influence on the lives of the people of Inverness – one only has to look at the list of churches in the City, past and present, to understand that – although nowadays that influence is dwindling slowly but steadily. The causes of that particular problem are not up for discussion in this book, although clearly it needs to be addressed if the decline is to be halted. The chronicle of the Church in Inverness is rich in history and, indeed, it is surprising how much one could write about, given the space to do so. I have included a short account of the history of each present Inverness church and, where appropriate, included a mention of those gone, but perhaps not forgotten.

The Kirk Session was a joint body of the Inverness charges, which were two in number prior to 1706 and three thereafter - these being the Old High, the West Church and St Mary's (Gaelic) Church. Until 1950 none of these churches had control over its own affairs, which were administered by the Session, as indeed were most of the charitable funds of the town. In 1624 a second minister was appointed in Inverness and he was given the "second charge", which eventually became the West Church; then in 1706 the Gaelic Church was built next to the Old High and this became the "third charge".

Whilst the Law Courts judged the townspeople on their secular misgivings, it was the Church which interpreted divine moral law – and it did so with a vengeance, ably supported and assisted by the Town Council.

If one stands on the east side of the Greig Street Bridge and looks around it is possible to spy 8 churches spread out on both sides of the river. There must be very few, if any, other cities in the world where one can do that – and spy 4 pubs and 4 licensed restaurants at the same time.

Old High Church

When Columba travelled up the Great Glen, in 563 A.D., on his famous journey from Iona to visit King Bridei at his headquarters in Inverness he also sought permission to build a church on some suitable location. The site he chose was St. Michael's Mount in Inverness, which is the present site of the Old High Church. It is reasonable to suppose that this small chapel would have been wooden in construction and fairly simply built, certainly not capable of enduring the elements for any considerable length of time. Little wonder then that no trace of it has ever been found. In later years, when such structures were replaced with more substantial stone buildings they were generally erected on the same sites as their predecessors. The Roman Catholic Church normally dedicated a new church to a saint, and in the case of the Old High it was the Virgin Mary. Some time in the middle to late 12th century William the Lion made a grant of "one plough of land in perpetual mortification" to the then priest in the Old High and the "Church of Saint Mary". It was not long afterwards that William granted the church and its revenues to the Monastery of Arbroath whose Abbot starved the Old High of funds. One wonders if there is a connection between this and the burning of part of the town by an armed band sent by the Abbot in 1372. Maintenance of the fabric of a church is always an expensive business and perhaps never more so than in the past. It is reported that in Queen Mary's time the wall surrounding the Old High was broken to such an extent that cows and horses wandered in to feed on the grass which surrounded the graves. In 1718 the Burgh applied for, and received, a Parliamentary sanction to levy a tax of two pence (Scots) on every pint of beer brewed in, or imported into, Inverness in order to pay for repairs to the Parish Church and the harbour – can you imagine the Church agreeing to such a levy nowadays. Of the original medieval stone built church only part of the 14th century tower remains, the remainder was demolished in 1769, when in a ruinous condition. The present building was constructed in 1770 with a parapet and spire being added to the tower. It is a plain, though attractive, rectangular building with galleries round three sides and an apse on the south side. When viewed from the west side of the river the church has a very balanced and arresting appearance which catches the eye and holds the attention.

For good reason then, this is the town church of Inverness, with the Minister being the Chaplain to the City. It has in its lifetime seen the Kirking of the Council on countless occasions, always on the Sunday following the Annual Meeting. Originally, the Town Council gathered at the Provost's residence every Sunday and then proceeded to walk, in procession, to the Old High where they sat according to rank in the centre of the gallery. The Provost and Magistrates had the privilege of armchairs, instead of pews, and each chair had a bible embossed with the Town Arms. After the service they retired to the Provost's house for refreshments before returning to church for the afternoon service. In 1775, there was a dispute between a tradesman and a merchant as to who should occupy the more "elevated" position in terms of rank. It became so impassioned that the next day a Council meeting was held and the seating arrangements were resolved by the forming of one long pew which seated everyone with equality. They also agreed to proceed to church from the Town House instead of the Provost's residence, a procedure which continued until 1894 when the weekly attendance changed to an annual appearance, which still takes place. The church contains a first edition copy of the King James Bible of 1611, held in a glass-topped case in front of the pulpit for all to see. This bible is known as the "He" bible because of the reference "and he went into the City" in Ruth 3; verse 15, instead of the more common translation "and she went into the City". The Old High Church bell continues to ring out curfew on weekdays as it has since 1720, with the exception of the World War II period. The bell, originally hand rung, was converted to electric drive in 1979.

In the 18th century it was commonplace for a coffin to be covered with a mortcloth whilst en route to the churchyard. The town possessed three which are described as "the best cloth, the next best cloth, and the old cloth", and the cost of hiring these depended on which one was chosen. The Guildry Craft also had a mortcloth which was of a better quality, being more decorative, than that of the town's "best" cloth. Since the latter proved more popular with mourners, and hence reduced the Council's income, they instructed the Guild to use it for their own members only. Despite their complaints the Council's mortcloths gathered sufficient income to pay the salary of the Grammar school's Master on more than one occasion.

The first Protestant Minister to be appointed was David Rag, in 1560, who was of dubious moral character as has already been outlined. His departure from the scene in 1565 saw the appointment of Thomas Howieson, a Burgh clerk, who had formerly been a priest. Howieson was also a schoolmaster and it is reported that he continued to teach after his appointment as minister. The Burgh Court ordained in 1564 that all citizens of Inverness should attend the Parish Church twice on every Sunday. This decree of Sunday (or Sabbath Day) observance took a firm hold in Inverness and remained strong until more recent times when it was gradually eroded away – sometimes for the best of reasons. I say that because in 1936 the Council agreed to open the baths in the public swimming pool so that citizens who did not have a bath at home could avail themselves of the facility prior to attending church. When the doors opened for that reason there then seemed little point in not opening the pool as well. In 1691 a Presbyterian Minister was appointed to the vacant post, but the Magistrates, favouring the Episcopacy candidate at the time, tried to prevent him from taking his post. Along with Duncan Forbes of Culloden, father of the famous Lord President Forbes, the new minister attempted to force his way into the church but was refused entry by a group of armed men. Following this the Government sent a regiment to Inverness to support the Presbyterians and the presentee was placed on the pulpit at the point of a bayonet. In its time the Old High has been used for Protestant and Episcopalian services and has always been known as the "English" church because no Gaelic was used in its services.

Following the Battle of Culloden the church was used as a prison and several Jacobite soldiers were executed in the graveyard adjoining the church. One English Officer stationed in Inverness at the time of post-Culloden occupation was Lieutenant Colonel James Wolfe, prior to his transfer to Canada, and he regularly attended services in the church.

In 1704 the General Assembly of the Church of Scotland passed an Act which saw the formation of a Kirk Session Library, and in 1706 it is recorded that the Library had in excess of 200 volumes valued at almost £800. At a loss as to where to store the books the Kirk Session placed them in a room at Dunbar's Hospital, and they may well have been used by the Grammar School. In 1792 when the Grammar School moved to New Street (Academy Street) to become the Inverness Academy the Library moved with it and remained in the Academy Hall until 1817, when it returned to Dunbar's Hospital. In 1845 it moved to the Session House of the Old High, when Dunbar's Hospital became a poorhouse, before transferring to the Female School on Academy Street. When this school closed the building housed a Kindergarten School before eventually becoming the Old High Church Hall. Here the Library remained until the Highland Council Library took it over in the 1970s.

East Church

Built in 1798 it was originally a Chapel of Ease for the Old High Church. In 1843 it became a Free Church but was rebuilt in 1853. It was considerably extended, in Victorian Gothic style, with the addition of a staircase and tower and an enlarged gallery, in 1897. The architect was Dr Alexander Ross whose work is well known and admired in Inverness. Little wonder he was called the "Christopher Wren of the Highlands". With the Union of Churches in 1929 it reverted to a Parish Church. At the rear of this church, on Margaret Street where the church hall now is, once stood a Roman Catholic Church. In 1829 a "no popery" demonstration aimed at Charles Grant MP, who was staying at the Caledonian Hotel, smashed the hotel windows before moving on to wreck the Chapel of this church. It was demolished when the church moved to Huntly Street in 1837.

West Church

Situated on the corner of Huntly Street and Greig Street this was the "second charge" of the Old High. It was built by Robert Caldwell, work starting in 1837 with the Church opening its doors six years later. It is a plain classical building with columns and a pediment. The main front is built in the form of a Classical temple. A square tower with an octagonal cupola rises above the triangular pediment. The tower has a dome on the top and the building faces on to the river. The church closed its doors in 2003 and was then converted into flats known as "Bell Tower".

Free Presbterian Church of Scotland

The Inverness congregation was first formed in 1893, the first minister, Rev. Allan Mackenzie being ordained in November of that year. Shortly afterwards a church was purchased in Fraser Street, costing £1100 and seating 450 people, sometime before May 1896. In July 1897, Mr Mackenzie and a number of his followers separated from the congregation, retaining the Fraser Street building. In May 1900 they were accepted into the Church of Scotland. A new church was built for the Free Presbyterian congregation, seating 700 people, and was opened on 12th January

1900 in North Church Place just off Chapel Street. The original building which is situated at the junction of Fraser Street and Bank Street is presently the Mustard Seed restaurant. Rev J.R. Mackay was inducted as minister on 24th January 1900, but left in 1918 to join the Free Church. He was succeeded as minister by Rev. Ewan MacQueen in 1919, but in 1938 he too left and formed a separate congregation in Inverness.

St Mary's (Gaelic) Church

Originally built for Gaelic speaking worshippers in 1649, it stands next to the Old High in Church Street and was rebuilt in 1792, with further reconstructions in 1822 and 1855. This is the third charge of the Old High and is a somewhat severe building with six high round-arched windows facing onto Church Street. When gas lighting was introduced to Church Street in 1827 this church was the first to regularly hold evening services, in English. The church had a noteworthy 17th century carved wooden pulpit called the "Black Pulpit" which was very ornate. It had been gifted to the church by William Robertson of Inshes. When the church moved, and the Free Church took over the building, the pulpit was removed and stored in the safe keeping of the Town Council, but vandals broke into the store and destroyed it. Thus a unique piece of Renaissance craftsmanship was lamentably lost to the town. The church transferred to Dalneigh as St Mary's, and the building in Church Street became Greyfriars Free Church but, alas, the Gaelic language did not transfer with the congregation. The church is now a second hand bookshop.

St Andrew's Cathedral

In the Scottish Episcopal Church the Bishops of Moray traditionally had their seat in Elgin. In 1850 the post of Bishop of Moray and Ross was vacant and two candidates were up for election – James MacKay of St John's, Inverness and Robert Eden of Leigh, Essex. In the ensuing election each candidate received four votes but when a second election was held some time later, Eden received five of the eight votes and became the new Bishop. In 1853 he proposed that the seat of the Bishopric be moved to Inverness and that a new

Cathedral should be built there. Initially his request fell on deaf ears but in 1864, when Caithness was added to the Diocese, it was viewed with more favour. Eden's conviction and enthusiasm were sufficient to

drive the project forward, and by late 1866 the Archbishop of Canterbury had laid the foundation stone for the new Cathedral; the first to be built in Britain since the Reformation. It is cruciform and Gothic Revival in style, with an arcaded nave, transepts, chancel and two western towers 100 feet high. The baptismal font is a copy of Thorwalden's font in Copenhagen Cathedral. Structural defects in the cast iron fleche saw it removed in 1961 and replaced with a copper cross. Designed by Dr Alexander Ross, who also planned the development of both Ardross Street and Terrace in empathy with the Cathedral, it was built at a cost of £20,000. It was not built exactly to plan because it originally had two spires a hundred feet high rising from the towers; the chancel was to have been some fifty feet longer with a semi-circular apse and an ambulatory with flying buttresses. A Cloister was also on the original plan. The building was dedicated in 1869 and consecrated in 1874. At that time the Episcopal congregation met in a small church in Bank Street, where the Y.M.C.A. building is situated, before transferring to the new and very spacious Cathedral.

The popular story, related by many in the past, that Inverness could not become a City because the Cathedral did not have its spires built was quite wrong, although also irrelevant nowadays. There are several sculpture heads carved inside the Cathedral, two of which belong to Ross and Eden. Another sculpture appears on the arch surrounding the transept window facing the river and is a wheel and a horse. The story relating to the sculpture says that the stone building blocks were raised by means of a pulley and wheel turned by a horse in the carving. The Bishop had a residence built shortly after the Cathedral which was called Eden Court (the Bishop's Palace) and later Bishop Eden's Episcopal School was built. When Eden Court was no longer used as the residence of Cathedral Bishops it was turned into a nurses' school and later a residential home for nurses. In 1976 when Eden Court Theatre was built the house was incorporated into the development.

St Columba High Church

This was originally known as the Free High Church and was built in 1843 between Fraser Street and Church Lane. The present building, built in 1852 on the site of a former brewery, is constructed in the Gothic Revival style and has a good spire, although the removal of the flying buttresses, in 1970, has spoiled the appearance of the church. Badly damaged by a fire during the Second World War and later restored by Leslie MacDougal, the interior of the church was dramatically altered thus changing its character. A church Mission Hall was built in Castle Street in 1932 and destroyed by a landslide several months later. The church was closed in 2010 in a move to reduce the number of congregations in the city centre. It was hoped, at the time of closure, that the church would relocate to the Holm area of the city.

St Stephen's Church

This very attractive looking church was built in 1896 and is linked with the Old High Church. Robert Carruthers was the architect and it is built in the Gothic style with a needle spire. It is situated on the crossroads of Old Edinburgh Road and Southside Road. It is in this church, in 1970, that I was married.

117

Crown Church

The building of a church in the Crown area of the town was first mooted around 1890, but abandoned because of indecision over a site for the building. However, six years later a further move was made and ground purchased for the building to be started. The foundation stone for the Crown Free Church was laid in 1897, a year after a preaching station was established in the Crown area. Great deliberations took place as to whether it was to remain a preaching station or become a church and finally concluded when the first minister was inducted in 1899. Four years later the building was completed, but without the spire because it was considered too costly at £1,000.

Queen Street Church

This church, which originally started out in Queen Street in 1837, was a simple barn which was later used as a school before being converted into houses and demolished in the 1960's. The second one was actually in King Street, built in 1864 in the Norman Revival style it eventually became a skating rink and then a warehouse. In 1868 a new manse was built in Kenneth Street, which backed onto the Church in King Street. The final version is now situated in Huntly Street and was built about 1895 by Pond MacDonald. Built in Italian Baroque style it has a tower with an ogee-conical spire and an impressive flight of steps leading to the entrance. At one time it had a lovely interior with an excellent pulpit. In 1971, the congregation joined with that of St Mark's West Church to form the Trinity Church and the Queen Street Church was sold. The church is now used as a the Funeral home of D. Chisholm &Son.

St Mary's and St Ninian's Roman Catholic Churches

It is documented that in 1810 a small congregation, mostly Gaelic speaking, assembled to celebrate Mass in a room in Margaret Street, known generally as "….. a place where Lord Lovat and the tinkers worshipped." We next hear of the group, seventeen years later, when St Mary's was established as a Mission. By 1831, the Margaret Street building was in a ruinous condition and the Catholic Directory reported that "……the poverty of the congregation is an obstacle to its being repaired or rebuilt." But by 1835 the Catholic Church had announced that it would build a new church in Inverness, and two years later St Mary's was opened; the first Catholic place of worship to be built in Inverness since the change of religion in the 16th century. The Gothic facade of the church, with the curious crocheted pinnacles and open parapets, may be asserted to be the finest example of revived Gothic of that period. According to the Inverness Courier (1837) the Architect was a Mr Robertson from Elgin. and is a good example of the Catholic Revival style.

By 1959 the congregation had swelled sufficiently for an additional church to be built. A house on Culduthel Road was purchased and converted into what is now St Ninian's.

St John's Episcopal Church

This church originally started out as a church on the Maggot Green and, at the beginning of the 19th century, moved to the north end of Church Street not far from Dunbar's Hospital and on the same side. In 1839 it then moved further along Church Street to beside the Market Hall entrance and was built in the Gothic style. Like St Mary's Catholic Church this one was also designed by Robertsons of Elgin and had some almost identical features. It also had a fan-vaulted roof with a tower which was incomplete. In 1853, when Bishop

Eden's Mission Chapel opened in Academy Street, the congregation of St John's split, and when the Inverness Cathedral was consecrated in 1874 the congregation split once again with many families leaving to support the Bishop. The Academy Street building was demolished in 1903 and the site used as a garage for a while; thereafter it became an auction room before being demolished in favour of an office block.

The struggling congregation then moved to its present location on Southside Road, to a new building on the site of the former Mission Church of St Columba, which was an outreach church of the Cathedral.

North Free Church

The original North Free Church was replaced by this one which is situated on Bank Street across Church Lane from the Old High. Built, in 1893, in the Gothic Revival style by architect Dr Ross the lines of the sides and buttresses of the tall spire (the highest in Inverness) contrasts unflatteringly with the Old High Church. The formation of the Free Church in 1843 saw a small congregation of members worship in the Wesleyan Church in Inglis Street for a period until the church was built, which only took seven months according to the records, although this is difficult to believe. Services were in English, with the East and North Churches retaining Gaelic services. Two years later the Free Church held its Assembly in a pavilion in Bell's (Farraline) Park where 2,500 members attended.

Methodist Church

John Wesley first visited Inverness in 1764 when he preached to a full High Church at an evening service. Six years later he repeated the task and that same year the Methodist Society rented a room off Academy Street for their use. In 1777 they appointed their first minister and the next seven years saw Wesley visit another twice and preach in the town. Their congregation grew in number and in 1797 they moved to a site at the corner of Academy Street and Inglis Street where they remained for the next 125 years. Situated in the middle of the north side of Union Street, opposite Lombard Street, a building once stood which was twice destroyed by fire. Initially it had shops on the ground floor and a Music Hall on the first floor but in 1898 it burned down. Rebuilt the following year, the Wesleyan Methodist Church moved into the first floor in 1922, but it too was burned down in 1961. The congregation met in the Town Hall and then the La Scala Cinema before moving into their new building in Huntly Street in 1965.

Trinity Church

The history of this church is somewhat complicated. Inverness Trinity Church came into being on the 11th May 1977 with the opening and dedication of the refurbished St. Mark's site. The congregation was formed as a result of the Union of Inverness Queen Street church with the congregation of Inverness Merkinch (St. Marks) in 1971 on the retirement of the minister of the Queen Street church. The former Queen Street Congregation was formed in 1837 when a church was built in Queen Street. The church then moved to King Street in 1864 and to Huntly Street/Balnain Street in 1869. In 1868 a new manse was built in Kenneth Street, which backed on to the Church Building in King Street, and this is now the manse of the United Congregations. The former Merkinch St. Mark's Congregation arose from a Mission Station created in 1861 and the building was completed in 1863. In 1866 the Mission was established as a Church Extension Charge. In 1939 a Hall was built in Thornbush Road as a Church extension designed to have a Church building added on the site, connected to the hall. This did not materialise due to the outbreak of World War II, so it became known as the Hall Church. The united church was first called St. Mark's (Queen Street and Merkinch) and it was decided that the church should be under one roof within seven years. This was achieved in six, with the opening of the refurbished and extended building in Huntly Place in 1977, when it was agreed to change the name to Inverness Trinity, as the three previous Congregations had become one. In 1982 a new hall, store and toilet accommodation was completed and a further extension was added in 1986 to provide a small meeting room and store.

St Michael and All Angels Church

This church has its origins on the east side of the River Ness, as the Chapel of the Holy Spirit on the Maggot Green. It began in 1877 when Canon Edward Medley, newly arrived on the clergy team of Inverness Cathedral, noticed "the overwhelming respectability of the congregation of the Cathedral, with scarcely a poor person amongst its numbers". He decided that something should be done and so, with the encouragement of Bishop Robert Eden, he began a church school in a rented cottage on the Maggot Green. Soon, so many children wanted to come to the classes, the cottage and an adjacent one had to be purchased to accommodate them all. By 1881 a chapel had been created in one of the cottages and the Bishop gave it the dedication of "The Mission Chapel of the Holy Spirit". Five years later, in 1886, money was raised to build a stone church in Factory Street, close to the Maggot Green and, around the same time, Canon Medley left Inverness to return to Norfolk. His work was continued by the clergy who followed him at the Chapel of the Holy Spirit – Bishop Eden himself after he retired in 1886 as Bishop of the Diocese; Father William Wilson; Father John Fergus and Father William Lachlan Mackintosh, who began his 35 year ministry there in 1891.

The area around the Maggot Green was subject to flooding from the River Ness and gradually the people moved to drier ground causing population growth on the west bank of the river. In 1902, when Canon Mackintosh was Rector, it was decided that the church should move too. Between 1903 and 1904 the building was dismantled stone by stone and taken across the river along with much of the internal furnishings, where it was rebuilt and consecrated as Saint Michael and All Angels on its present site in Abban Street under the guidance of architect Alexander Ross. One could say, therefore, that the church literally followed its people. A new High Alter was designed by Sir Ninian Comper, the well-known church architect, who took an interest in the church because his father, Reverend John

Comper, had been a Mission Priest in Inverness. During the time of the re-siting of the church, the congregation met in the Queen Street Church (now Chisholm's Funeral Directors). Some 20 years later, in 1923, Sir Ninian made further extensive improvements to the church where his influence is much in evidence throughout. Since its move across the river the church has had seven Rectors, three of whom each served for more than 30 years. Sir Ninian's famous signature of a strawberry can be seen in the window of the archangels, a memorial to Canon Mackintosh, and is also carved on the wooden font cover. He chose the strawberry as his signature in honour of his father who died whilst distributing strawberries to the poor in Aberdeen. It is interesting to note that Sir Ninian also designed windows in many churches throughout the UK including Westminster Abbey.

The church was extensively restored in 2002 with assistance from the Lottery Heritage Fund and Historic Scotland.

Chapter 7

Streets and Walks

The City of Inverness does not, in its architecture alone, overtly provide much evidence of its historic past, although there are many grand buildings still in existence. The ravages of destruction and rebuilding over the centuries, and particularly in the 1960s and '70s, have taken their toll on much of the past architectural beauty of the City. Replacing, in some cases, much of what was historic and appealing with that which is unattractive and ill fitting with the surrounding architecture. But, if one knows where to look, and takes the time to do so, there is still much to be discovered, and in doing so a wealth of antiquity can be opened up to the discerning viewer. If one carefully walks through the streets of the city looking upwards to the second storey of the buildings, and upwards, then one will see exactly what I mean.

A Royal Burgh since the 12th century, capital of the Highlands and holding an honourable place in the annuls of Scottish history, Inverness has much to offer the visitor as well as those who reside here. In times past it was the seat of justice from which the Highlands was governed as well as an outpost of Royal authority; more recently being the centre for development throughout the Highland area. The City's innate beauty is much enhanced by the River Ness and the way in which it winds its way through the City en route to the Firth. One can walk along the riverside on Ness Walk and Ness Bank in relative peace and quiet, and yet only be a few minutes from the busy City centre. I have (in my younger days) spent many a pleasant evening standing fishing in the river, around the "Little Isle Pool", with (in the distance) the Cathedral on my left and the Castle up on my right, coloured by the fading light of the sun, enjoying the beauty of my home town and realising why it was that I returned to settle here. It is on evenings such as these that one realises what a beautiful City Inverness really is. It is a pity that more of us do not make the effort, and take the time, to understand and enjoy it.

Having explored the City's early growth and development, and looked at the influence Education and the Church have had on its evolution and expansion, in this chapter I intend to convey the reader around the City exploring the streets and looking at what evidence remains of its historic past. Perhaps, on our journey around the City, you will allow me a little poetic licence at times, and forgive me for slipping into the past and referring to people and places which are no longer visible.

Before we begin the journey let us travel back in history to Medieval times. Do not imagine that the streets of the town looked anything like they do now. The houses would have been poorly assembled and built without regard for planning conformity or position, hence they would have been arranged in a "higgledy-piggledy" fashion and not in rows along a street – sometimes even jutting out into the roadway to form an obstruction. Most houses were low built of rubble and timber, thatched with turf or heather, and being of such poor construction that the gaps between the planks afforded little privacy between one room and another. The town merchants would have had "forestair" houses on two floors. The lower floor being their shop, probably with an earth floor, and the upper one being the dwelling. A wooden staircase would have led from the outside front of the house to the upper floor, there being no interior access from one floor to the other. The narrow streets, wynds and passageways would have had dungheaps and human excreta lying around as well as pigs and other livestock running wild through them. Manure from the stables or sties attached to many of the houses more often than not was just heaped onto the road and left to wash away in bad weather despite a law to say it had to be removed within 24 hours. These conditions were a haven for vermin which lived in the walls of the houses and the thatch of the roofs. In 1714 the Council employed a scavenger to keep the streets clean at £4 per year. By 1738 the streets were being cleaned free of charge in order to obtain the dung for manure by Robert Paterson of Bught. When Cumberland's soldiers were stationed in Inverness there were an additional 500 mounted troops contributing to the mess on the streets and extra sweepers were employed to keep the streets clear. The Council soon became aware that there was potential in the muck and having put the dung collection out to roup they promptly paid off the street cleaners thus saving a tidy sum annually. Notwithstanding, in the mid 19th century it was stated that it was a disgrace to Inverness that there were private slaughter houses existing all over the town, with the resulting stench in the streets.

With the passage of time, through the 15th and on into the 17th century, more conventionality would have entered into the building of dwellings around the main streets, which would have had a series of vennels, wynds and closes threading between the buildings, leading to courtyards and enclosures. They would still have been mere thatched cottages, with here and there a town mansion in the Flemish style belonging to one of the landed gentry. Don't forget that MacDonald of the Isles twice burned Inverness in the early 15th century so townspeople would have been wary of constructing an elaborate dwelling place for fear of it being destroyed. Windows would have been few and far between and none would have had glass in them, although some might have had shutters to keep out the cold wind. Rubbish would have been lying everywhere and rats commonplace. It is generally thought that the Duke of Cumberland, whilst stationed here after Culloden, was the first to order the streets to be swept clean on a regular basis, but as can be seen from the above, the Council had had it done some 30 years before his unwelcome arrival.

The streets themselves were simply constructed of compacted dirt which was often thick with mud and faeces, there being no drainage system. Although no pavements existed the centre of the road often had a line of stones for walking on in order to keep people clear from the filth on the streets. It was not until the latter part of the 17th century that the streets were levelled and paved. Rank clearly took precedence for the right to walk on the stone path because in 1565 the chief of the Gunn Clan was executed for not giving way to the Regent of Moray on the crown of the road. Street lighting was nonexistent and hence it was unsafe to move about after curfew without a lantern, both from the point of view of falling into the mire and also from the danger of being robbed. After curfew was rung out by the Old High Church each household had to provide a male for curfew watch. Some patrolled the streets whilst others were sent to Ballifeary and Clachnaharry to keep watch for marauding raiders from the clans – and others, who were not required that night, often retired to the warmth of a tavern to enjoy themselves.

The 18th and 19th centuries saw great improvements in the state of the streets and the buildings as well as the introduction of planning into the development and expansion of the town, although this was not always strictly adhered to. Thus the foundations of the City were laid and its people began to build and prosper from trade, industry and commerce, or at least some of them did.

The first streets of the town would certainly have centred on the early major buildings such as the Castle, the Blackfriars' Friary and the Parish Church. That would make Castle Street and Church Street the earliest, and later these would have been followed by High Street and Bridge Street, which would have lead to the river crossing.

126

Thereafter, the development of buildings would have determined the where the streets appeared. It is safe to imagine that the square enclosing the River Ness, Friars' Lane, Academy Street and High Street would have constituted the main part of Inverness, with a spur going off Castle Street. This then is where we should begin our journey.

Castle Street

Archaeological excavations in the late 20th century found evidence of human habitation in this area of the town as long ago as 7,000 B.C. It is likely that they were nomadic peoples and probably did not remain long in the area, although whatever it was that attracted them here also proved equally strong centuries later when other peoples populated the area. The construction of a castle on its present site would certainly have seen the first development of the town and the beginnings of dwellings seeking the protection of the castle's inhabitants. The formation of a street would quickly have followed and at this time Castle Street was called "Doomsdale" or "Overgait", its present name not coming into effect until around 1675. The name Doomsdale arises because there was a court held at the top of Castle Street, therefore the accused had to travel the length of the street, from the Tolbooth on Bridge Street, to be tried and then to await their judgement, or doom. Also, the first town gallows was situated somewhere around Muirfield and those who were condemned had to walk along the street to meet their fate. As the town grew so also did the street, and although nothing much in the way of important building would have existed prior to the MacDonalds burning the town in 1410 and 1429, thereafter it is recorded that both Robertson of Inshes and the Laird of Nairnside had houses on it. The Robertsons had property there from 1448 until the 1700's. Bridge Street and Church Street would both have had their share of important buildings at this time due to the proximity of the

Castle and the Exchange. In 1508, it is reported that a stone built house existed on Castle Street, probably one of the few in the town at that time.

As far as trade and commerce is concerned Castle Street was host to a range of different businesses in its time. The Laird of Nairnside had a brewery kiln alongside his residence and another brewer, called Martin Waus, was known in Castle Street in 1564. In 1757, Raining's School was built at the top of the stairway, originally called Barnhill Vennel but later called Raining Stairs, which leads from Castle Street to Ardconnel Street (which was originally called Barnhill, or Back of the Town). Much later, in 1775, the first bank in Inverness, a branch of the Bank of Scotland, was built in Castle Street; being followed in 1838 by the Caledonian Bank which later moved to High Street. The Post Office opened in 1790 at number 32, and passers by would have seen the post coach leave for Aberdeen every day until the Post Office moved in 1810. The recruiting station stood at the back of the town hall and was home to Sergeant Simon Fraser, who enlisted nearly a whole regiment in his time, and also to Red Rory the piper, who was very partial to a dram and who eventually perished of cold in the Crimea. Throughout its time the street has also played host to Myrtle's bakery; Forbes the Chemist; MacTavish the Ironmonger; J. MacNeill, the umbrella maker and repairer; and C. and J. MacDonald the fleshers. There were shops belonging to a cartwright, painter, stoneware merchant, draper, bookseller and stationer. Loch Fyne herring could be purchased at J. P. Brodie's in half firkins, firkins and quarter barrels. Alexander Smith had a hairdresser's shop and he was also the first person to introduce photography to Inverness. The Inverness Herald had its office there and the street also contained the residence of Phineas MacKintosh, four times Provost of the town. The "armourers and glovers" seemed to centre their trade in Castle Street, undoubtedly because of their proximity to the Castle.

The buildings at the bottom of the street, opposite the Town Hall were demolished in 1867 to make way for the Y.M.C.A. which had the three statues of Faith, Hope and Charity placed on the top. All to be demolished less than 100 years later for construction of the present building – another dreadful example of demolishing a wonderful building to replace it with a monstrosity. That same corner witnessed the erection of the first set of automatic traffic lights in Inverness. Until 1932 houses lined both sides of Castle Street, but that year saw a major landslide take place on the west side of the street.

Whilst cracks in the retaining wall, built by General Wade, and which supported the Castle Hill, were under investigation, the wall collapsed seriously damaging the houses and destroying the St Columba Church Mission Hall which had only been built several months previously. The remaining buildings on this side of the street, save the Town House, were demolished in the 1960s with the steep slope of the Castle Hill having now reverted to its original defensive function from the Middle Ages. Alongside these buildings ran a series of old closes connecting the street to the Castle Wynd. One, called Aboyne Court, was named after the Gordons of Huntly and Aboyne, because of their connection with the castle, and was later re-named Craggie's Close after John Fraser of Craggie. Others were called Macallan's, Scott's, Watson's, and Robertson's. Although a great deal of the east side of Castle Street has been rebuilt since the 1930s a few 18th century houses still remain.

In 1978 some of the buildings at the foot of the Rainings Stairs, opposite the Town Hall, were demolished. This led to excavations the following year, during which the original, and wider, cobbled road surface of Doomsdale was uncovered. In addition, the foundations of four early 13th to mid-15th century wood and wattle-and-clay buildings were found. There was evidence to suggest that these buildings had been destroyed by fire in the early part of the 15th century with subsequent rebuilding. Was this the work of the Lord of the Isles when he burned the town in 1410 and 1429, one wonders? A further discovery of Mesolithic flints pointed towards a settlement in this part of Inverness around 4000 B.C.

At the top of Castle Street, where the road forks into Old Edinburgh Road and Culduthel Road, stands Ardkeen Tower, which was built in 1834 and which I have described in Chapter 4. Diagonally across from it, on the corner of Old Edinburgh Road and Gordon Terrace, once stood Viewhill House, now a derelict building, which was built by Joseph Mitchell the son of John Mitchell who was Thomas Telford's Superintendent of Roads. For many years Viewhill House was a Youth Hostel but several years ago closed its doors and was boarded up. It was then purchased by a local builder with a view to turning it into flats, but alas in September 2007 it was mysteriously set on fire and irreparably damaged. Between then and the time of writing several schemes have been put forward for both its development and its demolition, although none have come to fruition. One current proposal, which I thoroughly approve of, is to restore and convert the property into 8 serviced apartments, with a permanent exhibition on the work of engineer Joseph Mitchell within the entrance hall, by the Highland Historic Buildings Trust. One hopes that it will come to pass.

Despite the fact that there were houses and businesses, including a brewery, on Castle Street the only way of obtaining water was to carry it from the river. In 1829, a reservoir was built at the top of Castle Street opposite Viewhill and water pumped up to it from the river, although Parliamentary approval had been obtained in 1808 to take water from Leys to serve the town.

At the bottom of the Castle Brae, where the Baptist Church (built in 1932) now stands, was the Overgait Port. It is here that the street was at its narrowest and this formed the gateway to the south, by way of Ness-side and Dores and also by Muirfield to Strathnairn and Strathdearn.

Bridge Street

With the exception of the Steeple and a couple of adjacent buildings running towards the river, this street has been wholly rebuilt – and most people would agree certainly not for the better, at least architecturally. Most of the demolition took place from the late 1950s through the 1960s and was carried out in order to widen Bridge Street, formerly called Brig Gait, and Bridgend, which was originally a very narrow street running down towards the river, and remained so even after it was first widened in 1817. At one time it contained several beautiful buildings as well as some town houses, almost all of which have now gone.

The south (or Castle) side of the street was part of the Royal Castlehill and was not built on until medieval times, probably because of the defensive slope. At that time the main access to the castle was from the town centre up Castle Wynd and through the castle gates. By the 16th century, some houses were beginning to appear on this side of the street and construction on this site continued through to the early 19th century, with some of the newer buildings retaining features from the earlier ones. Prior to demolition work in the 1960's this side of the street contained houses with closes leading to an occasional courtyard at the rear as well as larger buildings. The Albion Hotel once stood at number 11 with stairs leading up to it and an attractive courtyard, whilst the house next to it had a 16th century barrel-vaulted basement. Alongside was another building with a turnpike stairway which led to the upper floors. Further down the street, at number 23, was the Workmen's Club, built in 1871 by the architect John Rhind. It was a fine building with an attractive classical frontage. Between it and the adjoining building was a vennel called Watt's Close which led to Watt's Hotel, one of the town's few temperance hotels. It was in this area, during the rebuilding, that the base of a small round tower was discovered and is thought to have been part of the medieval defensive outworks of the castle.

At the bottom of the street stood the town house of the Robertsons of Inshes. This building projected out into the thoroughfare and also restricted access to the riverside so much that it was demolished in the 18th century. It was here, at the Laigh Council House, that the Town Council met, having previously met in the Parish Church. From here they moved to the first Town House in the late 17th century. Later, three two-storey houses were built on this site, facing the river, on a short street called Gordon Place which is now part of Castle Road. This road was constructed when the castle retaining wall was built in 1800 to replace a pathway along the riverside. A century later these buildings were replaced by a new Castle Tolmie, the previous one having been across the street on the corner of Bank Street, but it too was demolished for road improvements for the new bridge in 1959.

The original Castle Tolmie was thought to have been erected in 1678 for a Fraser family, since it had elaborately carved "fraises", or strawberry flowers, from the Fraser family coat of arms, in the stonework to the attic windows. Like the Robertsons of Inshes house, it projected out onto the road and restricted access to the river and along the riverside, a situation which was rectified in 1794 when the riverbank was widened and Bank Street formed. The house was demolished when the new bridge was being built after the flood in 1849. Slightly further up the street stood Queen Mary's House, one of the most historic in Inverness until it was sadly demolished in 1968.

131

Much altered during its lifetime this house was home to several wine and spirit merchants from the late 18th century until its demolition.

Still further on up the street is the Old Courthouse and beyond that the Steeple, both of which are fully described in Chapter 4. The courthouse and jail were first built on this site in 1732, prisoners having been locked in the Steeple prior to that. Some 50 years later, in 1787, a new jail was erected taking two years to complete, and an inscription stone to the erection can be seen in the Museum. This three storey Georgian fronted building is the one we see today although the ground level was altered in 1853 and converted into shops, the upper levels being used as offices. One end of the building is the Gellion's Hotel, named after the Gellion family who owned the hotel for the latter half of the 19th century. Careful inspection will show that there is a narrow close which runs from Bridge Street to form a link with Church Street, and which once formed an access to the rear of the hotel. The Steeple on the corner of Bridge Street and Church Street occupies a significant central position in the town, which reflects its importance. A steeple or tolbooth has stood in this position since around 1436 and, fortunately, has managed to escape the developers' 'axe' on more than one occasion. Spanning some 570 years of history, this edifice has been altered several times, and also rebuilt; the present 200-year old Steeple is the City's finest Georgian building.

<u>Church Street</u>

Originally called Kirkgate, then Kirk Street, before becoming Church Street, this is one of the oldest streets in Inverness. It probably owes its existence, at least initially, to the fact that it led from the Castle to the Parish Church and the Blackfriars' Friary, as well as to a ford over the river near the Friars' Shott.
It is here that the Friars could once be seen fishing for salmon in the river, their net no doubt catching sufficient numbers of fish to supplement their meagre diet. The fishing for salmon continued for several centuries after that on a commercial basis, both around the Friars' Shott and also at the mouth of the river. When the tide turned and the salmon started to enter the river a flat bottomed 'cobble'

would be rowed out from the Shott, with a man paying out a seine net from the rear, until it had almost crossed the river, then, using the current, the cobble would circle back across the river to a point slightly downstream from the Shott with the fish being caught in the resulting net bag. The cobble would then be beached and the end of the rope attached to a winch, called a 'crab', which would be used to haul in the catch.

There would have been houses on Church Street from an early date and they would probably have been owned by people of a "higher class". The working class people would have lived further away from the town centre. Their houses would have been smaller and cheaper. The Church Street houses would have been quite large, probably with servants quarters and a basement. Although most of the old buildings of any import are long gone from Church Street there are still a few remaining ones which are well worth exploring, including Abertarff House, Bow Court and Dunbar's Hospital all of which have been described in Chapter 4.

On the corner of Baron Taylor's Street, initially called Back or Black Vennel, and fronting on to Church Street, once stood the Northern Meeting Rooms. This large and somewhat plain building, built in 1790, had a columned portico which projected over the pavement. The Northern Meeting had been founded in 1788 and the construction of this building saw assemblies, banquets and balls which were second to none, not just in the Highlands but also much further afield. For nearly two centuries it provided the highlight of the "season" for Highland society, occasionally attracting members of the Royal family. The interior was lavishly decorated in great contrast to its exterior, yet befitting the type of occasions which were hosted there. It was demolished in 1963 and the beautiful chandeliers which hung in the ballroom are now to be found in the Town House. Opposite, on the corner of Bank Lane, formerly an extension of Back Vennel, stood the town house of the Frasers at number 23. A symmetrical Renaissance-style 18th century house it was sadly demolished in 1968 for a redevelopment scheme. Around 1830 it housed the Inverness Branch of the National Bank (which gave the lane its name) and had a small courtyard at its rear accessed from Bank Lane. It then became a solicitor's office before being knocked down. Across the Lane, on the north corner with Church Street (where the Ivy Restaurant now stands), was the Post Office from around 1820 to about 1840. Thereafter the building housed the Inverness Courier prior to its move to the bottom of Bank Lane. This Lane was also called School Vennel at one time due to the presence of a school situated at the corner of Bank Street and Bank Lane, where the Courier Office site was; fortunately this building has survived. Next door to this once stood the 19th century Parish Council Office with a columned, balustraded entrance porch and ogee dormer windows, but unfortunately it too was demolished in 1968.

Back on Church Street, next to the Post Office site, the two Masonic Lodges built a hotel in 1776, which was known as the Masons' Hotel. Some years later it was sold but the Masons continued to meet there until the hotel was demolished for rebuilding in 1966. In 1825 it had changed its name to the Caledonian Hotel, a name which remained, although the building was replaced, until recently. A hotel advert, published in 1893, boasted,

"This well-known First-Class Family Hotel is patronised by the Royal Family and most of the nobility of Europe. Having recently added fifty rooms, with numerous suites of apartments for families, and all handsomely refurbished throughout, it is now the largest and best appointed Hotel in Inverness, and universally acknowledged one of the most comfortable in Scotland"

Across the road, on the corner of Union Street, is a building designed by William Lawrie in 1863 and built in the Italianate style. When the site was being cleared for the construction of the building (a bank) the contractors found an old well, and it is reported that a well house once stood on this spot. Back across the street and further down is number 43 where once stood the town house of the Duffs of Drummuir, where Alexander Duff, Commissioner to the Estates for Inverness, and Lady Katherine lived. The house was demolished in 1843 and was more commonly known as Lady Drummuir's House (see Chapter 4). Adjoining this building was Cuthbert's Lodging, which belonged to David Cuthbert of Castlehill. The house was later owned and extended by Baillie Lachlan MacKintosh (a Jacobite Colonel) and his wife, before being demolished in 1865. On the opposite side of the street stood St John's Episcopal Church following its move from the bottom end of Church Street, near Dunbar's Hospital. The building was demolished in 1903 and the site used as a garage for a while; thereafter it became an auction room before being demolished in favour of an office block. At number 57 one finds a semi-circular stone arch which used to lead through to a flagstoned courtyard and an early 19th century house. This house, like many others on this side of Church Street, had its own orchard in a garden which reached down to the river. On the corner of Queensgate stood another town house, this one belonged to Baillie James Roy Dunbar of Dalcross and was built in 1699. The four dormer pediments which belonged to this house, demolished in 1900, were retained and incorporated into the present building.

Further down Church Street, on the north corner of Fraser Street, stands the former Commercial Bank building, now Hootanannay Café Bar. Next to it is the oldest secular building in Inverness, Abertarff House, built in 1593 as a town house and occupied, at various times, by the Shivas family of Kinmylies and Muirtown, the Warrands of Warrandfield and the Frasers of Lovat, it is a typical example of late 16th century building. The corble-stepped gables and the entry door of the tower show the influence of castellated architecture on town buildings of the time. On the opposite side of the street, at number 64, was the town house of the Frasers of Cromarty, later occupied by the Frasers of Bunchrew. Built in the Georgian style with a fine frontage it was sadly demolished in 1968. Next to it stood the Northern Hotel (about 1860) which changed its name to the Queen's Hotel towards the end of the 19th century before being purchased by the Cumming family and being renamed the Cumming's Hotel. This family owned the hotel for the first half of the 20th century and the name of the hotel remained until recently when it was refurbished and became The King's Highway. Further down, on the same side, is Bow Court built on ground gifted by Lady Drummuir to the Six Crafts or Incorporated Trades – Hammermen, Wrights, Shoemakers, Tailors, Skinners and Weavers - and to the Masons of Inverness. Across School Lane is Dunbar's Hospital, one of the most historic 17th century buildings left standing. Built by Alexander Dunbar of Barmuckety and Westfield, the house is of high architectural merit as described in Chapter 4.

On the opposite side of the street, on the corner of Church Lane (once called Church Vennel), stands the MacDougall Clansman Hotel. This was once the Free North Church manse and, on the same site, previously stood the medieval manse of the Vicar of St Mary's Parish Kirk. Further along on this side is the splendid looking Old High Church which stands on St Michael's Mound and overlooks the river. It is the town Parish Church and one sees it at its best when viewed from the Greig Street bridge. Next to it stands the Old Gaelic Church, latterly Greyfriars Free Church, which is now Leakey's book shop. Both these churches are fully described in Chapter 6. Further on, between Leakey's and Friars Street, once stood a plain fronted 19th century building which was demolished for street widening in 1975. Originally called Lowe's Building it was used as a drill hall for the Inverness Volunteer Companies after 1867 before becoming the Old Technical School in the 1890's. It was closed in 1937 when the new Technical School opened in Montague Row.

High Street and Eastgate

The most important building on High Street is the Town House which is a fine example of ornate Victorian Gothic architecture, the history of which is given in Chapter 4. Built in 1878 it has a splendid interior which boasts several fine paintings, portraits and busts, mostly by Scottish artists. Originally the site housed two buildings. One, on the corner of Castle Wynd, dated from 1630 and belonged to Forbes of Culloden before it became the Horns Hotel. This was the hotel that the Duke of Cumberland occupied, along with the Town House, as his headquarters following the Battle of Culloden. It also played host to Bishop Forbes during his Episcopal Visitation in 1770 and it was here that Boswell and Johnson stayed in 1773. Later the hotel changed its name to the Ettles Hotel, and in 1787 played host to Robert Burns when he visited Inverness. Another change of name, in the 19th century, saw it called the Commercial Hotel.

A larger building, standing next to it on the corner of Castle Street, was the 17th century town house of Lord Lovat. It was sold to the Council by David Cuthbert of Drakies and later demolished, along with the Commercial Hotel, to make way for a new Town House in 1878. The building was completed in 1882 and still stands today with the exception of a rather grand turret which once stood in the centre of the roof, but which was removed leaving only the base. To the left of the Town House entrance, and attached to the wall, is the Merkat Cross which was transferred there from the previous Town House building. First mentioned in 1456, the Cross originally stood in the middle of High Street (where the markets took place) but was destroyed during a clan raid in 1600. It was then given a new shaft and positioned on the Exchange outside the Town House. Street improvements in 1796 saw the Cross moved yet again to the front of the old Town House from where it was moved to its present position having been restored in 1900.

Incorporated into the base of the Merkat Cross is the Clachnacuddin Stone which at one time stood in the street, but the passage of time saw it vandalised (for the best of reasons – as will be explained later) and it was moved under the Forbes Fountain which stood outside the Town House. This fountain was presented to the town by Dr G. F. Forbes but was dismantled, during improvements to High Street, and a truncated version re-erected in Cavell Gardens. At that time the Clachnacuddin Stone was built-in to the base of the Merkat Cross where it can now be seen. Whilst largely ignored by most people today it was once beloved and respected by Invernessians. Those travelling to the four corners of the world would often chip off a piece of the stone to carry with them as a reminder of the town and would willingly identify themselves as "Clachnacuddin Boys". The name lives on by virtue of its identity with a local football team. Literally meaning "Stone of the Tubs" it was originally situated outside the Town House and used by local women to rest their washing tub on as they made their way to and from the river on washing day. Here they would stop and have a "blether", catching up on all the news with their friends and neighbours. Some people say that the stone has a pagan religious significance associated with baptism and also that it may have a prehistoric origin as a standing stone. Whether this is true or not still remains a mystery, although, personally, I think it is unlikely.

The Town House stands facing the Exchange, which for centuries was a focal point not just for the proclamation of events and happenings but also for celebration on special occasions. It was also where much of the town's business was conducted and once measured about 20 x 10 metres. When Lord Lovat married the Earl of Leven's daughter, in 1642, the Exchange was laid out with tables containing a generous spread for their entertainment. No doubt the 'common' townspeople saw none of it, though they probably watched with envy from nearby houses. This lavish exercise was repeated in 1650 when Montrose passed through the town on his way to Edinburgh to be executed. He was told by Provost Forbes, as he left, "My Lord, I am sorry for your circumstance", and he replied haughtily, "I am sorry for being the object of your pity". The Exchange was also a gathering point for townspeople when any Royalty visited the town, when parades or processions took place, when soldiers returned home from war, when jubilee celebrations were held and, more recently, at New Year when townsfolk gathered to "take in the bells". It also saw the darker side of life, however, and in 1746 the Duke of Cumberland gave orders for one Duncan MacRae of Kintail, suspected of being a spy, to be hanged from an apple tree growing in front of the Town Hall. Despite his protests of innocence, MacRae was stripped naked and left to hang on the tree for days until two beggars cut him down and buried him. According to local legend the tree never bore fruit again and eventually withered and died.

Across the street, on the corner with Church Street, stands the Athenaeum so called because it was a Literary Institute between 1815 and 1823. Originally built in 1812 and called Geddes's Building, this four-storey building was constructed in the Georgian style; the land was once said to have been owned, in the Middle Ages, by the Knights of St John of Jerusalem. The first floor was a meeting room at one time and adjacent to the windows can be seen Biblical texts inscribed on the stonework. Next to it stands a very dignified Classical building which was built in 1848, by architect Thomas MacKenzie of Elgin as the headquarters of the Caledonian Bank when it moved from Castle Street. This building, presently a restaurant/bar, is undoubtedly the most ornate and arguably one of the most attractive in Inverness. The ground floor has two splendidly carved archways at either end of the building and above is a grand portico with four fluted Roman Corinthian columns and two large urns. The columns support a massive pediment enclosing a group of richly sculptured allegorical figures which have been beautifully carved. The central figure is "Caledonia" holding the Roman fasces, a symbol of power, in her hand. To the left is "Plenty" pouring out the contents of a cornucopia, a reaper with an armful of corn and a shepherd and sheep; these figures are there to represent agriculture. To the right of centre is a figure representing the River Ness and also two figures rowing a boat; these are the symbolic representation of commerce. In 1907, the Caledonian Bank was taken over by the Bank of Scotland which remained in this building until 2004.

Back across the road again to the east corner of Castle Street and High Street. Here once stood another excellent architectural building, dating from 1868, which was well fitted to stand opposite the Bank of Scotland. Its tall Corinthian columns, balustrading, and bold classical appearance, complimented the Bank of Scotland building opposite and made an excellent corner piece for Castle Street. On the ground floor was MacKay's Clan Tartan Warehouse and above it the Y.M.C.A. Atop the building were three large statues known as Faith, Hope and Charity and they kept watch over all that happened in the Exchange for many generations. When the building was demolished in 1955 the statues were sold to a private collector in Orkney where they remained for many years only recently having been bought back from the owner.

The remainder of High Street, east of the junction with Castle Street, was originally called Eastgate until about 1900; with the present street we now call Eastgate being called Petty Street, until 1820, because it was here that the 'petty customs' were collected. Many of the buildings along both sides of High Street are fine, stone built 19th century Victorian structures, some more elaborate and ornate than others, and most with a bit of history attached to them. It would take too long to elaborate on each one individually so I will concentrate on the most historic of them. On the north side, at number 21, is a beautiful three-storey ornate Baronial Style building, built in 1878, for the Royal Tartan Warehouse and which has the Royal Arms carved on a central gable. Further along, at number 39, is a building erected in 1838 by Lord Lovat and some other lairds as the Union Hotel. It is from here that the stagecoach left for Aberdeen and Perth, as well as from the Caledonian Hotel, prior to the railway being built. During the building of this hotel workmen found part of a deer's horn, about 3 metres below the surface, which was covered in seashells, indicating that the sea had once reached this far into the town. From 1870 until 1978 it became the premises of the Highland Club, a social and residential organization used by local businessmen for lunch and by County Councillors for accommodation when attending Council meetings. The building next to it once housed the British Linen Bank and was substantially altered in the late 19th century with the addition of a new façade with Corinthian pilastrade, cornice and central pediment. Further east, between Inglis Street and Hamilton Street and facing onto Eastgate, is the old Clydesdale Bank building (formerly called the Town and Country Bank). This fine three-storey classical structure was built in 1845 and has a rounded corner entrance and an arched doorway. Hamilton Street was originally called Castle Raat (Roadway), the basis of the word 'Castle' is unknown but thought to refer, idiomatically, to some large house which once stood in the vicinity; its name was later changed to Theatre Lane because a Theatre was opened there in 1805.

In 1840, when a street called Hamilton Place (no longer there) was being constructed, the skeletons of a horse and its rider, wearing 17th century leather boots, were found in the ground near what once was the Eastgate entrance to the town. This does not mean, however, that there was once a 'Gate' or 'Door' which opened and closed in this part of the town as the 'gate', in Eastgate, refers to a way or street (gait). It is in the proximity of Hamilton Street that the old town ditch or 'fosse' was discovered during excavations in 1976, prior to the redevelopment of Eastgate. This ditch would have formed the first line of defence for the town and would have been supported by an inner, high timber palisade or 'pailing', which may have existed, at least in part, into the late 17th century. The ditch survived in this area until the 18th century and was used as a dump for refuse from the tanning works and the malt kilns as well as the town cess pit, hence the name "Foul Pool" which was sometimes used for this area. On hot days the smell must have been atrocious even to their accustomed noses.

On the opposite side of the street, at the east end, is the Market Brae Steps or Post Office Steps, so called because this is where the early 19th century Fish Market stood and also because the Post Office was sited just along from it at number 54, from 1844. This building,

140

started in 1843 and completed a year later, housed the Post Office until the new one was finished in Queensgate in 1890; it then became the Customs House – see Chapter 4.

Two vennels, Dr Grant's Close and the Meal Market Close, run from High Street through to Baron Taylor's Street (formerly Back Vennel, in the Middle Ages, and then Baron Taylor's Lane until the 1930's). The street was named after a lawyer, John Taylor, who owned a great deal of the property in the early 18th century and hence acquired the name "The Baron".

At the east end of High Street, opposite the Market Brae Steps, is Inglis Street which leads to Academy Street. Named after Provost William Inglis the street contains a number of notable 19th century buildings. On the east side is Hunter's Building, number 6; built in 1848 it is a good example of the Renaissance Style, while next to it is a Flemish Baronial Style building built in 1883. At the northeast end of the street once stood the Wesleyan Methodist Church with its striking rose window facing down Academy Street. The building was used by the Wesleyans for 125 years before they moved to Union Street in 1922. When road reconstruction took place in the 1970's the building was truncated and the rose window removed. Fortunately it is still in the keeping of the Town Council.

Academy Street, Union Street and Queensgate

Leaving Inglis Street and joining Academy Street, first laid out as New Street in 1765, one sees, directly opposite, the large area called Falcon Square, graced by a monument by local sculptor Gerald Laing, with the shopping centre beyond - which supports the Rotary Clock which was presented to the city by the Rotary Clubs of Inverness Culloden, Loch Ness and Inverness to celebrate the Rotary Centenary. This new replacement for a once much smaller square of the same name is one of the few modern 'improvements' which actually enhances the City, at least in my opinion, although it does seem to lack purpose at the moment. The building which stands on the square (housing Laura Ashley and Pizza Express) was dismantled and rebuilt at right angles to its original position using the same stone, and I think this also enhances the whole ambience of the area. Let's hope that the planners have, at last, wakened up to the importance of retaining the historical aspects of the City when changing and improving.

Prior to the arrival of the railway, the area east of here and as far as Loch Gorm was known as Dempster Gardens. Loch Gorm (The Green Loch) was a stagnant pool, often flooded at high tide, situated where Morrison's Supermarket is presently located in Millburn Road. It gave its name to the Lochgorm Inn, once situated beside the Cattle Mart, and also to a Furniture store on Millburn Road. It was in Dempster Gardens that any local feuds were settled by duelling, or other means, before the practice was stopped in the 1840s. Some twenty years later the area was built over and used as an industrial zone, catering for wholesale commerce and business connected with the new railhead. The narrow cobbled streets, containing warehouses and stores, were called First, Second, Third and Fourth Streets, all of which disappeared during the 1970s construction of the first Eastgate development works. First Street was also known as Washington Court, after the Washington Hotel on Hamilton Street, and the other three were usually collectively known as Dempster Gardens. Fourth Street was also known as Tobacco Street in the 1860s.

To the north of Falcon Square and facing onto Academy Street is a building with several steps leading up to it. This Georgian property was built in 1812, on the site of the old Inverness Brewery, by Sheriff-Substitute Edwards who had an area at the rear of the building, Edward's Court, called after him. It became the town house of the MacKintoshes of Aberarder, one of whom was twice Provost of the town, then of Colin Lyon MacKenzie, also Provost twice, and also of General John MacKenzie. It is the only remaining one of several similar residences, all with front steps and basements, which once stood on Academy Street.

Next to it is the entrance to the original Falcon Square and the way into the old Falcon Foundry, from which the square took its name, which was closed in the late 19th century. It is the office building of this old foundry which was demolished and then beautifully rebuilt on the new Falcon Square as part of the Eastgate development. The architects, Hurd Roland Partnership, have much to be proud of and, indeed, received an Inverness Civic Trust Award in 2005 for the project. At one time the square was the hub of the wholesale trade in

Inverness, and anything that people could eat, wear or use in their normal daily lives could be purchased there.

Continuing on, one comes to the old Station Hotel, now called the Royal Highland Hotel, situated on Station Square. Erected in 1859, this Italianate Style building's entrance was once centrally positioned, but alterations in 1898 included a new entrance, with Doric columned portico, positioned next to the Railway Station. The façade to the Station itself is relatively new and is, sadly, far less grandiose and imposing than the other buildings on the Square. Originally built by Joseph Mitchell in 1855 it blended in with the other buildings rather well, but was redesigned in 1968 in its present form. The Station *per se* has been much altered from the original layout for the Highland Railway devised by Joseph Mitchell and contains two plaques with coats of arms. One has the initials of the Inverness and Aberdeen Joint Railway with an inscription and the date 1858, and the other has a list of the Railway Directors. There is also a carved stone bearing the arms of Perth and Inverness and inscribed "Highland Railway". The north side of the Square contains the three-storey building which was the offices of the Highland Railway. Built in 1875 in Moray sandstone, the building has a beautifully ornate exterior and the entrance has Roman Doric columns. The Square also contains the statue of a Cameron Highlander, erected in 1891 in Portland Stone, having been sculpted by a Londoner, George Wade. The statue commemorates the men of the 79th Queen's Own Cameron Highlanders who died in the Egypt and Sudan Campaigns of 1882-85, and was unveiled by Lochiel, 24th Chief of Clan Cameron, on 14th July 1893 in front of a large crowd of townspeople, with the Square surrounded by the Queen's Own Cameron Highlanders. For many years thereafter it was surrounded by Hansom cabs as they waited to pick up a fare from the railway and the Station Hotel.

On the opposite side of the street from Station Square stands the old Royal Hotel (formerly Christie's Royal Hotel), which now houses the Clydesdale Bank. Built in 1864 it has a splendid Italianate façade and a columned entrance porch with a French style pavilion roof above the wallhead. Next to the hotel is the main entrance to the Victorian Market, or Arcade, which has a somewhat unique central position in the town with four entrances leading from each of the streets which surround it. The Market itself was originally built in 1869, by William Lawrie, and this triple arched Academy Street entrance has Corinthian columns with animal carvings on the keystones of the arches. The entrance and side windows are topped with balustrading and urns on two distinct levels making it a rather splendid entrance. The Arcade was rebuilt in 1891 following a fire, with the Union Street entrances being designed by Alexander Ross and MacBeth. The Market Hall and the Church Street entrance were built by John MacKenzie, Burgh Surveyor, whilst the Queensgate Arcade and entrance was designed by Duncan Cameron. The whole complex is an excellent example of Victorian design in pedestrian shopping, the architecture of which shows great character.

Opposite the Market entrance and slightly north of the Station Square (between the old Railway Offices and Strother's Lane) stands the original Royal Academy building at numbers 40-42. Built in 1792 to replace the Grammar School, it remained in use until 1896 when the Academy then moved to the Crown area before finally moving to its present Culduthel site. Unfortunately this was burnt down in late summer 2015. Behind the building was the school playground which was later built over and occupied by MacRae and Dick's garage before being reconstructed in its present form in the late 1990's. On the north corner of Strother's Lane and Academy Street stands the remains of the old La Scala cinema, now closed and reconstructed into office accommodation and flats, but once bustling with cinemagoers desperate to watch their favourite heroes and heroines on the 'silver screen'. Originally built in 1913, as Kelso's Cinema, it was constructed on the site of a house belonging to a prosperous merchant, Alexander Strother, who had the Lane named after him. The house fronted on to Academy Street around the late 19th century. From the 1970s for about 30 years, until the Riverside Screen opened in Eden Court, La Scala was Inverness's only cinema and was often filled to capacity with eager cinemagoers. In 1996, as it neared the end of its days, it hosted the world premier of "Loch Ness" starring Ted Danson and Joely Richardson. A celebrity audience including Bob Geldof, David Baddiel, Frank Skinner and Anneka Rice were watched entering the cinema by a large crowd of onlookers. When the Riverside Screen opened in 1998, however, attendances at La Scala tailed away and in January 2001 it opened its doors for the last time with a screening of "Casablanca". Thus ended the last of the Inverness cinemas, which had given countless hours of entertainment and pleasure to thousands of Invernessians over the previous century. Further along on the corner of Margaret Street is the East Church which was built in 1798 as a Chapel of Ease for the Old High Church. It was rebuilt in 1853 and extensively added to in 1897. Behind this church, on Margaret Street, where the East Church Hall now is, once stood the Secession

144

Church, erected in 1803. In 1820 it became a Roman Catholic Church but had its Chapel smashed by a "no popery" demonstration in 1829. This church moved to Huntly Street in 1837 as St Mary's RC Church.

Further up Margaret Street, past the recently rebuilt "Charlie's Café", is Farraline Park (once Bell's Park) and the bus station. Once a suitable site for a bus station, its recent renovation and re-instatement as one has done nothing to ease the transport difficulties in the City centre. When the Eastgate area was being redeveloped the bus station should have been re-sited there, and Farraline Park returned to a pleasant City centre park with associated restaurants, cafés and seating, where City centre workers could enjoy a quiet lunch break. Alas this is not to be – at least not yet. Standing in Farraline Park is one of the best classical buildings in the City – Dr Bell's Institution – which presently houses the Library. Designed by Archibald Simpson and built in 1841 in the Greek Revival style it has a central pedimented portico and Doric columns in Moray sandstone, with wreaths in the frieze instead of the usual triglyths. Dr Andrew Bell of Egmont, a Scottish educationist who developed the "Madras" monitoring system of instruction, was a Prebendary of Westminster who left his considerable fortune to educational institutes in Scotland. He bequeathed £10,000 to the magistrates of Inverness to fund a "charity" school and Dr Bell's Institute was built with the money. The present bus station was the playground of the school and the former Charlie's Café was one of the Gate Lodges to the grounds of the park. The school closed in 1937 and was amalgamated with the High School and Raining's School to form the Technical School. The building has had a number of uses since then including a theatre, police station and courthouse – a rather curious, but not inappropriate, mix of discipline and the arts! Behind the building stood the Inverness Reformatory or "Ragged School", built in 1858, until its demolition in the 1950s.

Returning to Academy Street, on the opposite side of the road is a large modern concrete block built in the early 1970's as an office block. From the late 1990's it lay empty for several years before being converted into a hotel. This ghastly building is flanked by much older, more attractive buildings, and stands on the site of the former Empire Theatre – once the Central Hall Picture House. Built in 1912 the Picture House was converted into a theatre, in 1934, following the destruction, by fire, of the town's Theatre Royal in Bank Street in 1931. As the town's only concert hall it was home to a multitude of acts and performers for 36 years before finally closing its doors in 1970 with a Gala Performance. For most of its last 20 years the theatre was managed by John Worth, who was himself a talented performer, and whose diligence and adroitness persuaded many excellent performers and shows to appear in Inverness. I was fortunate enough to have seen some, and was once at a performance of Lex MacLean where I laughed so much I nearly wet myself – the one and only time I found myself in that predicament I hasten to add.

Back across the street, on the corner of Rose Street, stands another Ross and MacBeth building, formerly known as the Rose Street Foundry, which stands on the site of the old Inverness Iron Works. Built in the French Renaissance style, in 1893, the gables have arched tympana decorated with coloured tile designs depicting various industrial activities. Sadly, it is being allowed to slowly decay with the inevitable loss of these wonderful decorations, unless something is done to stop it. In 1895, three local foundries and ironworks were amalgamated to form the Rose Street Foundry and Engineering Company, later to be called the A.I. Welders (where my father worked for many years). The remaining building was the offices of the company, the foundry itself closing down in 1992 and thereafter being demolished to make way for a supermarket. Rose Street, called after Rev. Robert Rose one time minister of the Old High Church, was originally the road along which herring was transported from the Longman Point to the town fish market, having been landed there by Black Isle fishermen. At that time it was called Scatgate (taxroad) because a "scat" or tax was levied on the fishermen's landings. The street was also known to local Gaels as the "gibbet street" (Sraid na Croiche) because it led to the public hanging site in the Longman.

The remaining buildings on both sides of the north end of Academy Street are not of major significance, although there is an interesting 18th century street-gable house (number 87), one of the last remaining in the City. Also worthy of note is the early 19th century two-storey terrace (numbers 91-107) featuring tripartite windows on the first floor. Houses like these would once have been more commonplace in the old part of the town.

Return to Station Square, where opposite it is to be found Union Street and some excellent examples of Victorian architecture. Forming a link between Academy Street and Church Street it was laid out in 1863 and follows the line of an old close called Ettles Court. The close was so named because of Ettles Hotel which stood there in the late 18th century. It was owned by a John Ettles who had once owned a hotel, of the same name, which stood on the Corner of Castle

Wynd next to the Town House. On the south side of Union Street, from the corner of Academy Street up to number 17, is an Italianate style three-storey building designed by William Lawrie in 1863. This elegant building is topped with a balustrade and most of it belonged, until recently, to Arnotts store.

Next to it, on the corner of Drummond Street, is the site of the United Presbyterian Church, erected there in 1864 and taken down in

1901 to make way for the present building, designed by William Carruthers and built for the Royal Bank. The architecture of this building, whilst in keeping with its neighbours, is clearly quite different. The United Church was not actually demolished, but rather it was removed to Alness and re-erected as a Masonic Lodge. On the opposite corner of Drummond Street and right up to Church Street is another magnificent building which was built as the Waverley Hotel, later called the Douglas Hotel. This is another of William Lawrie's buildings, dating from 1863, and originally it had a corner entrance. Virtually the whole of the north side of the street was designed by Alexander Ross and Joass with the buildings being a uniform three-storeys in height and sporting attractive balustrading. Built between 1863 and 1865 all these buildings, although individual in design, blend well together and collectively form a street of excellent architecture. This side of the street has, at its west end a beautiful corner building stretching partly down both Church Street and Union Street. Next to it is a large building stretching from number 46 to number 38, the rather grand arched entrance to which is midway along the building.

At the other end of the street, on the corner of Academy Street, stands the old Royal Hotel building, and next to it another rather grand design which stretches all the way up to the entrance to the Market, at number 22. This building had two entrances, one at number 10 (altered from the original) and the other at number 16. In between can be found a typical 1960s building which literally screams at the others in the street and looks totally out of place. The original 1865 building was a Music Hall, designed by Alexander Ross, but it burned down in 1898. Rebuilt the following year it became home to the Methodist Church in 1922, but was again burned down in 1961, after which the present building was erected.

There is a rather amusing story attached to this street and the two banks which once occupied buildings there. In 1975 an English firm was contracted to clean the stonework of the Royal Bank of Scotland, and in order to cause the least disruption the work was to be carried out on a Sunday – a plan which was frowned upon by the Church. The firm duly arrived, carried out the job and returned home. On Monday, however, on his arrival at the Bank, the Manager was less than pleased to see that nothing had been done. His wrath turned to amusement, however, when he noticed that the Bank of Scotland, just along the street, was sparkling clean. To the English firm's great embarrassment, and to the advantage of the Bank of Scotland, they had failed to differentiate between it and the Royal Bank of Scotland. The verdict of the more pious Invernessians was, "It serves them right for doing the work on the Sabbath."

The other street joining Academy Street and Church Street is Queensgate which was also laid out to a plan of Alexander Ross in 1884, when it was called Raigmore Street. On the north side, on the corner of Academy Street (numbers 2-8) is the old Royal Insurance Building. Built in 1894 in the Italianate style with arcaded shop fronts, the second floor windows have wrought iron railings on the balconies and more wrought iron atop the cornice of the roof. The entrance to the building is situated on the corner with Academy Street and on the top of the building, above the door, can be seen an emblem carved in stone with three lions in the centre and marked "The Lancashire Insurance Company". A similar building, built earlier in 1885 but without the stone carved corner piece, stands at the opposite end of the street on the corner of Church Street - at numbers 24-30.

Curiously enough it is in one of the offices of this building – number 28 – that Alexander Ross had his office. Between these two rather grand buildings once stood another equally ornate and majestic one which was built, by Ross of course, in 1888. It was the Post Office, built in the Italian Renaissance style in sandstone and well detailed, beautifully matching the buildings on either side and blending in with the others in the street. It took two years to complete and was damaged by an earthquake soon after its construction. It remained in use until 1966 when it was demolished and replaced by the present drab building which has no real character when compared to its neighbours. Why on earth the façade was not retained and the inside of the building altered to suit the needs of the time is a mystery to me, and no doubt to many others as well. On the opposite side of the street, on the corner of Academy Street, is another Ross building, numbers 1-13. This was built in the French Renaissance style but blends in very well with his other buildings. The remaining building on this side stretches all the way to Church Street and was erected around 1900 by W. J. Carruthers in contemporary English style. There is a rather obvious join to the two buildings between numbers 13 and 15, where two parallel cornice lines, half way up the building, and running towards Church Street, suddenly stop. That said, it is a very attractive building which once housed the Queensgate Hotel – the entrance to which can be seen at number 27. A fair part of this end of the street up to Church Street was rebuilt towards the end of the 20th century following a fire, and has been very sympathetically done.

The Glebe, the Maggot and the Longman

When the Blackfriars' Friary closed in 1567, land which had been used by the Friars to grow crops, and which lay northwest of the Friary, between Chapel Street and the river, as well as another "Green", was turned over to the town Parish Church. This became known as the Minister's Green, later being called the Minister's Glebe, giving name to Glebe Street. This Green should not, however, be confused with the 'Big Green' which lay across the river and stretched from Young Street to Abban Street. The Glebe was often used for recreational purposes but also had a Chapel dedicated to the Blessed Virgin Mary of the Green, which was usually called the Chapel on the Green, and it is this chapel which gave its name to Chapel Street and the Chapel Yard. The Chapel was very old and was certainly in existence in 1359, although it became ruinous after the Reformation (1560). The Church Manse was situated in a nearby street called Manse Place, which was renamed Gas Lane in the 19th century because the town's gas works stood there. The Chapel Yard served as a meeting place for town councillors long after the Medieval Chapel had disappeared. When Cromwell's army took the town the Chapel was destroyed and the stones later used in the construction of the Citadel, along with those of other ecclesiastical buildings in the area. The Chapel Yard has been a burial ground for several centuries – its origin probably being early to middle 16th century, although it could be older still. It contains the tombs and burial monuments of many notable old Inverness families, amongst them Fraser of Fairfield, Grant of Bught, Scott of Seabank, Inglis of Kingsmills, Forbes of Culloden and MacKintosh of Holm as well as the mausoleum of MacLeod of MacLeod (Clan Chief of Dunvegan). The earliest gravestone (still in existence) is for Hester Elliot (died 1604) who was the wife of the Minister from 1627-1635 and the great-grand niece of Mary Queen of Scots. In 1643 a Highland and an Irish Regiment were stationed in Inverness but the Parish Church and the Chapel were too small to accommodate them for services, so the Chapel Yard was used. A century later the Jacobites demolished some of the tombs belonging to the families of those who refused to declare for Prince Charlie. It is recorded that after the Battle of Culloden many of the

Royal Army were buried there, "in regular order two deep, with their officers at their heads." Much later, in the early 19th century, the Gaelic congregation used to assemble there on occasions when their church was too small to hold them. The burial ground was enclosed in 1784 although much of the present wall is 19th century. Entrance is by a gateway, built in 1795, leading off Chapel Street; the original arch of the entrance bore the motto, "Concordia Res Parvae Crescunt" (By Concord Small Things Do Increase). This cemetery is well worth a visit.

North of the Glebe and bounded by Shore Street and the river is an area known as the Maggot (Maggat), a very old name said to be a corruption of the name Margaret, there once being a chapel dedicated to St Margaret nearby. Another theory for the name is that it comes from the Gaelic "magh" (a plain, flat area). Whichever is correct there is no disputing that the delta of the river was originally much wider and the Maggot area would have been regularly flooded at high tide. The area was originally an island with the harbour situated on the north side in the Middle Ages. In 1530 James V granted a Charter to the Blackfriars in which the Maggot was described as an island. In the late 17th century it is recorded that a burial ground on the Maggot had its dead uncovered by high tides. A century later fishing boats could sail up to near Chapel Street, thus meaning that the Maggot was surrounded by water. One 16th century document refers to ships sailing up the river to lie at the "Stone of Inverness" which was probably a stone pillar situated in the Maggot.

By the middle of the 18th century the area had a number of "working class" houses built on it, which would have been of rough construction with thatched roofs. The people were attracted there because of the factories which had sprung up nearby in Glebe Street and Factory Street – a distillery, a thread manufacturer and a canvas and sailcloth factory. Later, when work in the factories became scarce, due to the changing economic climate, the area became rundown and fell into disrepute. One small, unpretentious building which faced onto the river was a schoolhouse presided over by Duncan MacKay, known as "Cripple Dunk." Although his pupils came from humble beginnings with no obvious advantages in life, his industrious teaching and their enthusiasm for learning turned a few into men with a future who ended their lives in much greater prosperity than they started out. The penny a week schooling fee was saved by many parents from their scanty earnings to enable their children to "learn and prosper", and to ensure that they had a good start in life very often paid great dividends, although the initial saving of it must have caused them great hardship.

Waterloo Place, formerly called Wellington Street, but renamed in honour of the Waterloo veterans of the town, once had several residences as well as a couple of Inns or Taverns. A house on the corner with Shore Street, now demolished, bore a tablet which read, "Be diligent working while it is day, the night cometh when no man can work". This is quite amusing since the Steam Generating Station, operated by the North of Scotland Electric Light and Power Company, produced electricity in the adjoining street, from 1905 to 1952, which clearly turned night into day for many workers. Further along the street towards the Waterloo Bridge is a small street of one storey Georgian terraced houses, called Portland Place. The houses have basements and a flight of steps leading to Roman columned porticos at the entrance doors. A date stone on the end house nearest to the bridge indicates that they were built in 1828.

The Waterloo Bridge was built in 1808 in timber, and because of the dark colour of the wood it was commonly known as the "Black Bridge." It was replaced by the present iron one, built in the Rose Street Foundry, in 1896. The bridge contains two plaques, one of which has the names of the engineers and contractors as well as the town coat of arms, whilst the other bears the names of the Provost and Town Council members of that time. Between here and the river once stood the Old Quay, the town's first proper harbour. Work commenced in 1675, using stone from the demolished Citadel, and took three years to complete. An earlier pier did exist around 1559 near Shore Street and was called the Auld Dyke or Churry Dyke (from curach for 'boat') but was not considered as a "harbour".

To the east lay the "Shiplands" or "Shipflats" adjacent to the Citadel area which once contained a farm of that name. During the late 18th and the 19th centuries the Citadel land was occupied by various industrial premises including a hemp manufacturer, a boat builder and a rope manufacturer. Between 1877 and 1930 a smallpox and cholera hospital existed there, the building being demolished in the 1960s. Slightly north of the Citadel was the pitch of the Citadel Football Club which had been founded in 1886 and was a founder member of the Highland League, along with the other three Inverness Clubs, in 1893. The Club was politely called the "Maroons" but less graciously named the "Sheep Bags" because of their ground's proximity to the slaughterhouse. They were a force to be reckoned with for most of their 50-year existence but increased travel costs saw the team "hang up their boots" around 1937. To the north east of the fort lay the area called "Lotlands", so named because the Town Council had 'lots' or 'feus' laid out there around 1770. Between the Citadel and the firth was an area of tidal islands and saltings known in the Middle Ages as the "Longman".

Around the middle of the 18th century the east bank of the river was built up to form an embankment thus preventing the area being flooded. This work was extended and by 1813 it had reached as far as blocking off the Lochgorm sea-inlet, thus ensuring that the whole Longman area was free of flooding. It was around this time, post 1800, that the hangman's "Gibbet Stance" was raised in this area, with the last hanging taking place in 1835. In the 1860's the Inverness Artillery Volunteers had a coastal battery and powder magazine in the Longman midst an area which by this time was mostly farmland. The Inverness Golf Club opened a 9-hole golf course here in 1893, prior to moving to their Culcabock site, and played here until 1939 when the Longman Municipal Aerodrome was enlarged as an RAF base during the Second World War. Two of the original hangers from this era still remain and are used as industrial buildings. The whole area now supports industrial buildings with the exception of the Inverness Caledonian Thistle Football Club.

Chapter 8

Communications

When one talks of communications, one thinks of a connecting route or link from one place to another, and when planning a journey one thinks, "How will I get there?" and, "How long will it take?" The answer to these questions nowadays, with our present transport systems, is probably, "Quite easily", and, "Not long". Go back several centuries in time, however, and the answer to these same questions would have been quite different indeed. Modes of transportation have, thankfully, changed and improved with the passage of time; starting out with the slow slog of foot travel and working through horse, coach, train, etc., to arrive at today's highly sophisticated and speedy methods of transportation. Of course, communication is not just concerned with the transportation of people. In earlier times, when the town was opening up to the outside world, merchants and tradespeople were also concerned with the transportation of goods into and out of the town, as indeed they still are. Even in those days the question, "How soon can you get it here?" would have been on the lips of every shopkeeper in the town. Improved speed of delivery, and the cost incurred, would have been as paramount then as it is today.

When nomadic travellers first arrived at the River Ness and looked for a crossing, they probably followed the animal tracks which led to and from the river, radiating out from it in all directions. From that day to this communication tracks have spread out from Inverness, widening and lengthening with the passage of time, bringing people to, and sending people from, the City in ever increasing numbers. The possible modes of transport slowly but inevitably increased as first the network of roads, then railways and finally the airport opened up the Highlands. Let us not forget the sea, however, which is one mode of transport where the numbers of travellers to and from Inverness has undoubtedly decreased over the years rather than increased. Let us now explore each one in turn and see how its impact has affected the City over the years.

Water

For centuries this was the easiest and cheapest form of transport, and was much used in all coastal towns and cities throughout the country. Inverness was no exception to this and, prior to the building of the Caledonian Canal, Inverness probably had closer links with the continent than it did with Glasgow and Liverpool. It is said that mountains divide people and seas unite them, and this was very much the case between Inverness and the east coast ports like Aberdeen and Leith.

In the City's early development one of the main thoroughfares was Church Street, not just because of the route to the Castle, from the Old High Church and the Blackfriars' Friary, but also because it led to the harbour and the lifeline of supplies brought in by ships on a daily basis. Cromwell probably chose the site of his Citadel for the same reasons – easy transportation of men and supplies to and from his fort. From the 17th century onwards ships have landed their goods in Inverness harbour for merchants and tradesmen alike, and have transported away the merchandise supplied to them for ports at home and abroad. In the first half of the 18th century Baillie John Steuart owned about a dozen ships, all less than 50 tons, with which he traded extensively both at home and abroad. Many of his merchant friends were in a similar position and altogether some three hundred ships must have been in the employment of these men. The vessels sailed wherever they could find trade – up the Pentland Firth; across the Minch to Stornoway; over the sea to Holland, Denmark, Norway and the Baltic ports; round Gibralter to the Mediterranean ports and the Adriatic. They generally sailed in convoy for fear of privateers from Sweden who were the scourge of the North Sea and the Baltic, and also from Moorish pirates who patrolled the Mediterranean and the Atlantic coasts of Morocco, Spain and Portugal. In addition, the ordinary perils of the sea took their toll on the shipping trade and it was not unusual for a merchant to suffer the loss of at least one ship a year, either lost or wrecked.

In 1717 one of Steuart's ships, the "Alexander", left Inverness with a cargo of herring to be sold in Cork. The vessel was then to proceed to La Rochelle, in France, for wine and brandy to take back to her home port. En route to Cork the ship was captured by a Swedish privateer commanded by an Englishman named Norcross, who started out with his prize for Gottenburg. Landing in France on the way home, Norcross was apprehended by the French authorities and sent to England. His crew sailed on without him and, with the "Alexander" in tow, headed for Gottenburg; but en route the Inverness lads attacked and overcame the Swedes landing the ships at a friendly Norwegian port. A Danish warship claimed the privateer and took her to Copenhagen, leaving the Inverness crew to sell their herring in the

Baltic before returning in triumph to Inverness in 1718. A century later piracy was still a problem on the high seas, but this time from American privateers, one of whom had a 200 ton vessel, the "Blockade of Rhode Island", which carried eighteen nine-pound guns, two twelve-pounders and one thirtytwo-pounder. She must have been a fearsome sight to see – especially if all you were trying to do was to take some salt herring to Ireland!

The term "Fair Trading" had a totally different meaning in the 18th century to that of the present day. In those days it meant smuggling, which was universally practised throughout Scotland. The 'war' with the Exciseman was seen as fair game and even gentlemen of rank and position joined in the smuggling trade with France, Holland and Spain. It is highly likely that Baillie Steuart and his friends were a part of this scene and just as likely that the Hanoverian officers who purchased the wine and brandy from them knew all too well that duty had not been paid on it. Wise merchants always had their ships insured against loss at sea but smuggled goods could not have been insured in the same way, so the loss of one of these ships was a costly business indeed. One supposes that profits from this trade must have been high enough to make the risk very worthwhile.

A pier was built in 1675 between the place where the Waterloo Bridge and the Railway Viaduct are now. The new Citadel Quay was built between 1725 and 1732 from a tax on ale brewed or sold in the town. Smaller boats would come up the River Ness as far as the Maggot and beach there whilst the larger ships tied up at the Shore Street and the Citadel Quays. A mid 18th century illustration shows women, with their skirts pulled up, wading into the water at the Maggot carrying their men on their backs out to their fishing boats. The construction of the Caledonian Canal, started in 1803, initially did much to increase trade, and in the first decade of the 19th century the harbour dues more than doubled. Huge amounts of supplies were brought in for the construction of the Canal, at least during its preliminary stages. For fear of competition from the Canal and the Muirtown Basin, the Citadel Quay was repaired and in 1813-17 Thornbush Quay was built so that boats of 250 tons could be taken. The completion of the Canal in 1822 did, however, have an adverse effect on the harbour and by 1826 the harbour dues had diminished considerably. The 1850s modernisation of the harbour, under Joseph Mitchell, gave it its present day shape, and river dredging allowed the larger vessels to gain access to its facilities, the dredged sand and gravel being used to shore up the harbour banks at the Capel Inch (below Thornbush Quay) and prevent flooding of that area. Another embankment was formed at the mouth of the river to reach Carnac Point to aid sailing vessels as they entered and left the harbour. Ships entering the river mouth would throw a rope from the vessel to a man at the Point who would then use three horses to take the boat "on tow" until it reached the Quay. A similar set-up was used to take the boat back out to the Firth, it being too dangerous to try and sail out from the Quay. After modernisation, the harbour again increased its business for a few years until the arrival of the railway which offered keen competition in the transportation of goods into and out of the town. Improvements to the Thornbush Quay at this time allowed larger coal-carrying vessels to dock, resulting in the harbour becoming the centre of the coal industry. By the early 20th century nearly 50,000 tons of coal was being imported and distributed from the harbour area. The inroads made by the railway slowly eroded the shipping industry. and by the late 19th century there were only five ship owners and five merchant traders registered. The back-bone of the sea trade had been broken.

Following an outbreak of plague on the continent in 1720 the harbour was closed to all foreign ships unless they spent 3 weeks in quarantine in Munlochy Bay. Some of the local merchants who were desperate for their goods, and clearly saw a way of avoiding the taxman, used to row out to the ships at Munlochy and try to smuggle the goods back to Inverness. When caught, they were arrested and, along with all their family, were locked up in their home for 3 weeks before being taken before the magistrates for sentencing. As a precaution against the plague, their boats and goods were burned. There is no doubt that, at this time, the Council took the threat of plague seriously, and dealt sternly with those who broke the quarantine. In 1847, control of the Harbour passed to the Inverness Harbour Trust, which was made up of 7 councillors, 5 merchants and 5 shipowners. Their work in 1850 gave the Harbour its present shape and the river was dredged until it was 21 feet deep and 120 feet wide, thus making it easier to enter.

As far back as 1804 passengers could embark at Inverness and sail to London on a journey lasting about 10-12 days for a very competitive price. Initially the ship sailed once every three weeks, but by the turn of the decade they were sailing every 10 days, sometimes more often. One report states that the ships left Inverness for London every three days, but I think that is unlikely. These vessels had a large single mast, as tall as a frigate's, and mainsails of a quarter of an acre in size, and must have been an impressive sight to see. The Inverness Packet called in at Fortrose, Cromarty, Invergordon, Findhorn, Burghead, Lossiemouth, Banff and Aberdeen en route to London. In 1823 Joseph Mitchell sailed from Aberdeen to London, cabin class. He got 4 meals a day and the journey, which cost 1 guinea, took 6 days. By 1847, however, the "Northern Star" left Thornbush Quay for London every alternate Monday between March and October, taking about three days and charging £4 for a cabin or £2 12s 6d steerage. The "Duke of Richmond" sailed for Leith (from Kessock) every Thursday and this was supplemented by a second steamer during the busiest part of the season, charging £1 8s for a cabin or 16s steerage. The "Maid of Morvern" also left Kessock for several Moray Firth ports every Monday and Wednesday, charging 5s for a cabin or 3s 6d for steerage to Burghead. As more and more people came to visit the Highlands by ship, coach and omnibus owners seized the opportunity and ran services for passengers to and from the local hotels - tourism was added to the list of local industries. It was a commonplace sight to see a phalanx of horse drawn cabs and coaches waiting at the pier to transport passengers on their onward journey. A similar sight could be seen at Muirtown when the Caledonian Canal was in full swing.

In the 1650s, Cromwell's government troops patrolled Loch Ness on a forty-ton ship, armed with four pieces of cannon, which was used to transport goods and provisions from one end of Loch Ness to the other. The ship had been built in Inverness and hauled overland, using log rollers, for six miles to Loch Ness, which must have been a mammoth task. One hundred and fifty years later Thomas Telford started work on the Caledonian Canal in an attempt to open up a safe east-west route for naval vessels during the Napoleonic Wars. From 1818 ships were sailing directly from Inverness to Fort Augustus with all sorts of cargoes, including passengers. By the time the Canal was finished, in 1822, at a cost of over £1,200,000, the War was over but the route made an enormous difference to transportation in the Highlands. Glasgow was now within easy reach of Inverness, Aberdeen, Dundee and the Baltic ports, and ships could sail safely from Wick to Ireland with salt herring. The days of the privateers were numbered. The "Culloden", the "Dolphin", the "Rob Roy" and the "Helen McGregor" all left from the Muirtown Locks on Monday and Thursday mornings for Glasgow charging £1.10s for a cabin and 10s steerage. Within twelve years, however, the canal was in serious need of repair with 23 miles on the point of collapse and it had to be closed. It took ten years and a further £150,000 to rectify the situation, reopening in 1847. On reopening there were 4 steamers which took passengers between Inverness and Glasgow at a cost of £1.10s for a cabin or 10 shillings for steerage. Coaches collected passengers at Muirtown to take them to Inverness. Another steamer, the Princess Beatrice" ran between Inverness and Liverpool.

The difficulties experienced by sailing ships with contrary winds on Loch Ness was overcome by the Canal Commissioners who provided steam tugs in the 1840s. By 1866, MacBrayne's paddle steamers, the "Gondolier" and the "Glengarry", provided a daily service between Muirtown and Banavie, along with the "Lochness", as often as not lurching to one side as they approached the pier, due to the passengers congregating at one side of the ship as they waited to alight. The "Gondolier" operated on this run for 73 years and was well known to generations of Highlanders, before being taken over by the Admiralty in 1939 and sunk, the following year, at Scapa Flow as a blockship for defence against submarines. The "Glengarry", formerly the "Edinburgh Castle", worked on the Clyde for two years before transferring to the Caledonian Canal in 1846. From 1866 she worked along with the "Gondolier" on Loch Ness before being disposed of in 1927, by which time she was the oldest operating steamship in the world with 83 years service. It is interesting to note that after a break of some 66 years, a new ferry service started operating in 2005 between Dochgarroch and Fort Augustus. The "Spirit of Skye" could whisk some 36 passengers the 30-mile trip in little over an hour and provided an excellent service to locals and tourists alike. Sadly it stopped after a few years and the boat was sold to Kazakhstan. In 1875 a regular steamer service, once a fortnight, ran from Liverpool to Leith, calling at Inverness and Aberdeen on route. Macbraynes steamers started, in 1883, sailing twice a week between Glasgow and Inverness, increasing in the summer months to everyday sailings. Progress ensured that iron hulled steamships gradually became larger and larger and the canal eventually became too small for them, whilst the perils of the Pentland Firth became less daunting.

Competition from bus and rail travel gradually overcame sea transportation and did much to kill off passenger ships, but it did not stem the public's desire to travel on water. The "Princess Louise", followed by the "Scot II" and then the Jacobite Cruises have maintained pleasure boats on the Canal right up to the present day, and it is also a fairly common sight to see motor cruisers and ocean-going yachts passing along the Canal in increasing numbers. It seems that despite the improvements in speed of travel, people still want to "mess about in boats". The "Scott II" has had a number of different roles in its over-70-year association with the Canal – as icebreaker, tug, cruise boat and more recently as a floating restaurant. It spent the last few years lying rusting in the Muirtown Basin after its owners, British Waterways, abandoned a botched renovation attempt. Fortunately it has now been purchased privately and has been restored to its former glory.

I could not finish this chapter without a mention of the famous Kessock Ferry which transported people, goods, animals and anything else it could carry between south and north Kessock for many generations. Surprisingly, not much has been written about the Ferry and finding information on its origin and boats, and people who worked on them, was quite difficult. The right to have a Ferry was granted to the Burgh in the Great Charter of 1591, but at some stage this found its way into private ownership, not unlike many other of the town assets.

The Kessock Ferry started through necessity, as probably all ferries do. The transportation of livestock, goods and people from the Black Isle to the markets in Inverness was initially its prime task. From that day, until the Kessock Bridge was opened in 1982, the Ferry operated successfully, although at times somewhat erratically; continually weaving its way back and forth between Inverness and the Black Isle every 30 minutes or so. For many passengers it was like a sea voyage – the only one some would ever experience – and for many others it heralded a day out at the beach in Rosemarkie, perhaps the only 'holiday' they ever took.

Initially operated by sail, the Ferry would load pigs, sheep, the occasional cattle, and whatever else was being taken to market in Inverness from the Black Isle, and convey them and their drover to South Kessock. At this point there would probably have been much noise and confusion as people and animals were taken off the boat and mixed with those waiting to alight on the next crossing. The drover would be tasked with rounding up his animals and driving them up the pier to Kessock Road and onward towards market. Assuming he wished to arrive at the market at a respectable time, his early morning start from wherever on the Black Isle. the distance he travelled would have given him a thirst by the time he reached the Kessock Inn and he may well have been tempted to have a quick dram before continuing his journey. If this was the case he may have parted with a farthing or so to the local 'ferry' boys to keep an eye on his animals until he had quenched his thirst. If he were wise he would not emerge from the Inn the "worse for wear" after an unexpectedly protracted delay – although he would not have been the first to find himself in such a position.

In 1825 the Ferry was sold, along with the estates of Redcastle, to Sir William Fettes for £135,000. Much of the credit for modernising the Ferry must go to him, for within three years of its purchase he had a steam vessel operating from new piers and had an Inn built at North Kessock. By 1844, passenger traffic was 'considerable' and the Burgh subsidised, to the amount of £10, a new bus service between the town and the Ferry terminal – this was the first public bus service in Inverness. The tariffs charged for the transportation of animals had long been a bone of contention and in 1887 there was great objection to paying 6d for a cow, 1d for a sheep and 2d for carrying 'small pigs in bags'. The outcome of this argument is not recorded but it was one which had been frequently raised in the past.

Much later, in 1939, the Ferry was purchased jointly by the Town Council and Ross and Cromarty County Council and eventually passed on to the newly formed Highland Regional Council in 1975. I can recall two of the boats used in my day and, indeed, distinctly remember, as a young boy, using the "Eilean Dubh" as a passenger on many occasions, although I recollect that her dubious reliability earned her the nickname 'ailing doo'. The cost for a car in those days was 3s for the half-mile journey. In 1967 the "Rosehaugh" took over from the "Eilean Dubh" thus enabling cars to be driven on and off without manoeuvring. The "Eilean Dubh" became the relief boat at that point and when the Ferry ceased it served as a tender for oil rigs in the Cromarty Firth.

Roads

In the 17th and 18th centuries, travelling over land was far less speedy than by water. Whereas the latter had a ready-made surface to travel on there were no roads to speak of in the Highlands until the middle of the 18th century. Indeed, it took well into the 19th century for road surfaces to be suitable for more 'modern' forms of transport. One could almost have traced future movement in and around Inverness by looking for the original tracks made by the early settlers as they passed by. The route through the Great Glen and the "Via Regis" (King's Road) along the east towards Moray and Aberdeen being two good examples. People who need to travel from one place to another will always find the most suitable route to follow, and in many instances it is from these tracks that the early roads took their line. School architects should never design paths in a school environment because very often they are not used by the pupils. Children walk from one place to another by the simplest route – often this does not involve circling round objects. My advice would be to leave paths out of the equation for a few months and then return to see all the tracks the pupils have formed – that is where the paths should be laid. In the same way the paths around the town, and into and out of it, would have slowly become more established as the town grew and enlarged.

In the 11th century when MacBeth became King and took over the Castle at Inverness, he no doubt followed a well-established route to Inverness from the east. Although it was probably fit only for horse, cattle and foot passengers, at that time in history that was all that was required. Even in the middle of the 17th century when Cromwellian troops occupied the town it is unlikely that the roads were much better. They were probably wider and well trodden due to increased traffic, but would still have been a mire when the weather was at its worst. In those days most travel took place during the summer months; very few people ventured far in the winter for obvious reasons. Even as late as the 1740s Lord Lovat took 11 days to travel to Edinburgh, the coach breaking its axle three times on the way, and Johnson and Boswell reported that they could find no road fit for wheeled vehicles north of Inverness in 1773 – although they may well have been comparing our roads with those in London.

When George Wade reported his findings to the English Parliament in the 1720s and was then hastily dispatched to the Highlands to undertake a road building programme, that heralded the beginning of improved transportation by road in the Highlands. Initially, his roads were constructed for military purposes, and simply connected forts and outposts in order to facilitate troop movements and provide routes for supplies to be transported. Later, other links were added and thus began the infrastructure which formed the backbone of Highland routes – many of which are still in existence today, at least in part.

Between 1725 and 1727 Wade worked on and completed the road from Fort William to Inverness, and in the ensuing years connected Inverness with the south of Scotland, over the Drumochter Pass, and various garrisons throughout the Highlands. The stronghold at Fort Augustus was started in 1728 and Ruthven barracks was built in 1734, both of which had good roads leading to them from Inverness. These roads were between 3.5 and 5 metres wide and excavated down to the gravel sub-soil before being topped with graded stones. The earth from the excavation was thrown up on either side of the road to form a bank. Wade's departure from the scene in 1740, when he returned to London, did not mean the end of road building, however. Major William Caulfield took up where Wade had left off and between 1740 and 1767 he planned about 900 miles of military roads. He had been Wade's principal assistant for some time and in 1732 was promoted to Inspector of Roads. Two years later he settled in Cradlehall, outside Inverness, and continued his road making from there until his death in 1767. In almost thirty years he built roads from Coupar Angus to Fort George, Stirling to Fort William, Contin to Poolewe and several others as well. Despite Wade's reputation, Caulfeild was second only to Thomas Telford for the work that he did on Highland roads. It perhaps puts things into perspective, however, to say that even then a candid assessment of the average speed of travel along Highland roads would have been around 2 m.p.h. – not exactly 'flying' but still an improvement. In 1785, responsibility for Highland roads passed from the military to civil engineers and the days of the great Scottish road builders had arrived. Thomas Telford, Joseph Mitchell and J. L. Macadam took up the challenge with relish and transformed road travel over the following decades.

Thomas Telford was born in 1757 in Dumfries-shire, the posthumous son of a shepherd. He left school at the age of 14 to become a stonemason and through his ability and his desire to better himself he changed from stonemason to engineer and attained the post of Surveyor of Public Works by the age of 31 years. Five years later he built the Ellsmere Canal, including the spectacular Pontcysylite Aqueduct, which Sir Walter Scott described as the most impressive work of art he had ever seen. In 1801 the Government asked Telford to survey the roads across Scotland, and over the 20 years from 1804 Telford built over 920 miles of road and 120 bridges throughout the Highlands. He also built many harbours and jetties all over Scotland as well as the Caledonian Canal and some 32 churches in the Highlands and Islands. He was a man of vision and design so far in advance of the technology available to him at that time that his name is held in awe even by modern bridge and road builders.

Trained by Thomas Telford, Joseph Mitchell succeeded his father as Chief Inspector and Superintendent of Highland Roads and Bridges. He is chiefly remembered as the projector of the Highland Railway, which threads its way through the glens north of Perth on its way to Inverness, although he also constructed harbours along the

Highland coast. As one of the young civil engineers trained to carry out Telford's numerous projects he was also concerned with roads and bridges, and here he succeeded his father who had devoted years of his life to this work. Mitchell's father, John, had been Thomas Telford's Superintendent of Roads and had lived in Telford Street. Joseph spent his boyhood years here and attended the Royal Academy before going on to enjoy a distinguished career as an engineer and eventually replacing his father as Superintendent of Roads. He built and lived in Viewhill House, at the top of Castle Street, and served on the Town Council. His portrait hangs in the Town House.

Macadam was the Surveyor General of Roads from 1827 and, although his contribution to road building in the Highlands was minor compared to the others, he is better known for inventing the road surfacing method which bears his name – tarmacadam or tarmac - where the graded road surface is coated with tar and rolled firm to form a weather-proof surface.

Prior to the 1740s all mail was transported by horse post, which was slow and expensive. About this time a direct mail coach to Edinburgh was introduced and for the next 120 years, until the Inverness and Perth Railway was completed by Joseph Mitchell, Invernessians enjoyed a steady introduction of new coach routes to towns and cities north and south of Inverness. In 1803, a new Edinburgh run was started with onward transmission of packages and letters to London. This was gradually followed with routes to Aberdeen, Tain, Wick, Thurso, Perth, Fort William and Glasgow. Most of these runs would have left Inverness, initially, once or twice a week and gradually increased in frequency as travel time shortened. The 1809 run to Perth originally took three days to complete but this was gradually reduced to 16 hours – leaving Inverness at 5am and arriving in Perth at 9pm. By the middle of the 19th century daily coaches were commonplace, with the cost to Perth being £2 5s inside and £1 12s outside, to Aberdeen being £2 inside and £1 1s outside and to Tain £1 inside and £0 14s outside.

The run to the beach at Nairn was also popular, undertaken by the "Star" which left for Elgin daily. In the summer months there was an extra coach put on to Nairn to meet the demand. The question, "How long will it take to get there?", was often on the lips of the traveller who, even then, was interested in travelling as swiftly as possible to his destination.

To begin with coaches were pretty basic affairs and not luxurious in any way whatsoever. The ride would have been pretty bumpy as the roads were rough and potholed and those who could only afford to travel outside had to endure the ravages of the wind and the weather, in all seasons. The stops, at Inns along the way, in order to change horses and obtain some sustenance, would have been fairly frequent on long journeys and generally speaking the experience would not have been a pleasant one, particularly for the fairer sex. The passage of time, public demand and increased competition for routes gradually saw an improvement in conditions, and towards the end of the coaching hey-day these journeys were completed in relative comfort with fine coaches and handsome horses travelling at around 10 mph. Most coaches ran to time, despite the hazards of broken wheels and axles, potholes, lame horses and difficult passengers, with the coachmen travelling several thousand miles each year on their individual routes.

When Mitchell completed his Inverness and Perth Railway (Highland Railway) in 1863 the days of long distance travel by coach were over. The "smooth passage" in the railway carriage and the quickness of travel was a far greater attraction to the traveller, and although coach travel still flourished outwith these new rail routes the late 19th century saw the demise of the stagecoach. Despite the introduction of the internal combustion engine in the 1880s the automobile did not become frequently used in Inverness until after the First World War, and did not become common place until after the Second World War. Up until the mid 1920s MacRae and Dick's horse drawn cabs could be seen in the streets of Inverness but were eventually replaced with Highland Omnibuses. Out with the old and in with the new.

The 20th century saw the gradual increase of motorised transport and the inevitable improvement in the road network throughout the Highlands. The City also saw changes, with streets being realigned and one-way traffic systems being introduced to cope with the ever increasing volume of vehicles. Curiously enough, the question "How long will it take to get there?" is still relevant today, but for a different reason. In the late 19th century travelling was slow because the roads and transportation systems dictated it, today we are slowing down again because the volume of traffic on the roads is so great – hopefully we will not end up where we started, travelling at an average speed of 5 mph, unless of course the powers that be decide that the A9 traffic should travel even slower.

Rail

During the 1840s the railway routes connecting Glasgow and Edinburgh to London were completed, and routes north to Perth (1848) and Aberdeen (1850) opened. A railway route connecting Inverness to the south had been proposed, by the Great North of Scotland Railway Company, as early as 1845, but took a rather circuitous route along the east coast to Aberdeen, thus avoiding the crossing of any mountain barrier and its associated steep gradients. An alternative route, linking Inverness to Aberdeen, was proposed by the Inverness and Elgin Junction Company. Neither scheme was greeted with great enthusiasm in Inverness, however, because of the seemingly unnecessarily long detour via Aberdeen.

In 1845, Joseph Mitchell produced a bold scheme with a more direct route south across the Grampians via Elgin, which not only had the obvious disadvantage of having to overcome steep inclines, but also travelled through sparsely populated countryside with little hope of revenue for the railway. To raise the required capital shares were first successfully sold in Edinburgh, before 48,000 shares, at £2 10s each, were issued in London and "sold like wild-fire". Despite the valiant efforts of Mitchell and a number of prominent citizens from the North, the proposal was turned down by Parliament. Mitchell was thoroughly disheartened by the attitude adopted by some Parliamentarians who had ridiculed his idea and likened him to Napoleon and Hannibal for attempting to build a railway over a 1450-foot summit. Discouraged at the termination of his labours he may have been down but he was not beaten. In 1854, the Inverness and Nairn Railway Company cut the first sod for a line between these two towns and the occasion was marked in true Highland style with a holiday being declared and a crowd of over 8,000 people turning up to watch. The line was completely isolated from any other line in Scotland, and hence all necessary equipment for its construction had to be brought in by sea. Despite this difficulty the line opened a year later when more than half the population of the town gathered at the railway station, which was resplendent with flags and bunting, and the line was soon extended further east to Keith. Joseph Mitchell designed and built the Railway Station in 1855 and the Station Hotel was added in 1859. The Inverness and Nairn Railway was taken over by the Inverness and Aberdeen Railway Company in 1861.

By the late 1850s railway engineering and engine design had both advanced sufficiently to make the direct route to Perth, from

Inverness, more feasible. The Inverness and Perth Junction Railway proposed a new route (very similar to Mitchell's original proposal) across the Grampians and, despite strong opposition, this time it was accepted. The route went through Forres and then proceeded to Kingussie before descending to Dunkeld and finally Perth. Joseph Mitchell was appointed as engineer for the route which finally opened in 1863. Two years later the Inverness and Perth Junction, and the Inverness and Aberdeen Junction Railways amalgamated to form the Highland Railway Company, which made its headquarters in the Station Square in Inverness where it remained until the Company became part of the London Midland and Scottish Railway (LMS) in 1923. The result of this more direct route south was shorter travelling times and lower fares which were appealing to both passengers and companies who transported goods by rail. The time of the railway had arrived and the Highland Railway Company flourished.

People further north began to see the advantages and possibilities of the railway and by 1860 the Inverness and Ross-shire Company had a proposal for a line to Dingwall which opened two years later. This line not only had to span the River Ness and the Caledonian Canal but also the Rivers Beauly and Conon. The introduction of this new line north saw an extension to the Station in Inverness in order to cope with the new lines and the increased traffic.

In 1883, the Glasgow and North Western Railway proposed a route from Glasgow to Inverness via Fort William, which was some 50 miles shorter than the Perth route. The Highland Railway Company successfully convinced Parliament that there was insufficient business to support two routes, and the scheme was turned down. Competition between various companies for a west coast route to Inverness continued over the next three decades, and even after it was completed it was never financially successful. By 1884, a mere thirty years after the first sod was cut in Inverness the Highland Railway Company operated from Aberdeen in the east, to Wick and Thurso in the north, to Kyle of Lochalsh in the west, and to Perth in the south. That same year they decided to shorten the route to Perth and take the line directly to Carrbridge from Inverness. They were in no hurry to complete the work, however, because it was not finished until 1898, although it did include the viaducts at Slochd, Tomatin and Culloden, all impressive engineering feats.

Although the introduction of the railway age was somewhat gradual in Inverness and the surrounding area, nonetheless the social implications were enormous. By the mid 19th century over six hundred companies were registered in Scotland with a united capital of £563,203,000. There was a frenzy of speculation throughout the country which brought ruin to some and fortunes to others over the years. The boom years of 1845 and 1846 were followed by a crash in 1847 which spread ruin throughout the country. Shareholders who had speculatively bought into Railway companies found their stocks unsaleable as these companies suspended operations. The crash was short lived, however, principally due to the need, and demand, for rail links throughout Scotland, and particularly so in the North where the condition of the roads hampered the swift transportation of goods.

Huge numbers of labourers followed the construction of the railways and usually spent their wages liberally in local communities, especially the Inns and taverns. Since the roads were not particularly suitable for the transportation of heavy goods, the construction of a Railway Station usually had beneficial economic results, with whole communities centring themselves on country stations. By the time the Highland Railway Company was formed the train from Inverness took six hours to Perth – eight hours quicker than the mail coach at that time – whilst one could travel to Glasgow in under nine hours and reach London in 18 hours. Commerce was not slow in taking advantage of these improved travel times and the railways steadily improved their share of trade, usually at the expense of the shipping industry. At that time the Moray Firth teemed with fish of all kinds, most of which had to be cured before being transported by boat to markets in the south of Scotland, London and the Baltic states. Rail transportation allowed the fish to be sent as far as London in a fresh state, thus realizing a higher price. Since, at that time, around 60,000 tons of fish were caught annually in the Moray Firth area this amounted to a huge investment. Whilst good quality Cod in Inverness sold for around 8p, in the London fish market it could realize 9s, and fishmongers were not slow to realise this. The meat trade also benefited from rail transport with a meat train leaving Elgin for London each day. Trade is a two-way thing, of course, and shopkeepers in Inverness began to stock up with goods which were hitherto unknown in this area – much to the surprise, at times, of visitors from London.

Travel over large distances was easier and indeed cheaper than ever before and people took advantage of it. Tourism, and its associated industries, began to become a part of Highland life. The number of hotels and shops catering for tourists increased, and shooting and fishing holidays were advertised as were excursions by coach and rail. In the summer of 1876 the Highland Railway treated its workmen and their wives and families to their annual outing to Aberdeen. Some 900 passengers left Inverness at 5 a.m., returning after 11 p.m., and they included the band of the Artillery Volunteers who preceded the group on the march from the station to the Drill Hall where games were played. A group of 435 passengers from Dundee reciprocated at a cost of 7s for a third class fare and spent the day in Inverness. Visits of this type would, no doubt, have been a boon to the local shopkeepers and also to the local pubs. No doubt the return journeys on such visits were fraught with the difficulties of fractious children and fathers who had over indulged. Despite the boom in railway travel the standard of comfort on the railways was not particularly good. Third class passengers had to sit on wooden benches, ten to a compartment, whilst first class passengers had padded seats and were only eight to a compartment. There was no heating or refreshments available, although rugs and pillows could be hired for the journey. Eventually the needs of passengers were taken into consideration and the level of comfort improved with the introduction of heating and refreshment facilities in the early 1900s. (Perhaps someone should tell ScotRail for the trains north of Perth).

The upsurge in rail travel, both passenger and goods, had its down side, of course, and that was to herald the demise of sea traffic which had been at its zenith in the mid 19th century. The Lochgorm Locomotive Works was built in 1864, on the site of the Loch of that name in Eastgate, and carriage and wagon shops were later built at Needlefield in the Longman area. The Highland Railway was one of the biggest employers in the town with a paint shop staff of around 50 men, not to mention the other tradesmen and railway employees.

Air

In 1933, Captain Fresson registered Highland Airways Limited, which was to operate an air service from the Longman, throughout northern Scotland. The following year he inaugurated the first regular British internal air mail service when he piloted a DH Dragon Moth G-ACCE to Kirkwall carrying around 2,000 letters. That same year saw the formation of Northern and Scottish Airways Limited, which amalgamated with Fresson's company in 1937 to form Scottish Airways Limited. This new company was used to match up the interests of British Airways with those of the LMS Railway Company and David MacBrayne Limited.

169

In an area as geographically challenging as the Highlands it is perhaps not surprising that air travel arrived here as early as it did. Where mountains and water have to be negotiated the benefits of air travel are fairly obvious, although the drawbacks of low population numbers and the lack of suitable land for airports are equally apparent. The transportation of mail and people to and from the Islands to the north and west of Inverness, though small in number, had great benefits for travellers. When British European Airways (BEA) was set up in 1946 and given the task of operating all UK services, rapid development followed with the airfield having moved from the Longman out to the RAF airfield at Dalcross.

Throughout the 1960s and beyond much controversy has surrounded flights from Inverness to London and other parts of the UK, with Scottish Airways and Loganair pioneering many of the routes. The same issues, we are told, continue to plague today's flights as they did in those days – lack of viable numbers of passengers. Although one wonders why the 'cheap fare' airlines are so successful if this is indeed the case.

Chapter 9

Folklore and Myth

Folklore is generally accepted as being the unwritten literature of a particular people or place as expressed in tales, songs, etc. This being the case, Inverness has plenty of it, culminating in the existence of "Nessie" the Loch Ness Monster. I have included only a few of these stories for fear of overburdening the chapter with romantic tales rather than factual information on Inverness itself. It is all too easy, when one starts to explore the myths and legends of this area, to become embroiled in the superstitious beliefs, which have become entangled with the true folklore of the past. Since some of the stories have an element of truth attached to them, no matter how small, it should be the task of the storyteller to unravel the tale and try to isolate the truth – but then in doing so the tale loses a great deal of interest and excitement. Let us then simply look at the stories as they are told and secretly believe what we feel is the element of truth contained within them. My own mother had a plethora of sayings and stories surrounding all sorts of daily happenings, including the weather, when to plant things in the garden, and why animals did certain things, which, as a youngster, I actually believed were true. But then if one says them often enough the law of averages suggests that it is bound to be right some of the time. If one uses a discerning eye and an imaginative mind when reading the stories, one should be able to separate sheer superstition and romantic folklore from any element of truth contained in them. Whatever route is chosen the tales themselves are very entertaining.

The Fiddlers of Tomnahurich

Two fiddlers from Strathspey, Farquhar Grant and Thomas Cumming, had spent one Saturday performing on the streets of Inverness in order to raise some money to support their families. At the end of it they had little reward to show for their day's work and, as dusk fell, they glumly made their way across the Ness Bridge to their lodgings. Half way across the bridge they were accosted by a small man dressed in a red tam-o'-shanter and a green jerkin and breeches who inquired after their families, much to the surprise of the fiddlers who did not know him. When they explained to the man that they had fallen on bad times he took pity on them and invited them to come and play at a party he was giving, for which they would be well rewarded. The two fiddlers willingly followed him to the Tomnahurich Hill, which they all proceeded to climb. Near the top of the hill he opened a door, which the fiddlers had never seen before, and ushered them in to what they assumed was his house. They then passed along a long tunnel which led to a large brightly lit hall where they were greeted by a number of people who welcomed them and urged them to start playing their fiddles. As the night wore on the fiddlers played reel after reel and the dance was in full swing. There was a splendid feast laid out and ale a-plenty, which pleased the fiddlers no end and encouraged them to play all the more.

As evening turned into day their host approached them and, thanking them for their night's work, handed them a bag of gold and wished them well as he ushered them out of the house. Happily the two musicians wove their way down the hill and headed back into Inverness, but soon became conscious that they were the centre of attention to all they met. The townspeople, who were dressed in strange clothes, looked at them and laughed as they passed by, leaving the fiddlers puzzled as to what was wrong. They were further perplexed when they arrived in the town to find unfamiliar sights before their eyes, the old wooden bridge had changed into a stone one and so had some of the houses changed from hovels into new stone buildings. Disturbed by what they saw they headed for Strathspey, but on their arrival they recognised nobody and nobody seemed to know them. Fearing that they were bewitched they headed for the parish church to see the minister, only to find that some of the headstones bore the names of people they knew and had spoken to only the day before. When they reached the church they threw open the door and stepped in, only to find that they did not recognise the minister. In desperation they sat down to consider their plight as the minister opened his bible and began to read to the congregation from it. As soon as the minister mentioned the name of God their bag of gold turned to leaves and they themselves dropped to the floor as dust, much to the consternation of the congregation.

It would appear that the fiddlers had been playing for no ordinary people, but for fairies, and not just for one night, but for 100 years. Now legend has it that had the fiddlers carried a piece of iron the fairies would not have touched them, as they are powerless against this metal.

Farquhar of Invertromie

The glens and moors of Badenoch were once the domain of a fierce baron called the Red Comyn. Most of the land was forested or fit only for sheep, although there were a few pockets which were farmed. One such farmer was a giant of a man called Big Farquhar who stood over eight feet tall and was quite capable of felling ten assailants with one blow of his cudgel. For reasons unknown his wife left him and went to live with Donald Dhu, a widower with nine sons, whose home was in Glentromie. Affronted by this slur to his manhood, Farquhar took up with a lady called Grace from Red Comyn's court. When Red Comyn heard of the liaison he was furious and summoned the two of them to appear before him. Convinced that the pair were not willing to part company Red Comyn gave Farquhar the choice of marrying Grace or being hanged. Farquhar chose the route of least resistance and agreed to marry her.

Initially, all was well as Grace was well connected and through this Farquhar found favour at court. After a while some of his animals began to disappear, so Farquhar resolved to catch the culprits red-handed. He lay in wait for them one night and caught and killed three of them as they stole his animals. Unfortunately for him the marauders turned out to be members of Red Comyn's court. Warned by Grace's brother to flee for his life, Farquhar fled to Donald Dhu's house in Glentromie where he spent his time lounging about being attended to by his former wife. This was more that Donald Dhu could take so he summoned his sons and they agreed to kill Farquhar. Their plot was overheard by a pedlar friend of Farquhar's who immediately warned him of their scheme. Helped by his mother, Farquhar murdered Donald Dhu and his nine sons and piled their heads into a cairn on a nearby hillock – now called Ceann na Torr (The Head of the Hillock). Fearing reprisals Farquhar gathered all his animals and his goods together and fled along with his mother to his son's house in Lochaber.

Loch na Sanais

There was once a smith who lived at Kilvean near Torvean. He had a beautiful daughter who was deeply in love with a penniless, but handsome, young man from Dochfour. Her father, however, had other ideas as to whom she should marry and had selected a rich merchant, which would suit his own financial situation very well.

Despite his frequent attempts to persuade his daughter to marry the merchant, she would have none of it; so her father decided that the only course of action would be to give the young man a beating in an attempt to frighten him away from his daughter. One day the merchant and a friend ambushed the young man close to a loch with a view to carrying out their dastardly deed. They got more than they bargained for, however, because the young man was too powerful for them and gave the two of them a sound thrashing instead. When he was told of the outcome of their endeavours the smith was furious and sought out the merchant to have words with him. He met up with him and they decided to hatch a new plot. Whilst they walked together past a loch, they were noticed by the smith's daughter, who concealed herself in the bushes to hide from them. As they passed close by her she heard her father whispering to the merchant that the young man would have to be killed if the merchant was to win his daughter's hand in marriage. Terrified by what she had heard she leapt up and ran all the way to Dochfour to warn her lad of the plan her father and the merchant were arranging. To escape from the impending doom the two of them decided to elope. When the local people found out what had happened they named the loch "Loch na Sanais" (loch of the whisper).

The Kingussie Boatman

At one time the only means of crossing the River Spey at Ruthven was either to use the boat or to ford the river. The latter was, at times, extremely dangerous and the former cost a penny, payable to the boatman who always held himself in readiness for a fare. During one Communion celebration at Kingussie, when the river was in flood, the boatman was in great demand and, being a dishonest and corrupt character, he decided to cash in on the situation. He started to demand sixpence for the crossing and refused to take those who either would not, or could not, pay. Consequently, a number of people missed Communion, including an old woman of over 90 years of age, who had never missed a Communion in over 50 years. She pleaded in vain with the boatman to take her across but he flatly refused unless she paid her sixpence fare. Even when she promised to pay the outstanding amount at a later date he refused to take her. Heartbroken she returned home to her croft.

When she was missed from church over the next few days her elder called on her to find out why she had not attended the service. He found her in bed and near to her end. She explained to him what had happened and made a prediction as to what would happen to the boatman because of his greed. On his return to Kingussie the elder sought out the boatman, lambasted him for his treatment of the old woman, and warned him of her prediction, saying that he would be deprived of his living, his house and his land; in addition he would die an unnatural death, and his body would be devoured by beasts.

A year later a wooden bridge was built across the Spey at Ruthven and the boatman lost his job, his house and his land. He was forced to do whatever odd jobs he could find in the area, occasionally being employed by a miller to clean out a pigsty and do some work about the mill. One wet day the miller told him to shut the water off the mill as it was high with the rain. To do this the boatman had to walk across a narrow plank from the loft of the mill to the sluice. The miller noticed that the water was shut off but could not find the boatman anywhere. Some time later he found the pigs devouring his body. He had slipped from the wet plank and fallen into the pigsty where the pigs had set upon him.

The Clootie Well

This well, also known as St Mary's Well, is situated beside the mausoleum of the Forbes of Culloden just above Culloden House and is reputed to have magical properties and healing powers. St Mary is supposed to have lived nearby in the Culloden area and to have travelled through the countryside healing the sick and helping the poor. She always carried with her a supply of water from the well, which she liberally administered to those who were ill. The outcome, more often than not, was that the person recovered from the illness and as a result of this curative powers have been attributed to the well water. To activate the spell it is necessary to be present at the well on the morning of the 1st of May when the first rays of the sun shine on the well. A cloth, or "cloot", is then dipped into the water and hung on a nearby tree in order that the sun's rays will dry it. A silver coin is then deposited in the well and a sip of water taken from it. The story says that any disease suffered by the donor will slowly dissipate as the "cloot" dries in the wind and rain and eventually rots. Anyone removing a "cloot" from the tree will take on the ill that it represented. Several other wells with supposed powers also exist in the area. One, called Eppie's Well, is nearby the Clootie Well, whilst another is on the Fortrose road on the Black Isle and a third, called Tober Voorie, is situated at Tarradale in Ross-shire.

At the turn of the 20th century the pilgrimage to the Clootie Well was supported by thousands of people from Inverness and Nairn and was quite a family day out. Initially, people walked from the town out to Culloden usually taking a picnic and not returning until the evening. The largest crowd recorded was in 1946, after the end of the war, when close on 3,000 people were taken there by MacRae and Dick's and Alexander's buses. The Inverness Courier of that week reported that:

"Six Cameron Highlanders, now demobbed, met at the Well in fulfilment of a resolution made at Sfax (in Tunisia) during the North African campaign. When they reached a well in an olive grove at Sfax, they decided that, as it was the first Sunday in May, they would have a ceremony similar to that observed annually at the "Clootie" Well at Culloden. They drank the water, expressed the wish that they would meet again at the Culloden Well and tied bits of cloth to the olive trees. The wish came true, for Alexander Mackenzie, Robert Mackintosh, Robert Nairn, Alex Patience, Duncan Mackay and John Johnstone were at the Culloden Well on Sunday to drink the water."

The Stolen Family

A young man whose wife had not long given birth to a baby came home one day to find them missing. He searched high and low but no trace of either of them could be found. It was suspected that the fairies had stolen them away, as they were particularly fond of young children. The bereft father wandered around the countryside seeking out his wife and child, when suddenly he was confronted by the apparition of his wife who told him that that very night the fairies were to ride in procession throughout the land, and would pass by his house after dark. She added that if he ever wanted to see them again he would have to rush out of the house as the procession passed and throw his wife's wedding gown over her shoulders. That way the fairies would leave them alone and the family would be reunited. The husband was terrified, and to overcome this he invited his neighbours to sit with him and wait for the procession to arrive. The room abounded with stories of fairies and the power they could wield over humans. Eventually the sound of horses' hooves approached the house and the husband rose with the gown ready to throw over his wife. By this time, however, the neighbours were afraid that something might happen to them for assisting him and they pounced on him and held him down. The sound of the process died away into the distance along with the wailing of a woman's voice. The man's wife and child were never heard of again.

The Kingussie Witch

An infamous witch once lived on a croft called Bean-an-Lagain, near Kingussie. She took great pleasure in plundering her neighbour's animal stock much to their continual annoyance. One day a crofter found one of her sheep eating his corn so he tied the animal up until she paid for the damage it had done. The witch was furious at his demand and, after settling up with the crofter, she vowed a terrible revenge on him. Within a few weeks the crofter fell ill and died and shortly afterwards his barn burned down. Next his house was troubled by a large black cat which so terrified his wife that she and her family up and left the croft.

A new crofter took over the place and tried everything he knew to ward off the cat, but without success. He tied a sprig of bog myrtle to his cows, placed rowan branches on his byre, and nailed a horseshoe to his house door. Nothing seemed to deter the cat and his chickens and eggs continued to disappear. The crofter suspected that the cat was actually the witch in disguise and so he placed a silver button in his gun and fired it at the cat, hitting it on one of its hind legs. The next time the crofter saw the witch she was limping which confirmed his suspicions. His smile, however, betrayed him and did not go unnoticed by the witch.

A few days later he was sitting at his fireside when a large black hen appeared beside him. His dogs growled fiercely and the crofter became alarmed as they slowly backed away from the hen. As he watched, the hen grew larger and larger until eventually it turned into the witch. She demanded that he tied up his dogs but he told her that he had nothing to tie them up with. She pulled some hairs from her head and gave them to him saying that he should use these to tie up the dogs. As he placed them on the sleeve of his jacket she sprang at him and screamed, "Tighten hairs, cut and strangle", but as she did so his faithful dogs set upon her and chased her from the house. One of the dogs did not return home that night and so the next day the crofter set off to look for it. He found it dead not far from the croft with a piece of human flesh in its mouth and on returning home was informed by a neighbour that the witch had been found dead at home. Her body was carried to the top of a hill and burned, but to this day, despite attempts to plant trees on the spot, not one will take root.

The Witches of Millburn

In the early 18th century there lived in a bothy in the Mill Burn area of the town two sisters who were supposed to be witches. One day some children who were playing in the burn found a doll, which had pins sticking into it. This was a well-known spell of a witch and was supposed to place a curse on a victim, sometimes resulting in their death. One of the children was the grandchild of one of the sisters, known as Creibh Mhor, and unfortunately she admitted to the others that she had seen her grandmother making the doll. As soon as word of this reached the authorities the woman was arrested and tortured in order to extract a confession of her guilt. She refused to confess and so her sister was also imprisoned and tortured. The sister confessed to them both being witches under the strain of the torture, and added that the effigy was supposed to be that of Cuthbert of Castlehill. This sealed the fate of the sisters who were sentenced to burn at the stake. As one of the witches watched her sister being consumed by the flames she cursed both Baillie David Fraser and the Cuthberts, before she too was dispatched to meet her maker. In keeping with the curse Fraser sold no more goods from his shop and some time later George Cuthbert fell from his horse and was killed.

Witches probably fared better in Inverness than in many other places throughout the country, despite the publication of the "Malleus Maleficarum" (The Witch Hammer) by Kramer and Sprenger in 1486. This guidebook for "Inquisitors" was designed to aid them in identifying, prosecuting and dispatching all witches, and was probably responsible for seeing several thousand old women, midwives, Jews, and gypsies put to their death throughout the country. Anyone who did not fit into the contemporary view of a pious Christian was suspect, and easily branded a witch - usually to devastating effect. Indeed, this situation was exacerbated in 1563, by a law, passed by Mary Queen of Scots, which stated that witches, and those who helped or consulted them, would be dealt with severely, thus enabling anyone who had a grudge against a neighbour to name them and have them tried as a witch. This did occur in Inverness, but initially the Council only saw fit to have those found "wanting" simply receive a rebuke by the minister in the Parish Church, the Old High, and force them to ask their fellow citizens for forgiveness. They were also refused the right to trade within the Burgh boundaries.

Almost 150 years later, in 1604, James VI decreed that witches were sorcerers who made a pact with the devil himself and that nobody should "suffer a witch to live". This changed the situation completely, and the number of prosecutions of 'witches,' throughout Scotland grew steadily as the century progressed. The 1640 General Assembly actively encouraged ministers to search out and punish all witches – and they did so with fervour. In the Inverness area, however, the Council and the Church continued to spare many of the accused the agonies of torture and a fiery death – instead, they continued to parade them before the Presbytery, the case of one Robert Stuart, in 1603, being an exception. He was accused of several charges of witchcraft and found guilty, being burned at the stake at the Haugh Head.

The Reverend James Fraser of Kirkhill, who showed great interest in the witchcraft trials of his day, tells of a Mr Paterson who arrived in Inverness in 1662 as a witch hunter. Commonly known as "The Pricker", Paterson would first strip his victims, and then shave them over, men and women alike, before rubbing his hands over their bodies. As he did so he would slip a brass pin into their flesh and then ask them to find it. They were generally so terrified of him that they never felt the pin enter their bodies, and indeed, few ever found it. Those that didn't succeed in finding the pin were found guilty and subjected to torture by Paterson before being thrown into prison. The curious thing is that Paterson was later found out to be a woman – but only after she had imprisoned many locals for being involved in witchcraft.

Formation of Loch Ness

A holy man once lived in a bothy in the neighbourhood of Dores. He was fortunate enough to have a spring of fine clear water outside his house, which in those days was of great value, if for no other reason than the fact that it prevented having to tramp great distances for water. Being kind hearted and wishing his neighbours good fortune he offered them the use of the well, on condition that they always closed the wooden lid when they had drawn the water they needed. One day a young mother approached the well and, laying her child down on the grass, she lifted the lid off the spring. Laying the lid down on the grass beside the child she proceeded to fill her pitcher with water. As the pitcher was slowly filling she looked at the child and noticed that an adder was approaching it, so she ran and picked the child up and fled from the well leaving the trapdoor open and the pitcher slowly filling. The water gradually rose over the top of the pitcher, and spilling out of the well it trickled down the slope until Loch Ness was formed.

Atholl Treachery

Dalwhinnie (The Dell of Meeting) was a place often used by clan chiefs to meet and sort out their differences, sometimes ending in bloodshed as graves in the hillside can witness. On one such occasion a meeting was arranged by Atholl, who invited Lochiel to meet him with only two attendants, to resolve a matter. Lochiel did not trust Atholl and consulted the prophetess of the district. She warned him to be careful as his life was in danger so he arranged for two hundred of his men to hide in the hills near the meeting place and await his signal if the need arose. When Lochiel arrived at the scene with his attendants Atholl was waiting for him with only two men as promised. Lochiel felt ashamed that he had not trusted Atholl, who was being very friendly towards him during their meeting, and became concerned that his men should be detected on the hillside. Atholl's cloak fell from his shoulders and, as if by accident, he slipped it on again inside out. Immediately, a group of Atholl men bearing arms appeared nearby. When Lochiel demanded to know what was happening, Atholl replied, "These are Atholl sheep coming to eat Lochaber grass." At that Lochiel raised his bonnet and waived it in the air and his men appeared on the hillside. Atholl was taken aback and shouted at Lochiel, "What have we here?" With a smile on his lips Lochiel replied, "Only Lochaber dogs ready to worry Atholl sheep. Draw, traitor, and defend your life." A bloody conflict ensued at which Lochiel was the victor. The graves of the Atholl men can be seen to this day to the west of Dalwhinnie.

Coinneach Odhar - The Brahan Seer

The second sight (Da Shealladh, or two sights) is recognised as the ability to see things which will occur in the future, that others cannot. It distinguishes between the world we all see with our eyes and the world visible only to those known as visionaries or seers. If any people have been afflicted with the second sight then it must surely be the Scots. Never regarded as witchcraft in Scotland it was always seen more as a curse than a blessing.

Commonly believed to be a Lewisman, born in Baile na Cille in the first half of the 17th century, Coinneach Odhar, also known as Kenneth Mackenzie, the Brahan Seer, received his second sight from an action of his mother's. She was making her way home from helping with a birth, and passed a graveyard on a certain night when ghosts rise from their graves to wander the earth. Being a brave, and inquisitive, woman she sat down at the graveside of a young girl and waited for her to return. When the spectre of the girl appeared, Coinneach Odhar's mother barred her way and asked where she had been. The girl was terrified because if she did not regain her lair before the sun rose she would suffer dire consequences. The girl explained to the woman that she was a Danish Princess who had been drowned at sea and her body washed ashore in Scotland. That night she had returned to Denmark to see if she could view her family. Coinneach Odhar's mother demanded a tribute from the girl for allowing her to pass to safety and the girl offered her the second sight. The woman accepted, but asked the girl to give it to her son instead. Later that day Coinneach Odhar stopped his work in the fields and lay down to rest. When he awoke he found a curious bluish-black stone by his side with a small hole in it. He picked it up and when he looked through it he found that he could see into the future, something that stayed with him all his life and, indeed was the cause of his death.

After leaving Lewis he eventually moved east, and around 1665 was working at Brahan Castle, 3.5 miles south-east of Dingwall, for the Earl of Seaforth. His wife, the Countess Isabella, who was said to be the ugliest woman in Scotland, asked Coinneach Odhar's advice on where her husband was, and whom he was with. She was re-assured that her husband was well and on his way home from a trip abroad. Believing her husband to be with another woman she threatened to have Coinneach Odhar killed if he did not tell her all he knew. Never having much time for nobility and their demands he said to her, "Your husband is this moment with another who is fairer than yourself. She could hardly be other." On hearing his reply she had him arrested for witchcraft, and screaming that she and her husband had been insulted she ordered that he be dragged into the courtyard of the castle where a barrel of tar was boiling. Realising his fate, Coinneach Odhar threw his stone aside, where it landed in the water-filled hoof-print of a cow, and made his last prophecy, in which he predicted the downfall of the House of Seaforth which was to come true, in uncanny detail, many years later, when all his sons died before him. He was then thrust head first into the boiling tar. Later, looking for the stone Coinneach Odhar had cast aside, his murderers found water coming from the spot – some say that the water eventually became Loch Ussie.

There is no written evidence that Coinneach Odhar ever existed in the seventeenth century, and yet many of the prophecies attributed to him have come to pass and are well remembered throughout the Highlands. Those still unfulfilled are, in many quarters, waited with apprehension. Although the 17th century is a well-documented period in Scottish history there is no reference to him whatsoever in contemporary writings. Alexander Brodie of Brodie, who kept very detailed journals between 1652 and 1685, did not mention him at all; nor does the Reverend James Fraser of Kirkhill in his Wardlaw Manuscript, although he showed great interest in the witchcraft trials of the day. There was, however, a Kennoch Owir (possibly an English clerk's transcription of Coinneach Odhar) who was arrested for witchcraft in 1577 in connection with the Munro witchcraft trials. He would no doubt have been burned at Chanonry since it is in the seat of the diocese of Ross. The cathedral records for that period are missing, however, and it is not possible to check the accuracy of the tale. Since the title of Earl of Seaforth did not exist until 1623 it seems highly unlikely that Kennoch Owir was the same person as Coinneach Odhar. Who then was the Brahan seer? There can be no doubt what Lieutenant-General Lord Francis Humberston Mackenzie thought as he watched, down to the last detail, the awesome prophecy come true, 150 years after it was uttered. Nor was there any doubt in the minds of those who erected the commemorative stone at Chanonry Point.

Although Coinneach Odhar did not come from Inverness, nor, as far as I am aware, ever live in the town, some of his prophecies involve Inverness and I have, therefore, included him in this section. In his lifetime he made a number of predictions, some of which have come to pass, some which are yet awaited and a few of which had catastrophic consequences for those involved. If you are tempted to laugh it all away, then ponder this. He once claimed that, "A village of four churches will get another spire, and a ship will come from the sky and moor at it." Needless to say, at the time of the prediction he was laughed at, but this unlikely event happened in 1932 when an airship made an emergency landing and was tied up to the spire of the new church. He also claimed that the overturning of a great stone near Inverness would presage the end of the world. "When the stone is turned for the third time, the end will follow in a week." The stone was first turned over by a blacksmith, as a demonstration of his strength, in 1789. It was then turned again by another strongman in 1932. The stone is now surrounded by an iron cage and set in concrete – after all, one can't be too careful with these things ....

Prediction

"The day is coming when fire and water will run in streams side by side through the streets of Inverness."

Explanation

This was the Brahan Seer's first attempt to see into the future and the account was somewhat garbled. It is generally taken to foresee the arrival of piped water and gas to the streets of Inverness.

Prediction

"The day is coming when long strings of chariots without horse or bridle shall charge from Inverness to the Muir of Ord and there will be soldiers in the chariots."

Explanation

This clearly refers to a train with railway carriages, although it is not clear why he referred to soldiers on the train, rather than people.

Prediction

"I see the Fairy Hill under lock and key with the spirits of the dead secured within."

Explanation

This undoubtedly refers to the use of Tomnahurich Hill as a burial ground. The cemetery is surrounded by a fence, the gates of which are kept locked at night.

Prediction

"The time will come when full-rigged ships with sails unfurled will be seen sailing east and west by the back of Tomnahurich Hill."

Explanation

This prediction foresees the route of the Caledonian Canal and those which first used it in the middle of the 19th century would certainly have had sails.

Prediction

"The day is coming when two false teachers shall come from across the seas. At the same time there will be nine bridges in Inverness. The streets will be full of ministers without grace and women without shame."

Explanation

There is doubt as to whether this prophecy has been fulfilled yet. Some say that the two false teachers were the evangelists Moody and Sankey who attempted to transform the religion of the Highlands, without success. Whether, or not, there are nine bridges in Inverness depends on two things. One, counting the Islands bridges as two rather than one crossing of the river; and two, whether one includes the Kessock Bridge. If one includes both of these, then look out for "ministers who were without grace" and "women without shame".

Prediction

"The day is coming when the bridge that spans the River Ness will be swept away while crowded with people. I see a man on a white horse and a woman great with child falling into the water."

Explanation

In April 1665 the bridge at the bottom of Bridge Street was undergoing repairs by a joiner when he inadvertently sawed through a main beam. The bridge, which had some 200 men, women and children on it at the time, collapsed and threw all the people into the river. Although there were a number of injuries sustained nobody was killed. There were several horsemen on the bridge at the time, one of whom was riding a grey stallion.

Prediction

"Oh, Drumossie Moor, my heart is aching for thee, for the day is coming when thy black wilderness will flow with the best of Highland blood. I pray to God that I may not be spared to witness that day for it will be a fearful time. Heads lie lopped off in the heather; limbs lie severed and lost; mercy has altogether deserted mankind while brother savages brother. Red coats are stained black with blood; red blood chokes the flower of the clans. The roar of the great guns has woken the dead in hell while the living weep in the glens. Children rise up against children, old men cut out the hearts of their companions. Oh God, oh Culloden, I am dying with your dead; I am stricken with your injured. Let me die before that day, oh let me die."

Explanation

This prediction was made on Drumossie Moor almost 100 years before the Battle of Culloden. Coinneach Odhar had visited Forbes of Culloden who had angered him and he was in a black mood before he fell into a trance on Drumossie.

Chapter 10

Notables and Characters of Old Inverness

People have one thing in common; they are all different. The citizens of Inverness, past and present, are no exception to this. From its earliest days Inverness has been subject to a particularly rich variety of cultural influences. Though the population is famous for its sense of 'Highland belonging' one must bear in mind that it has grown from a melting pot of Irish, Welsh and Norse influences, with a mixture of European enrichment thrown in. Despite the fact that from the 18th century onwards the indigenous population was continually being 'watered down' by Lowlanders, and others from further afield, a strong Highland or Gaelic culture remained, at grass roots level at least, for the next two centuries. It is the 'Highlandness' of the people, encompassing their strength of character, determination, hunger to succeed and open honesty, which made them what they are, and which ensured that those who travelled to the four corners of the world to seek their fortunes would succeed so well in what they did. The Highland clearances may have been aimed at deporting the population for the material gain of the landlords who participated in it, but it also ensured that Highlanders were spread around the globe to work their magic wherever they landed. Many an Invernessian left home to seek his fortune in the new world and ended up holding a position of high esteem in his adopted country – history bears witness to this many times over.

Of course not all successful Invernessians left home to make their mark on life, many remained here and spent their lives, or at least some of it, contributing to the success of the town. I have outlined the lives of some of these notables in this section, although clearly it has not been possible to include everyone who might merit inclusion. One must also bear in mind that success is a journey, not a destination – so do not be surprised if some of the characters are not life's 'favourite sons'. Many have contributed to the colourful past of Inverness in all sorts of interesting ways – some have been financially successful, some have built great buildings, whilst others, with a less fortunate start in life, have contributed in their own special way to the history of the City. So, as well as the more notable citizens of the past one will also read of the 'characters' whose individuality seemed to be moulded in a different pattern to that of other people, and whose worth was measured on another plane from that of the ordinary citizen. They are all worthy of mention in their own special way.

Cuthbert of Castlehill and Drakies

The first known Cuthbert in Inverness married a 'lady of the auld castle', in 1368, and inherited large tracts of land, which his family retained for the next three centuries. This family was once one of the most powerful and influential in Inverness, and their importance extended well beyond the boundaries of the town. Colbert, a Prime Minister to Louis XIV of France, went to the extent of obtaining an Act of Parliament to claim descent from the Cuthberts, which shows the extent of their influence in Scotland at that time, and another descendant fought at the Battle of Harlaw in 1411. Some time in the 16th century the family managed to acquire the lands of Drakies, which had been granted to the Burgh in the Charter of 1591.

The first member of the family to become Provost of the town was George, in 1556, and for 60 of the next 130 years a Cuthbert was Provost of the town, with other relations often holding different offices at the same time. It was this same George Cuthbert to whom the Prior of the Friary handed over the Dominican Friars' valuables and papers to, in 1554, and whose widow denied all knowledge of them after his death. Curiously, he also managed to acquire all the Friary lands as well as the Friary itself for his own profit despite the fact that they were given to the town for the relief of the poor. Almost a century later, in 1644, another relative, John Cuthbert of Castlehill, was given command of a troop of Inverness militia, made up of eighty of the best musketeers from the town, who went to confront the Irish who had landed in support of Montrose. Some 30 years later Margaret Cuthbert of Castlehill bequeathed the land of the Chapel Yard to the town, for the purpose of a burial ground, after seeing bodies on the Maggot exposed by the rising tide.

The last Cuthbert to be Provost was John, in the late 17th century, and shortly afterwards his Drakies side of the family died out, with all lands and possessions going to the Castlehill side. But in 1748 George of Castlehill, Sheriff Depute of Inverness-shire, fell foul of a curse from the Witch of Millburn and fell to his death from his horse. From that point onward the fortunes of the Cuthbert's rapidly declined. One Lewis Cuthbert, former Provost Marshall of Jamaica, and whose brother was the Bishop of Rodez, returned to Inverness with a view to recovering the family fortunes but without success, and he died in modest circumstances. The family lived on in the area but the glory days were long gone, and in 1783 the last of the line to receive any kind of public office was Alexander Cuthbert, who became a freeman of the Burgh.

Lady Anne Mackintosh

Anne Farquharson of Invercauld was 20 years old when she married Angus, the 22nd MacKintosh of MacKintosh, who was more than twice her age at the time. With her husband away pursuing his military career with the Government forces this very beautiful young woman was left to fend for herself much of the time. Her sympathies lay firmly with those of her Jacobite father, rather than with those of her husband. So when news reached her in July, 1745, that the Young Pretender had landed in Scotland she embraced his cause with enthusiasm. Returning home she rejected her husband's political loyalty and set about encouraging his clansmen to support the Prince. With a purse full of money and a sweet smile "Colonel Anne", as she came to be known, had within 15 days won over some 600 of the MacKintosh clan and placed Alexander MacGillivray of Dunmaglass

 at the head of her troops. It was reported that he was in love with her and willingly took the position. On 16th February, 1746, the Prince stayed with her at Moy Hall and some reports suggest that she offered herself to him with the grace and nobility of her position. Lord Loudoun, commander of the Government forces in Inverness, learnt of the Prince's whereabouts and set out to capture him with around 1,700 men, but his journey to Moy was noticed and reported to Anne, whereupon she immediately sent her blacksmith, Donald Fraser, and four servants to watch the approaching troops. Fraser deployed his small band and told them to fire at the Hanoverians whilst he shouted, "Advance, advance lads, I think we have the dogs now!" The Government troops thought they were caught in a trap by the Jacobite army and turned and fled back to Inverness. This action, known as the "Rout of Moy" ensured the Prince's safety for the calamity of Culloden.

Prince Charlie rallied his forces and pursued Loudoun to Inverness expecting to meet him in battle – only to find the town deserted of troops and Loudoun heading north. They eventually met at Dornoch where a skirmish took place resulting in the MacKintosh

being captured along with some Government troops. The MacKintosh was ignominiously handed over into the custody of Colonel Anne to be detained in his own ancestral home. It is said that their meeting was cold and formal. She greeted him saying, "Your servant, Captain", and he replied, "Your servant, Colonel".

The day following the battle of Culloden, Anne was captured and taken to Inverness where her deeds were well documented amongst the Government forces. It is said that when she was arrested the soldiers could not believe that the slight girl they saw before them was the warrior they were seeking. She spent six weeks in the guardroom at Inverness and during that time softened the hearts of all who met her bar General Hawley, who would have hanged her had he had his way. According to letters written by the Government officers of the time, Anne had many visitors to her cell to "drink tea" – the most frequent being Lord Loudoun who, it is thought, had an affair with her.

In 1750, Anne went to London where she was much sought after by 'society' who were eager to catch a glimpse of the legendary Highland rebel. An apocryphal story relates how she met the Duke of Cumberland at a ball where he asked her to dance to the tune "Up and waur them a', Willie". She obliged, but at the end of the dance asked him to dance to her tune, which he foolishly agreed to – it turned out to be "The auld Stuarts back again" much to his embarrassment.

When her husband died in 1770, she went to live in the Lowlands although a letter to Provost MacKintosh in Inverness suggests that her heart was still in the Highlands – "I beg my best compliments to your family, and all my friends in Inverness. I shall ever remember the place and them with the greatest affection."

Charles Grant MP

One of Inverness's famous sons he was born at Aldourie in March 1746, just before the Battle of Culloden. His father fought for the Jacobites in the battle and, although seriously wounded, he was taken by friends and hidden from Cumberland's soldiers until it was safe for him to return home. No longer able to farm after Culloden he joined the Government forces and spent most of his life serving abroad. His wife was left to raise their children in her father's home. When Charles was old enough he became assistant to a merchant and ship owner in Cromarty who taught him a great deal about business matters. Five years later Charles went to London to work in the counting house of his father's cousin, Alexander Grant, who had served with Clive in India and who was now an East India Merchant. Two years later, at the age of 21 years, he left for Bengal in India to work for a Richard Becher, a member of the India Council. Suffering ill health in 1770 he returned to London for a short spell and, during his convalescence he married a seventeen-year-old girl, Jane Fraser, from Balnain. He returned to India with his bride in 1773 and spent a further seventeen years there before his wife's ill health forced them to returning home, in 1790. In the interim Charles had made his fortune through hard work and devotion to duty.

He had risen steadily in the ranks whilst in India, mainly because he was found to be honest and trustworthy, attributes which were in short supply at that time in the Indian Service. Had he not been forced to return to this country through his wife's ill health it is said that he would have become Governor General. On his return to India in 1773 he was made a Director of the East India Company and later became its Chairman. A deeply religious man, he founded and financed several churches in India and at home and is attributed as having established the first Sunday School in Inverness.

He was elected MP for Inverness-shire from 1802 to 1818, having beaten Fraser of Lovat and Forbes of Culloden in the contest. Widely recognised as an excellent MP, he willingly supported schemes which benefited the Highlands including the Caledonian Canal and general improvements in transport.

Charles Grant Jnr

Two of his three sons, all born in India, also followed him into Parliament and were prominent in public affairs. Charles, born in 1778, and Robert, a year later, entered Cambridge together, and gaining outstanding academic distinction they were both called to the Bar in 1807. Charles entered Parliament in 1811 and became Lord of the Treasury two years later before taking up his father's constituency on his retirement in 1818. The following year he became Chief Secretary for Ireland and a Privy Councillor. Holding several other offices, he resigned in 1827, only to return three years later as Colonial Secretary and be raised to the peerage as Lord Glenelg. In 1829, whilst he was staying in the Caledonian Hotel, a "no popery" demonstration in the town burned his effigy on the Exchange, smashed the hotel windows and then went on to wreck the Catholic Chapel on Margaret Street. A few months later, in a change of fortune, he was chaired through the streets of Inverness with music and banners because of his support for Reform. Charles retired from office in 1839.

Robert Grant

His brother Robert did not enter Parliament until 1818 when he represented Elgin for eight years before moving to Inverness. Unlike the Magistrates of Inverness, Robert supported Reform, and when the 1830 election was called the Magistrates nominated Baillie of Leys instead of Robert. This decision made Robert's defeat in the election almost inevitable so he transferred to Norwich where he was elected with a large majority. He resigned from politics in 1834 to become Governor of Bombay and also received a Knighthood. A poet of some repute, his best known composition is "O Worship the King, all-glorious above", sometimes known as the 'Inverness Hymn'.

Captain Hugh Edward Walker

Born in Yorkshire in 1865, Walker was educated at Eton and Sandhurst before taking a commission in the Royal Welsh Fusiliers. He fought in Burma in 1885 but did not see active service in the First World War. Captain Walker and his wife came to Inverness in 1919 and took up residence in Kingsmills House (the former Kingsmills Hotel) as tenant of its then owner, Alexander Fraser. Six years later he purchased Kingsmills House from Fraser for the extremely reasonable sum of £5,750 – considering that it included in the price a large garden with a peach house, greenhouses, summer house, gardener's cottage, garage, stables, wash house, a boat and the Mill Dam which fed the King's Mill Granary. Captain Walker had a kind, generous nature, and in the sixteen years he spent in Inverness, before his death in 1935, he succeeded in doing a great deal of good work in a very unpretentious and unassuming way. During that time he served as President of the Inverness Thistle Football Club as well as Northern Counties Cricket Club and the Inverness Horticultural Society. He was also a prominent Rotarian, chief lay elector of St John's Church and Assistant County Commissioner of the Boy Scouts. His funeral was attended by a large number of mourners and he was survived by his wife, Marjory – daughter of the 21st Baron Forbes of Brux – his son and three daughters.

Walker always had a keen interest in sport and young people and as a consequence he donated the park, bounded by Kingsmills Road and Damfield Road, as a playing field for the Boy Scouts and the Boys Brigade. The park was named after him, Walker Park, and, in line with his instructions, the Council planted trees and shrubs along its perimeter. It is interesting that, to this day, the park remains an open recreational ground as intended by Walker.

Opposite to Walker Park, on the other side of Kingsmills Road, stands Fraser Park, which was donated to the Town by **Fraser of Maryfield.** It was designed to have hockey pitches, a football pitch, tennis courts and a bowling green as well as a pavilion. Mrs Fraser of Maryfield declared the area open in June 1935 by throwing the first bowl and serving the first ball, in the tennis court, before the assembled crowd adjourned to the pavilion for tea. Thus the Town gained two excellent recreational areas thanks to the generosity of two of its prominent citizens.

Anne MacKay

During the aftermath of Culloden when Cumberland's men were rounding up stray Jacobites and imprisoning them wherever they could find a suitable spot, two men, Robert Nairn and Ranald Macdonald of Bellfinlay, found themselves locked in the cellar of Anne MacKay's house. Originally from Skye, and MacLeod by name, she had lived in Inverness for some time and was clearly a Jacobite supporter. For a whole year she provided the two men with food and clothing and generally made sure that they were as comfortable as possible – despite Macdonald's broken leg. She eventually agreed, with other Jacobite sympathisers, to enter into a plot to free Nairn – Macdonald's leg forbidding him to be part of the plan. She smuggled some food and clothing into his cell and enticed the guard away from the entrance and up a nearby close long enough for Nairn to effect his escape, which was not noticed until the following morning when there was an almighty hue and cry. MacKay was apprehended and dragged before Colonel Leighton for questioning. Since she could not speak any English, Baillie Fraser was instructed to question her in the "Irish tongue". She refused an offer of 10 guineas, a fairly substantial sum of money, to divulge who her accomplices were and, as punishment for her silence, was summarily dispatched to a house full of soldiers with orders that she was not to sit or lie down for three days and nights. Thereafter, she was sent to prison for seven weeks where she contracted swelling of her legs which she never recovered from. During her stay in prison a soldier's wife was put in with her to intoxicate her and try to make her confess to being a Jacobite. Anne was up to the challenge, however, being both loyal to her clan and also to the Jacobite cause, she replied, "I like the Duke for I be a MacLeod, and MacLeod's do not like Charley". Unable to break her and make her confess, Leighton was minded to have her banished from the town, but Provost Fraser managed to persuade him to have her released instead. Shortly after her release from prison some soldiers beat up her son so badly that he died three days afterwards. A very sad end to a tale of bravery and loyalty.

Alexander Ross

Although his name is usually strongly associated with the Highlands, the architect Alexander Ross was born in Huntly Hill, Stracathro, Angus, in 1834, the son of James Ross, architect, who was then aged about 53. His father brought the family to Inverness around 1838 and they lived in Church Street, where his father had his business office. He was educated at Inverness Royal Academy and Bell's Institution, and on leaving, about 1848, he was apprenticed to a building contractor to gain practical experience before being articled to his father. It is unlikely that either of these apprenticeships could have been the usual length of time as it is written that he left his father's office to gain practical experience as 'a clerk of works in a contractor's firm'. He returned to his father as assistant before taking over the practice at the age of 19 when his father died in 1853. A younger brother, James, who predeceased him, had been a solicitor in Inverness.

In 1859 he formed a partnership with an old school friend, William Joass, and in the same year enlisted in the Volunteers with the Inverness Garrison Artillery of which he was later to become colonel. A few years later, in 1863, he joined the exclusive St John's Masonic

Lodge, Inverness. The following year he married Mary Ann Carnaby Finlayson, daughter of Sir Alexander Matheson's factor on Harris, an influential match which brought the factorship of Matheson's Inverness estate in 1868. The partnership of Ross & Joass was dissolved in 1865, Joass thereafter practising independently in Dingwall. The following year Ross secured the commission for the new St Andrew's Cathedral in Inverness and this, in turn, resulted in his being nominated to take part in a limited competition for the design of St Mary's Episcopal Cathedral in Edinburgh, in 1872. His triple-spired design was mistaken for that of William Burges' while that of Burges was wrongly assumed to be Ross's. Both architects issued disclaimers, thus effectively identifying their correct design. Ross's scheme, nevertheless, attracted the admiration of the Trustees although it eventually lost out to George Gilbert Scott by only one vote. Scott was then asked to add western spires to his own design similar to that of Ross's. This provoked a reaction from Ross who wrote objecting to Scott's appointment. This appeal to the Trustees was unsuccessful and the competition damaged Ross's reputation when rumours began to circulate that Ross's design had been made by an ex-assistant of Burges', the London architect George Freeth Roper to whom the design of St Andrew's Cathedral in Inverness had been farmed out in 1866.

Despite all of this, the Bishop of Brechin gave Ross his support and his lodge made him master from 1873 to 1876. In addition, Ross was elected to the Town Council of Inverness in 1881, and served as provost from 1889 to 1895. The University of Aberdeen conferred the degree of LLD on him in 1891, by which date Ross's practice had grown very considerably, particularly with new schools and schoolhouses, of which he was said to have built 450 for the school boards from 1872 onwards. It was probably because of school work in the remoter areas of the Highlands, including long journeys by steamer, mail coach and gig, that Ross opened a branch office in Oban in 1880, having five years earlier entered into a partnership with David Mackintosh. It was Mackintosh who ran the branch office, but sometime after 1883, when the demands of the school boards had been largely met, the partnership was dissolved, Mackintosh thereafter continued to run the Oban practice independently, just as Joass had done in Dingwall. In 1887 Ross entered into a third and much longer running partnership with Robert John Macbeth who had worked for firms in Elgin and Aberdeen before joining Ross's practice in 1880.

Ross was admitted FRIBA in 1893 and his nomination papers state that by this date he had "spent a good deal of time in travelling and study, visiting Germany, France, Italy, Greece, Egypt, Palestine." A formal Jubilee dinner at the Palace Hotel was hosted by Inverness and District Building Trades Federation to mark his half centenary in practice in March 1904, the event being marked by the presentation of a gold watch and silver candelabra.

The partnership with MacBeth was dissolved the following year as Ross wanted to take his son John Alistair Ross, born 1882, into partnership. Ross continued the practice through the First World War while his son served with the Royal Artillery, eventually reaching the rank of Major. Alexander Ross retired in 1923 and remained quite remarkably active until he died on 19 May 1925 at the age of ninety, still supervising work in his garden until the previous day. His funeral was held in St Andrews Cathedral, where he was a member of the congregation and he was buried at Tomnahurich with Masonic rites. He left moveable estate of £2,670 but probably had significant property holdings in addition.

Ross had extensive public and business interests during his lifetime and was conservative in politics. He was a director of the Northern Infirmary, the Inverness College, the Caledonian Bank, the Lancashire Assurance Company and Inverness tweed mills, as well as being a major shareholder of the Rose Street Foundry. He was one of the founders of the Inverness Scientific Society and Field Club, assisting in its publications as antiquarian and geologist, and the Gaelic Society of Inverness, always wearing full Highland dress on any occasion that was at all formal. Ross came to be known as "The Christopher Wren of the Highlands", because of his outstanding architectural achievements.

William Inglis of Kinmylies

William Inglis (1747-1801) was a prosperous merchant and banker in Inverness. He bought the small estate of Kingsmills in 1786, the original house of which was ultimately incorporated into the Kingsmills Hotel when it was built. Inglis entered the Town Council at an early age and was made a Baillie at the age of 33 years. In 1791, as Dean of Guild, he was responsible for raising funds to build a new jail, courthouse and steeple, and was the cashier for the Court House and Jail accounts. He was also the driving force behind the establishment of Inverness Royal Academy and the Northern Infirmary, both of which received funds from planters in Guyana, hence establishing a connection with the slave trade.

One of the most influential figures in the Burgh, he was made Honorary Treasurer of the Burgh in 1775. In 1797 Inglis was elected provost, a post he held until 1800, and his portrait hangs in the Main Hall of Inverness Town House, although the artist is unknown. Provost Inglis is particularly remembered for having entertained Robert Burns to supper at his home in Kingsmills in September 1787. Under Provost Inglis' administration many of the buildings in Inverness, which had fallen into ruin since the Jacobite Rebellion, were repaired or rebuilt, and in 1800 he persuaded the Council to build a retaining wall at the foot of the castle. Inglis Street, named after him, used to be the crowded link between the town's meal market and the cattle market. The street, along with Academy Street and Eastgate, was also the site of the town's annual Martinmas Market, held in November. This was more commonly called 'The Cheese Market' as locally made cheese and butter were sold at this annual fair. William Inglis committed suicide on 14th February 1801. *"Provost Inglis, whom we all respected and esteemed, has destroyed himself; a sudden shock, occasioned by the elopement of his Banking clerk, who was also the active partner in the wine business, acting on a Plethoric [red faced, florid] Habit and a mind which felt severely any shock . . . He threw himself into the Ness from the middle arch [of the bridge] at half ebb in the morning of the 14th at ½ past 3 in the morning."* Although he died two years before the opening of the Northern Infirmary,William Inglis' name appeared prominently on the facade of the building. In 2009 a plaque was placed on the building acknowledging for the first time the source of much of the funds.

William Inglis' brother, George, left the town for Bristol shortly afterwards

"rather than give to some envious narrow minded wretches in this little community the malignant satisfaction of triumphing in the adversity of our family."

Another brother, Alexander, had a daughter who married Dr James Robertson of Aultnaskiach, also a provost of Inverness. Alexander's granddaughter was Dr Elsie Inglis, one of Edinburgh's best-known medical women. She specialised in the care of women and children, but also set up the Scottish Women's Hospital which sent hospital units to France, Greece and Serbia during World War I. Another member of the family, Dr John Inglis Nicol, served as provost from 1840 to 1843.

William's brothers George and Hugh were also involved in the slave trade and in the family owned plantations in Demerara, Guyana. Hugh captained the *Maria*, which traded between Bristol and St Kitts and George's son, also called Hugh, later managed their Demerara plantations. By 1798 the family owned two adjoining plantations on the Demerara coast, *Bellefield* and *Phoenix Park*, each of 250 acres and growing cotton. Hugh left Demerara in 1804 and returned to Inverness but was again in the colony in 1806. George Inglis was a partner of Evan Baillie, an Inverness-born slave trader based in Bristol. He was originally from Dochfour and was the owner of nearly 2000 slaves, as well as being an MP for Bristol. He opposed the campaign to abolish the slave trade because he believed that it would inevitably lead to a demand to free the slaves on West Indian plantations.

Sir James MacKintosh of Kyllachy

James MacKintosh (1765 – 1832) was born at Aldourie and both his parents were from old Highland families. His mother died while he was still a child and his father was frequently abroad, so he was brought up by his grandmother whilst attending Fortrose Academy. A bright boy, he frequently encouraged his classmates to join him in debates and, at the age of 13 years, proclaimed himself a Whig. He went to Kings College, Aberdeen, in 1780, gaining his degree in 1787. A year later he moved to London and married Catherine Stuart. They had a son, who died in infancy, and three daughters. His efforts in journalism became fairly profitable, although he appeared to be more interested in political events than his professional prospects. His wife died in 1797 and the following year he married Catherine Allen, sister-in-law of Joshua Wedgewood. They had 2 sons, one of whom died in infancy, and 2 daughters.

MacKintosh became absorbed by the French Revolution and in 1791 he published "Vindiciae Gallicae", a defence of the French Revolution, which won him the admiration and friendship of some of the most distinguished men of the time. The success of this book encouraged him to give up medicine and change to the legal profession and he was called to the bar in 1795 and gained a considerable reputation. His greatest public efforts in the legal field were his lectures at Lincoln's Inn, and the resulting fame helped open doors for him later in life. Mackintosh was also famed for his speech in 1803 defending Jean Gabriel Peltier, a French refugee, against a libel suit instigated by Napoleon. He was knighted the same year.

In 1804 he sold his Kyllachy estate to Provost Phineas MacKintosh for £9,000, although most of the money was eaten up in loans that had been previously drawn on the estate in anticipation of its sale. Although the estate remained in MacKintosh hands, by the sale  to Phineas Mackintosh, there is little evidence that this was James MacKintosh's intention, or that the sale held much interest for him beyond pecuniary gain. To Sir James himself, the sale of Kyllachy offered a means of affording the life to which he aspired, one that was marked by a sense of belonging to the centres of metropolitan power. With little to gain from his own networks of kin and clan, MacKintosh moved away from the Highlands to form other relationships that would provide him with a greater chance of access for social and political power. In 1804 he took up a post as Chief Judge of Bombay. He didn't take to India, where he became quite ill, and was glad to leave for home in 1811. He entered Parliament, as a Whig, in 1813, representing Nairn until 1818. From 1818 to 1824 he was professor of law and politics in the East India Company's College in Haileybury, then he returned to Parliament to represent Knaresborough till his death in 1832. MacKintosh stood against the famous novelist Sir Walter Scott in the election for Rector of Glasgow University in 1822. The vote was tied and the outgoing Rector, Francis Jeffrey, gave his casting vote to Sir James. He was made a privy councillor in 1828 and appointed Commissioner for the affairs of India under the Whig administration of 1830. His "History of the Revolution in England" was not published until 2 years after his death and was proclaimed as the best history ever written of the reign of James II.

MacKintosh's premature death, at the age of sixty-six, was due to a chicken bone becoming stuck in his throat causing him to choke. Although the bone was eventually removed, his suffering continued until he died a month later. He was buried in Hampstead churchyard having spent much of his later life in London. .

John Mitchell

John Mitchell moved to Inverness from Fort Augustus to take up the position of General Inspector of Roads and the family lived in Telford Street. His house was in a row of Redcastle stone houses which were built for Caledonian Canal contractors and which are still standing today. Joseph spent his boyhood years here and attended the Royal Academy before going on to enjoy a distinguished career as an engineer. He studied under Thomas Telford and was responsible for building the railway between Inverness and Perth, which greatly improved communications to the Highlands. Joseph was associated with improvements to the harbour, giving it its present shape, and also the road network, having by this time taken over from his father as Superintendent of Roads. He served on the Town Council, his portrait hangs in the Town House, and was a Director of the Caledonian Bank in Inverness as well as a prominent member of the Institute of Civil Engineers in London. When he died in 1883 his body was brought back from London to Viewhill villa in Inverness before being buried in Tomnahurich cemetery. In his will he left generous sums of money to both the Soup Kitchen and the Coal Fund in Inverness, having previously given a donation to establish a town library. Joseph Mitchell wrote "Reminiscences of my Life in the Highlands", in two volumes, which gives a wonderful account of his work and the people of this area.

Phineas MacKintosh of Drummond – "Phinny Fool"

Phineas MacKintosh was born in 1725, the son of a landed proprietor. His parents had lost a number of children in infancy and resolved not to call him by a traditional family name, so they chose a name from the Bible. He served as Provost four times between 1770 and 1791 and his portrait hangs in the Town house. Phineas lived with his sister, Catherine, in a large house near the foot of Castle Street, the entrance to which was off a courtyard. He was an eccentric who was well known as the host of large and costly dinner parties to which all the gentlemen of 'position' were invited. The best fare was always to be had at Phinny's table along with the choicest wines and the dinner lasted for several hours. It is said that when he came to count the cost of these evenings he would wring his hands and wail and cry, although it seemed to have been soon forgotten.

If anything was served at table that he didn't care for himself he would have it removed before anyone could taste it saying "I am for none. Take it away". The highlight of these evenings appears to have been his after dinner toasts and speeches which were given in crambo, (a form of verse speech) part of his everyday conversation, often less than complimentary to his guests although they seemed to take it in good part. The evening often finished up with Phinny under the table, having taken too much of his own wine. Although he had a good staff of servants, on the day of a party he was often seen running about the house in a white apron doing some of the domestic tasks himself and issuing orders to everyone. For fear of incurring the wrath of the minister, Phinney did not have dinner parties on a Sunday. Instead he would invite someone home from church to lunch with him. On one occasion when the Sunday lunch was mistakenly burnt he was heard running about the house screaming at the servants that they would all end up in jail.

He was fond of attending the various cattle markets and when there he generally drank too much whisky, ending with him making purchases which he regretted the following day. On one occasion he purchased a bull which was delivered to his house and Phinny wakened up the following morning to the sound of the bull roaring.

He was a tall, stout gentleman with a bad leg which he dragged as he walked, thus he tended to drive about in a high gig drawn by a fine horse. It was said that he had had a toe amputated and that he kept it in spirits on his mantelpiece. When he attended the Northern Meeting Balls he always wore a scarlet waistcoat embroidered with gold thread and with bright buttons on his coat. One presumes that he didn't do a lot of dancing !!

It is said that he made his money in the West Indies but it is difficult to imagine that someone with his 'shortcomings' could have acquired it by his own efforts. It seems more likely that he inherited it in some way. Perhaps he was not as eccentric as he made out, however, because it would appear that during his time as Provost he was involved in some shady dealings. In 1783, the land of Drummond, owned by the Burgh, was sold well below value to Phineas, and in 1796 land called Campfield, which adjoined

Drummond, and which also belonged to the Burgh, was acquired by him. The land was described in the council minutes as being barren, which was substantially untrue, and was therefore sold at less than its true value. It was also alleged that a higher offer for the land was refused. In 1804 he purchased the Kyllachy estate from Sir James MacKintosh for £9,000 so he must indeed have been a man of some means.

Characters in Inverness

There were many local characters and eccentrics that were often seen in and around Inverness over the centuries. Some of which I had heard about from my parents, although I had never seen them, and a few who I remember myself.

"Cappy Eppie" (I think Euphemia was her real name) always wore a man's cap, or a battered straw hat, as she wandered round the town with her melodeon under her arm. She couldn't actually play it but she loved the noise it made as she pushed the bellows in and out. One story relates that "Cappy Eppie" went into a dance hall in Elgin while a fancy dress ball was on and she was given the first prize for being dressed as "Cappy Eppie".

"Rory the Bird" was an inmate of the Poorhouse (later Hilton Hospital) and he was known to all in the town. He shuffled round the town all day greeting everyone and asking after them often remarking "aye, aye, how are you, och aye".

"Feeto Cher" was another character who wandered aimlessly around the town. When he walked his feet pointed at a quarter to three and every now and then he would stop in front of a woman, irrespective of age, and say, "Now here's a beautiful gyurl".

"Forty Pockets" was a very well known character about town. He got his name from the endless layers of coats and jackets that he wore, and when offered another jacket or a coat he simply wore it on top of what he already had. Originally from the Merkinch area he wandered the streets looking in the bins until the late 1950s. When he had money, which was seldom, he would spend the night in a lodging house for poor people in North Church Place. He slept rough in the Leachkin area and, I believe, delivered the papers in that area too. Sadly, he ended up as an inmate in Craig Dunain. Whilst there he still wore an oversized brown coat that was always checked last thing at night and which was usually full of "stolen goods". His 'tale' lives on, however, as he has been commemorated on the newly decorated wall of Crown Road. Fiddlers were common in and around the town also. **"Aberfoyle"** was a lame fiddler who broke his leg between the pier and Kessock Ferry after playing at a wedding party on the Black Isle. **"John Fowler"** would play at "penny reels" when everyone who went paid a penny for the dance. **"Blind Willie"** would also play for those "penny reels". **"Corn in Egypt"** was another fiddler whose real name was John MacRae. The boys called him by his nickname, which made him so angry that he would chase them. He was always accompanied by his daughter on the "boss" fiddle.

Another Inverness fiddler was **Jocky Cumming** who was in the Inverness Militia, but he joined the band and played in orchestras, especially at the Northern Meeting Balls. He was also a composer of reels and Strathspeys. Once he had an invitation to play at Buckingham Palace, and set off for London by sea, but there he got mixed up with bad characters, who took everything worth any money from him. He wandered around London for weeks until he met someone from Inverness, who paid for his return. He lived only for four weeks after his return, probably through lack of food and exposure while in London.

Chapter 11

Markets and Fairs

One of the Charters granted to the Burgh of Inverness by King William the Lion (1165 – 1214) gave the burgesses the right to hold weekly markets as well as a number of other rights. The Great Charter of 1591, granted by James VI, and which confirmed all previous charters and defined the properties and privileges of the burgh, reaffirmed this and stated that Inverness had trading and market rights over other northern burghs including Tain, Dingwall and Cromarty. The Charter states that markets were to be held on Wednesdays and Saturdays and, in addition, eight fairs could be held in any year, and last for up to eight days each. One on Palm Sunday, St Andrew's Fair on 7th July, Marymas on 15th August, Roodmas in September, Martinmas on 10th November, Saint Thomas Fair in December, Peter Fair on 1st February, and Saint Mark's Fair on 25th April. Such events played a very important part in the life of the ordinary working man and his family, often forming a welcome relief from the humdrum of everyday life and the struggle for survival. Many were associated with religious beliefs and for the poorer, often illiterate, townspeople these days fashioned reference points for them to measure their way throughout the year. The Burgh Court records indicate that there were other individual days which were also celebrated, such as Ash Wednesday, St Boniface Fair, St Boniface Day, Lammas, Yule, Letter Mary Day, Hallowmas, Mary Day, St Thomas's Eve, Feast of Midsummer, St Colme's Day, Rood Day, Roodmas, Munroe's Fair, Feast of Hallowmas, Fasterns Eve, Pasch, Andrewmas, Coan Fair, Corpus Christie Day, Michaelmas, Beltane, St Duthus Day, Uphalye Day, Pardoun Fair and Bryde Day. There certainly seems to have been plenty of them and, as we shall see later, no shortage of stalls selling goods or the people to buy them.

The area outside the Town Hall, known as the Exchange, once measured 20 x 10 metres and was used to proclaim events of special interest to the townspeople. An ideal place for townswomen to gather and have a gossip and for their men to buy snuff or tobacco from the numerous stalls which abounded on the street. Here too could be seen the people who had been sentenced to the pillory or tied to the whipping post for punishment – often receiving taunts and jibes from the local boys. It was also used as a market area and, indeed, at one time the markets stretched along the full length of High Street with the

Market Cross standing in the middle of the street. The first mention of the Cross, in this position, was in 1456, indicating that markets were held along the length of the High Street at that time. The Cross was destroyed during a clan raid in 1600 but, following the addition of a new shaft, it was repositioned on the Exchange where it stood for almost 200 years. In 1796 it was again moved, this time to the front of the old Town House where it stood alongside the Clachnacuddin stone before its final move to its present position, when the present Town House was built in 1882. Market days were not restricted to Wednesdays and Saturdays, as the Charter indicates, but at various times in the Town's history they appear to have taken place on most days of the week. Neither were the markets limited to the constraints of High Street but also appeared on Eastgate, Inglis Street, Academy Street, Bridge Street and Bank Street, depending on the type of market it was.

Throughout the history of the town, High Street has been the main area for traders and merchants. Its length once consisted of dwelling houses with ground floor stalls which opened onto the street and displayed the wares of the merchants who lived there. On market days the street would also be lined with another row of stalls where the country people would exhibit their produce and merchandise. On such days the street must have been bustling with people crowding round stalls, buying and bargaining for goods, with stallholders shouting for custom and children running about and being "tutted" at by the adults they annoyed with their antics. There were candy stalls which the 'Clach' boys delighted in tasting; gingerbread stalls with birds and other animals which smelled divinely of the peppery stuff they were made of; cheap jewellery stalls from which the town boys treated their lasses; boot and shoe stalls run by the cobblers from the Black Isle; farmers' stalls with butter, milk, eggs, cream, cheese, chickens, ducks, vegetables and fruit from their crofts and farms; stalls with old women selling stockings, wool, rolls of plaiding and homespun thread. Sandie Smith had a ballad stall opposite the High Street Post Office and sold his copies to anyone who was interested in them. Wicker baskets were sold by a 'foreigner' who always had a stall on the corner of Inglis Street. Nearby one would find pails and washing-tubs for sale and laid out on the street for all to see. Ballad singers and fiddlers plied their trade at strategic points along the street hoping to pick up a few pence as their raucous melodies competed with the shouts of the traders. Penny wheels and other amusements were ever present to test the resolve of young and old alike and to part them from their hard earned pennies. The taverns and inns around the town also did a good trade with beer and whisky flowing from 'early morn to dewy eve'. Market days usually saw a confrontation between the town boys and their country counterparts who were to be found at the family stalls on the High Street. One such altercation, which took place in 1738, found a MacLean lad from Glenurquhart being set upon by several town boys. He was their match, however, and soundly thrashed them before they cried out for reinforcements. Seeing the number he was faced with MacLean shouted out for clan support, a cry which could not be resisted by the then Town Provost, also a MacLean, who joined in the scuffle knocking several of the boys aside before being recognised and the trouble suppressed. Fighting amongst the boys of the town was not uncommon and some reports are given of schools fighting each other, quite apart from class fights and street fights.

By the middle of the 19th century the markets had become organised, and designated areas were set aside for the various producers to display their goods. On Tuesdays and Fridays a dairy market took place on the exchange and farmers would send their milk, butter, poultry, eggs, etc. to be sold there, competing against each other for the custom of the townspeople. On the same days a fruit and vegetable market was held on Academy Street with the farmers selling their wares from their carts directly to the people. A butcher's market (flesh market) was initially situated on Eastgate (Petty Street) not far from the foot of Stephen's Brae, but as the butchers gradually acquired shops within the town centre, the market changed to a slaughter house. A fish market was situated at the east end of High Street beside the foot of the Market Brae Steps, but the smell eventually became too much for the townspeople and it was shifted further out to Eastgate where the Butchers' Market was. On the site of the Fish Market, and that of an old building whose ground floor had been a Meal Market, was built the Post Office in 1844, and the building later became the Customs House. At the top of Stephen's Brae, stretching over towards Castle Street, there was a cattle market but, as the area was being developed, the residents found it very disagreeable and it was eventually shifted to the lands beside the Loch Gorm, which had been reclaimed once the embankment was built at the Longman in 1738.

On one market day, in 1668, a country woman was selling cheese and bread to the men who were attending the Cattle Market when one fellow, Finlay Dow by name, lifted up one of the cheeses and asked her how much she wanted for it. On hearing her reply he dropped the cheese, either by design or fault, which rolled down the slope towards the Castle. The woman informed him that he would now have to pay for the cheese but he told her, in no uncertain terms, that he would not. A man who had overheard the quarrel took a firm hold of Finlay and removed his bonnet as a guarantee of payment for the cheese. Finlay's friend now entered the fray and informed the man that he should free Finlay as the matter was none of his concern. The man refused and the matter then led to blows, soon encompassing more and more people until the whole hill was involved. After some time, as the fight spread and grew worse, the Town Guard was called out and John Reed, the Captain, tried without success to mediate in the argument. Swords were drawn and guns presented to the crowd in an attempt to maintain order with a few being wounded in the fray. Provost Cuthbert was summoned and appeared, complete with sword and targe, accompanied by a band of supporters. At this the guard, under pressure from the crowd, fired some rounds into the mob, killing two of them and wounding about 10 others, thus restoring peace.

A Horse Market was held in the Kingsmills area, on what is now the second tee of the Golf Course. The New Market Inn was named because of this market but has always been known locally as the "Fluke Inn". This is because the Kingsmills Burn had a ford across the road at this point and the road was called Fluke Street (from the Gaelic "fliuch" meaning "wet"). The Burn was inclined to overflow at one point and a flood in 1800 saw the spate cause great damage to property in Fluke Street, such that the area from the Millburn Roundabout to the sea had two feet of debris covering it. The body of a woman was discovered in Viewfield House the day after the flood subsided and it was supposed that she had been carried away by the water and drowned. Her identity has never been discovered.

As the popularity of the Friday Market grew in Inverness so did the cost of having a stall, much to the dissatisfaction of some of the country people – especially those from the Glenurquhart area. There already existed a Goat Market at Cnoc-nan-Gobhar (Hill of the Goats) near Tomnahurich, and they decided to set up their stalls there on a Thursday instead of attending the town Friday Market. Since the area was outside the Burgh grounds they did not have to pay stallholders charges. Gradually this market grew into a regular Cattle Market and then began to sell all kinds of farm produce, much to the annoyance of the farmers who used the Friday Market. The Town Magistrates were petitioned to have the Thursday Market stopped but were less then willing to do so. Next the Lairds of Grant and Glenurquhart were asked for assistance and responded by threatening to dismiss any farmer who traded at Cnoc-nan-Gobhar. Thus the Thursday Market ceased to exist and the Glenurquhart farmers were forced to compete with the other farmers at the Friday Market.

By this time there were five annual Fairs which were announced on the Exchange on Wednesdays and held on the two following days – Candlemas Fair in February, Whitsuntide Market in May, St Andrew's Fair in July, Marymas Fair in August and Martinmas Fair in November. On these same market days a Cattle Market was held on the Shore Street side of the Waterloo Bridge, later moving to the Capel Inch on the opposite side of the river, as a Horse and Cattle Market. On the last Fridays of April and October Feeing Markets were held when local lads and lasses put themselves up for hire as servants in the big town and country houses. As a result of the Highland Clearances another fair appeared on the scene, the Wool Fair, which took place on the second Thursday in July and the two following days. This Fair was extremely successful and so widely known that it was accepted as the gauge for sheep prices throughout Scotland. At its height it sold around 100,000 stones of wool and about the same number of sheep each year.

Initially, the country people would have flocked to these fairs to sell and barter their home-made cloth, tartan, farm produce and other goods, but the passage of time saw town shopkeepers stocking more and more as improved transportation made it easier to obtain goods from further afield, and 'country' goods became harder to sell. Eventually little business was done in local goods and the markets became less of an attraction for town and country people alike. By 1869, the Victorian Market was built with the main entrance on Academy Street adorned with the sculptured heads of sheep and cattle. Although some of the fairs and markets survived for many years after that, they all gradually faded into extinction. Only the Marymas Fair still exists, having been resurrected some years back, although it bears little resemblance to its original form.

We now have a once monthly "Farmers' Market" in the city, but how nice it would be to have a street market once a week – perhaps on the little used Falcon Square.

Chapter 12

Trade and Commerce

The location of Inverness, sitting astride the River Ness as it enters the Moray Firth and at the crossroads of east-west and north-south passage ways, dictates that it should have both strategical and tactical importance as a City. This remained the case throughout the City's history and, even today, it retains its status as an important administrative capital at the hub of transportation services for the Highlands. The emergence of the castle, initially to defend the river crossing, forged the way for the inevitable materialisation of houses around it, seeking its protection. As the need for defence diminished with the passage of time, the houses spread ever further from the protection of the castle, eventually crossing the river. As the population continued to grow, so did the necessity to supply food and goods to satisfy the demands of the townspeople. Initially a self-sufficient community, the continued growth of the town would have determined the need for commerce and industry to emerge and for a suitable transportation system to supply that growth. The town's coastal situation, with a river estuary wide enough, and sufficiently deep, to allow ships to enter, made it ideal for maritime transportation; the roads at that time being highly unsuitable for any form of transportation where time was a consideration.

It has long been debated whether the harbour grew because of the position of the town, or whether the town grew because the harbour was there to service it. Doubtless, one is a consequence of the other and collectively they provide the essence for development. Landowners and clan chiefs, educated in the town, freely mixed with the town's burghers and merchants, often discussing the needs and aspirations of the town and the necessity for improvement in its housing, transport, commerce, etc. These were the people who travelled far and wide, not just to England but also to the continent, and came into contact with other merchants looking for new business opportunities and partners. Hence the business net of trade and commerce connected with the town grew ever larger and wider with the passage of time.

The type of commerce and industry which forms within a community is often a factor of its location and the resources it has access to, and Inverness was no exception to that rule. It should be no surprise, then, to learn that the fishing, shipping and shipbuilding industries, and their associated trades, flourished in the town's early days, and that the multitude of merchandise which could be transported here, by ship, from ports near and far, formed the raw materials for the industries which grew up around the town. From about the 16th century the only people who were allowed to deal in raw materials, and manufacture items, were the Burgesses or members of the Merchant's Guilds. To become a Burgess you had to own a rood of land in the Burgh and pay the King 5d a year for it as well as live in the Burgh and help to keep watch in the town. On being admitted to the Guild you had to swear to be faithful to the Crown, and the Burgh, and treat your fellow Burgesses to a banquet of spice and wine as well as pay a fee of 20 merks to the town Treasurer. Others would be licensed to be stallholders for the sale of merchandise.

Bootholders were a lower class of person who paid for the right to work leather and make shoes. The Great Charter of 1591 stated that "no ship break bulk between Tarbetness and Inverness", thus giving the town the sole right, over towns to the north and east, to land goods from shipping. This ensured that the town had a busy port with goods being imported and exported not just for Inverness itself but also for the wider community. Both the Council and seafarers must have taken this right seriously because there are few records of it ever being breached. In 1609, however, Robert Henderson, sailing out of Leith, had his ship and its cargo confiscated for breaking bulk at Petty, and again in 1648 a Dundee Master was fined by the Council for landing cargo between Tarbetness and Inverness. The hinterland, surrounding the town, had a plethora of farms and crofts which produced a wide range of commodities and merchandise, in particular, wool, hides and barley – all essential elements for some of the towns manufacturing processes. The town merchants made good use of all that was valuable to their businesses, whilst the remainder was left for individuals to peddle at the markets. Most "common" people would have manufactured some of their own clothing – spinning and weaving the linen before tailoring the clothes – whilst the farmers and crofters also produced beef, pork, mutton, potatoes, oats, wheat, butter, honey, milk, cream, eggs, chickens, ducks, geese and rabbits, with many distilling their own whisky, so long as they could avoid the clutches of the excise man.

Make no mistake, life for most people in those days was hard. With work being scarce and wages low it was not easy even for tradesmen to make a decent living. There were no Trades Unions to look after the wellbeing of workers and the Guilds which did exist were for the protection of the employers. Once a man was employed, especially a craftsman, he was tied to the employer until released – if he chose to leave without the consent of the employer then it was unlikely that he would find further employment, and even probable that he would be prosecuted by the Burgh Courts.

From earliest times ship-building has played a predominant role in the history of Inverness, with at least three shipyards being situated along the length of the lower reaches of the river at any one time. Oak wood was floated down the river from Loch Ness and Fir from Glenmoriston and Strathglass by way of the River Beauly. The industry continued up until the middle of the 19th century, although by that time construction was limited to small boats and dinghies. The earliest record of a ship being built in Inverness is for the Comte de St Pol et Blois, Hugh de Chatellar, in 1249, when he commissioned a ship "of great size" to take him to the Crusades with Louis IX of France. It is undoubtedly a testimonial to the widely recognised skills of the shipwrights of Inverness, and the excellent reputation they must have enjoyed, that de Chatellar should choose here, rather than a shipyard in France, England or Spain, for the building of his ship. It was said that an Inverness ship's carpenter could command a job anywhere and hold his own with any other, at home or abroad. Thirty-one years later another French Count commissioned a ship in Inverness, following the wrecking of his vessel in the Orkney Islands. One would suspect, therefore, that the Inverness shipyards had a good reputation, which was worldwide rather than just local or national. It would not have been difficult to obtain the necessary timber for the construction of these ships, since the forests around Struy and Glenstrathfarrar were well stocked with excellent fir and oak trees. Any additional hardwood could easily have been obtained from south of the border, if needed. It is recorded that the Inverness yards received large orders for ships in the 14th century, from the government of Denmark, thus confirming that their fine reputation was international indeed.

Captain George Scott, later Vice-Admiral Scott, came to Inverness in 1643 for a ship to fight the Turks. He took his own carpenters with him, for some strange reason, and Lord Lovat supplied him with oak and fir from Glenmoriston, to construct a huge ship which took over two years to build. It set sail the day before the Battle of Auldearn and was anchored off Nairn, with a clear view of the Battle when it took place. Scott took his war frigate to the

Mediterranean Sea and served Venice where he became Vice-Admiral of the Venetian fleet and was the terror of the Mohammedan sailors. Ten years later, in 1655, Cromwell had a forty-ton frigate built for use on Loch Ness. The ship, carrying sixty men and armed with four pieces of cannon, was used to carry provisions from one end of the loch to the other. There being no canal at that time, the ship had to be hauled overland, using log rollers, for the six miles from Inverness to Loch Ness. It must have been a mammoth task for the soldiers and sailors who carried it out, as it is recorded that they broke three seven inch cables in the process. In 1670, Captain Pot, from the Royal Naval dockyard at Chatham, came to Inverness in search of timber for ships' masts. He obtained two shiploads of suitable fir trees from nearby forests, which were duly shipped back to London for use in the yards there.

These are only a few of the vessels which were built on the Ness shipyards over a space of about six centuries. There were also passenger schooners for the Inverness-London trade, the "Caledonia" being among them; smacks which journeyed from Inverness to Leith with passengers and goods; fishing vessels for the in-shore and sea-going trade; cargo boats for the merchants of the town and sea-faring ships to carry goods to and from continental, Baltic and Mediterranean ports. One report, from the early 19th century, states that a shipyard on the Ness had one ship ready for launching and another two at an advanced stage of construction, indicating that, even then, the industry was in a healthy state. In their heyday these yards must have employed a huge number of tradesmen and would probably have been one of the major employers of their time.

The obvious success of the shipbuilding industry would naturally have encouraged the development of other, associated, trades. Not surprisingly, therefore, Inverness was also noted for sailmaking, which was carried out in the Rope and Sail Works (sometimes referred to in the records as the Rope and Hempen-cloth Manufactory), built in 1765 and situated at the Citadel. The clock tower, which is sited near where Cromwell's Citadel was built, and was once thought to be the only remaining part of it, is actually the clock tower of this Rope and Sail Works. The sailcloth was manufactured there too, on looms, and the sails made to order for the local yards as well as those further afield. Judging by the number of people employed in the factory there was plenty of work for them to do, making and repairing sails for the ships which used the port. In another part of the Works all kinds of ropes were fabricated, from fine twine right up to ships' mooring cables, with hemp which was generally imported from the Baltic. At the beginning of the 20th century this factory employed around ninety people with a tradesman earning about 12s a week, the boys getting 2s and the girls slightly less, all of them working ten hours a day, six days a week.

The fishing industry was also a lucrative trade at one time, with a fleet of boats working out of the town. Prior to the late 17th century, when the first harbour was built, boats simply beached at the Longman, or the Maggot, depending how far up the river they could come, and unloaded their catch – which would have consisted of herring, cod, mackerel, haddock, whiting, skate, turbot and salmon. Thereafter, when the harbour was constructed, the port became busier as boats could more easily unload their catches and decrease their time at the quayside. The fish would either go to the market in Inverness or be repacked in larger boats and taken to the markets in England, Ireland and the continent. Salmon fishing in the River Ness was also a profitable business and was pursued commercially right into the 20th century. When the Lords of Justiciary visited the town on their circuit, in May, it was not unusual for them to be hospitably entertained in the Islands to fresh caught salmon from the river. There were salmon nets situated near to the mouth of the river, as well as the net fishing at the Friars' Shott, and this ensured a ready supply of fresh salmon for the townspeople in addition to that which was sold further afield.

Large fishing boats usually beached at the Longman and unloaded their cargo, which would then be transported into town via Rose Street, at that time called Scatgate (derived from the word 'scat' or tax) because all the fish landed was taxed. Another name for Scatgate was "Herring Way" because large amounts of herring came into the town via that route from the Longman. When the first quay in the harbour was built, in 1675, using some of the stones from the Chapel on the Green and paid for using income from Shore Dues, it meant that ships no longer had to beach at Longman Point, or further upstream at the Maggot, to unload their cargoes. The quay was situated to the east of where the Black Bridge is now, and on towards what is now Shore Street, with access to it by a track leading from the end of Church Street. It took almost 150 years for this track to be upgraded to something resembling a road. Some fishing boats, up to the end of the 18th century, continued past the quay on to the end of Chapel Street to discharge their catches.

By 1718 the harbour was in a very dilapidated state and in dire need of repair. The Town Council moved to raise the funds and obtained a Parliamentary Act, allowing them to levy a tax of one-sixth of a penny on every pint of beer sold within the Burgh, the income from which was to be used to build a harbour and a church. The Council were aided in the obtaining of the Act by Sir John Barnard, Lord Mayor of London, whose portrait hangs in the Town House as a reminder. There is no record of whether a church was built or not, but a new quay, named the Citadel Quay, which could take ships of up to 150 tons, was constructed in 1738. The harbour was further developed on the opposite side of the river, in the Thornbush area, although the east side of the river remained the main part of the harbour. Thus sailing vessels unloaded at either Clachnaharry, Muirtown, Thornbush or the Citadel Quay, around which were built storage sheds for merchants and wholesalers.

Up to the middle of the 18th century the harbour witnessed the passage of practically all trade in and out of the town, thereafter seeing a slow decline until the advent of the railways finally saw its demise as the main transportation system. Although coal was shipped into the harbour in the early 1720s the merchant responsible ran into financial difficulties and this, coupled with the Jacobite rebellion, saw little mention of it until the 1770s when it again begins to be landed, this time in ever increasing quantities. At one time one of the largest imports into the town, the amount of coal now imported is very small indeed. By the beginning of the 19th century the London trade had become more regular and structured with sailings every three days, arriving in London about two weeks later. It is recorded that there were about 9 boats, manned by 6 men each, carrying fish, skins from goat, roe deer, fox, hare, rabbit and otter, along with other goods for the London markets. They returned with 'luxury' and other goods for sale within the town. The advent of the Railway in the middle of the 19th century saw the decline of the harbour as a major import centre, although pig-iron, wine, bacon, boots and shoes, linen and woollen drapery, hardware, china and glass all feature on the records. The bulk transport of goods such as timber and coal still remained in its domain. Its main exports at that time were grain, potatoes, wool, sailcloth, ropes, cast-iron, dairy produce, leather, and malt liquors. Nowadays it deals largely with the importing of petroleum and the importing and exporting of timber products, although other cargoes do continue to be handled in smaller quantities.

Malting was for generations the main employment of the town, which enjoyed almost a monopoly in the trade, supplying all the northern counties as well as the Hebrides and Orkney with malt. By the end of the 17th century almost half the buildings in the town were involved in the trade with malting-houses, kilns, and granaries abounding. By the time Cumberland arrived, in the aftermath of Culloden, the trade had died and the town was a mass of empty and dilapidated buildings associated with malting. At its peak the malting business employed around 10,000 people and had its centre in Inverness, but eventually lost the trade to places like Forfarshire. It was around this time that the two hemp factories, which were also large employers, were also nearing the end of their existence. The town must have looked a sorry sight indeed.

Following the Battle of Culloden, although the clan chiefs found their status profoundly changed, the economy of the Highlands did not collapse. In fact there were positive signs to the contrary. By 1755 more than half the population of Scotland lived north of the Tay, with about one third of these being resident in the Highlands. By 1830 the Highland population had increased by 50 per cent, probably as a result of increasing prosperity. Such numbers had forced the traditional foods of oatmeal, cheese and meat to be supplemented with potatoes, a situation which the Highland chiefs and landowners were quick to cash in on. By 1800, potatoes provided about 80 per cent of the diet of Highlanders, thus allowing landowners to make substantial profits selling their other products of meal, cheese, meat and leather to the occupying army. Seaweed and kelp, which was easily come by, when dried and burned left an ash which was in great demand by the glass and soap industries. In 1720 the ash sold at £2 per ton and by 1800 it had risen to £22 per ton, a situation which earned MacDonald of Clanranald £98,000 annually. Such wealth inevitably found its way into the pockets of the Inverness merchants, by way of trade, and continued to do so until the price of kelp crashed around 1815, which helped spark the Highland clearances. The middle of the 19th century saw potato blight strike twice with devastating effect on the poor, both within and outwith the town, a situation which was only made worse by the crop failures of the late 1840s. It was at times of hardship like these, that the 'country' people drifted into the town to find work and settle down and, indeed, one notes that the town's population increased significantly over these decades.

In addition to the industries mentioned above, Inverness also had large works in connection with the Highland Railway, two large wood yards and saw-mills, a rope works, two breweries, three distilleries, several polished granite and marble works, a tannery, a tobacco manufacturers, and several foundries.

Chapter 13

Other Things and People

The Caledonian Canal

    The Caledonian Canal, like the Forth and Clyde Canal, came into being because of the necessity for seagoing ships to safely and quickly traverse the east/west coasts of Scotland without having to take the dangerous, and considerably longer, Pentland Firth route round the north of Scotland. As well as economic reasons for the building of the canal, however, there were also social conditions which made its inception and construction acceptable. By 1800 the glens of Scotland were being mercilessly cleared to make way for sheep farms, with the local people being thrown off their land and encouraged to

emigrate. This raised genuine concern throughout the country about conditions in the Highlands, and it was generally thought that improved communications would benefit the area. The construction of a canal through the Great Glen had been proposed several times during the previous century, but to no avail. The government of the time was not, however, thinking solely, if indeed at all, of the good this canal would do for trade in the north of Scotland. Their decision was greatly influenced by the fact that in 1803, when the canal was started, we were engaged in the Napoleonic Wars, and the canal would provide safe passage for Royal Navy ships between the North Sea and the Atlantic.

    At the beginning of the 19th century the British government feared further unrest and uprising in the Highlands and asked Thomas Telford, in 1801 and again in 1802, to survey the Highland area and report on his proposals for action. Telford's principal recommendations were for the construction of a number of new roads and bridges – for which he is well known – and also for the building of a canal which would link Inverness with Fort William, passing through Loch Ness, Loch Oich and Loch Lochy. If implemented, these proposals would provide a series of links, road and water, between forts, and enable better communications and troop transportation in times of trouble. As far as the canal was concerned, Telford knew that most of the merchant ships using it would be associated with trade in the Baltic and Scandinavian countries and would, therefore, be fairly large, as indeed would the Navy ships. This meant that the canal would necessarily have to be made wider and deeper than the Forth and Clyde Canal, thus making the construction a far more difficult task than any of those undertaken previously. He stated that the work would be complex and take around twenty years to complete, employing some 3,000 Highlanders – people who would probably otherwise have emigrated.

In 1803 an Act was passed authorising the construction of the Caledonian Canal. In that same year Thomas Telford was appointed as the principal engineer for the project, at a rate of 3 guineas a day plus travelling expenses, and William Jessop was appointed as the consulting engineer. Telford and Jessop immediately started work and within a few months Jessop had costed the project at £474,500 excluding the purchase of any land. In 1805 two resident engineers, John Telford (no relation) and Matthew Davidson, were appointed by Telford to help with the increasing workload. That same year Jessop and Telford decided that the Corpach sea-lock should have a basin and the locks there arranged in a staircase flight to save money. It was reported around this time that the eastern end of the canal employed about 500 workers, mainly from the Moray Firth area, and the western end had 400, including 300 from Appin, Arisaig, Kintyre, Morar and Skye, in addition to some crofters who had been thrown off their land at Loch Arkaig by Cameron of Lochiel.

By 1811 the eight-lock staircase at Banavie was built, and two years later the four-rise staircase at Muirtown, in Inverness, was completed. Things were progressing very well and both Telford and Jessop were pleased at the pace of progress. By 1818 things were not going quite so well, however. Telford was having difficult and protracted negotiations with MacDonald of Clanranald and McDonell of Glengarry about the course of navigation through Loch Oich. At the same time he was wrestling with the increased prices of food and labour and the unexpected cost of additional land purchase. These problems were compounded by an increase in the number of sections of the canal requiring clay lining, the difficulties of transporting and assembling dredgers in remote parts of the Highlands, and also the complications of cutting through rock in some parts of the country. Notwithstanding all these setbacks, in 1818 the eastern section of the canal was opened thus allowing ships passage from the North Sea through Inverness to Fort Augustus. The following year the sea-lock and entrance basin at Corpach near Fort William had opened, and the year after that saw the five-lock staircase at Fort Augustus completed. By 1822 the canal was finally opened throughout its length with much jubilation and celebration by all concerned, although it was still not at its full depth.

The design of the canal was a notable feature in that it had three sections of staircase locks – that is to say that the top gate on one lock forms the bottom gate of the next, and so on. These were at Muirtown (4 locks), Fort Augustus (5 locks) and Banavie (8 locks) – the latter becoming known as Neptune's Staircase. Whilst the staircase locks were cheaper to build than a flight of locks with basins in between, they do cause a hold-up in traffic flow at busy times, as passage through them can be slow.

Within four years of its completion there were difficulties. In 1826 the Gairlochy regulating-lock was causing trouble because of premature decay. Telford put this down to the use of inferior stone being used in its construction – there being no better stone available at the time of building. By the time 1847 had arrived the canal was in serious need of repair with 23 miles of it on the point of collapse. In January 1849 the canal burst its banks in Inverness and raised the level of the water in the River Ness to such an extent that the main bridge in the town was destroyed and large areas around the river were flooded. It took ten years and £300,000 to rectify the difficulties with the canal and to complete it to its design specification.

Like all its predecessors the Caledonian Canal was built with picks and shovels and the blood, sweat and tears of thousands of workers. The living conditions of the workers were poor to say the least and they frequently complained about both the wages and the food they were given. That said, it is reported that when the men were paid at the end of the month, unless their wives were there to claim a share, they "took to drinking and quarrelling, and spent as much money on whisky as would have fed them comfortably for a whole month."

Unlike many of the other canals in Scotland, the Caledonian Canal is still in use to this day, providing safe passage for yachts, fishing boats, commercial traffic and leisure boats all year round. It is indeed a wonderful feat of engineering skill, and a tribute to Telford and Jessop, that it remains in use after almost 200 years.

Fort George

Since the Middle Ages the Highlands of Scotland had given the English government varying degrees of concern on an ongoing basis. The way of life of the Highlanders, and the anxiety it often caused their neighbours, did not sit comfortably with government; nor did the general alarm it often caused south of the border. Cromwell's military occupation of the Highlands had caused serious disaffection, and when one coupled that with the general unruliness of the Highlanders, it was too much to bear. The English government built a large fort at Inverness and another, smaller one, at Inverlochy. Nothing like this had been seen in the Highlands before and did little to ease the feelings north of the border. Cromwell's fort was dismantled after the restoration of Charles II, but when William III came to the throne he enforced his authority over the Highlands with an army. The Inverlochy fort was rebuilt, and named Fort William after him, and whilst the one at Inverness remained in ruins he, instead, strengthened the ancient castle in Inverness.

When George I came to the throne he was welcomed in Scotland by the 1715 Jacobite uprising and support for the exiled James VII. Following the Jacobite defeat, four infantry barracks were constructed to augment the forts at Inverness Castle and Fort William.

These were at the south end of Loch Ness (near where Fort Augustus was later built), Ruthven near Kingussie, Bernera in Glenelg, and Inversnaid in Stirlingshire. Despite this, Jacobite disaffection continued north of the border and in 1724 General Wade was asked to survey the situation and report to parliament. This resulted in the construction of Fort Augustus to replace the nearby barracks, new works undertaken at Inverness Castle (which became the first Fort George), and a number of military roads joining the forts. Wade now had a string of forts between Inverness and Fort William with good road communication links between them, thus securing the strategically important Great Glen.

True to form, the Highlanders were not impressed by the government's efforts to curtail their activities. Prince Charlie's commanders realised that their freedom to manoeuvre during their campaign would be restricted by these forts and early in 1746 they took action. Inverness fell easily and at Fort Augustus a cannon ball fell on the powder magazine and the fort immediately surrendered. The battle for Fort William was far from easy, however, due far more to the courage of the troops than the fort's defences, and it was only two weeks before Culloden that the siege was raised. The destruction of two of their forts was a humiliating experience for the Hanoverians and only served to prove that all the measures they had put in place to curb the Highlanders had proved ineffective. A mistake which would not be repeated by George II.

In 1746 an Irish engineer submitted plans for the reconstruction of Cromwell's fort in Inverness, and the following year William Skinner, military engineer for the Highlands, also submitted plans. Skinner's plans were accepted and William Adam was awarded the building contract. Just before work commenced the reconstruction of the Citadel fort the Inverness Burgh Council claimed a large sum in compensation for loss of harbour dues because of the closeness of the new fort to the landing docks. The government, unwilling to pay compensation, abandoned the scheme and a new site was sought for the fort. By 1747 Skinner had identified a spit of land near Ardersier on the Moray Firth as a suitable site.

The new site was spacious and its isolation on a promontory made it highly suitable for the purpose. The only high ground was to the east but it was 1.6 km away and, at that time, it would make the fort beyond the range of any enemy guns. The shape of the land suggested to Skinner that the sea defences could be confined to the encircling rampart, whilst the main defence, landward, could be concentrated on the front of the fort. Here the main rampart formed the innermost line of defence, beyond which a complex arrangement of outworks could keep a besieger at a distance and delay his advance. The internal buildings were to hold two infantry battalions (1600 men) and an artillery unit. When under attack the garrison could retire to vaulted barrack rooms which were built under the rampart, where they would be safe from attack from mortars and guns. The cost of construction was estimated at £92,673 19s 1d but actually ended up costing more than twice that amount.

William Skinner died in 1748, the same year as the work was started, but the contract remained with his family firm and was taken over by his eldest son, John. Skinner's death was not the only problem facing the firm, however. Whereas there were plenty of labourers for the earthmoving which was all done by hand, and indeed the military could easily help out if required, there were few local tradesmen available and so most of them had to be taken from the Lowlands of Scotland. In addition almost all the building materials had to be taken in by sea, the roads not being suitable for such heavy loads. This was by far the biggest construction job the Highlands had ever seen, only eclipsed by the building of the Caledonian Canal in the next century. The government was wary of further uprisings and hence, whilst building work progressed, the site had to be secured against attack. In 1750 a temporary palisade was erected around the site and the fort kept in a state of readiness at all times, but with enough buildings for a small town spread over 42 acres this was not an easy task. Building began on the east side whilst a pier was built on the south side to land materials from ships. At the height of the construction around 1,000 men were employed in building and earthmoving works at the site. By 1753 the defences had been reinforced with a ravelin, which acted as a redoubt while the main rampart was being built. Eight guns were placed there and eight more put on the mounds of earth which were raised for the bastions. By 1757 the defences were well advanced, the internal buildings were under construction and the accommodation was ready for use. Progress was at last being made when three years later the fort received its main armament. A further three years saw the start of the last building to be undertaken, the chapel, as well as the replacement of temporary structures with permanent bridges over the ditches. Whilst the actual target completion date is unknown it was obvious that the sheer scale of the project and its complexity had forced work to fall behind schedule and pushed the budget to well over £200,000 – more than Scotland's GNP for 1750 – an enormous sum of money.

By the time the fort was finished in 1770 the threat of Jacobite disaffection had dissipated to nothing more than a romantic notion, and the fort was viewed as a costly mistake. In fairness to the government of the time, however, who, other than Cumberland, would have guessed that his murderous military regime (coupled with social and economic change) would have pacified the Highlanders quite as much as it did. Three years later, when Johnson and Boswell arrived in Inverness the 37th Foot were stationed at the fort. The 73rd Highland Regiment of Foot, ancestors of the Royal Highland Fusiliers, embarked at the fort in 1778 after being raised at Elgin. In fact most of the Highland Regiments which were embodied in the later part of the 18th century spent time there, and in the following century, 1881, the fort became the depot of the Seaforth Highlanders, then formed by amalgamation of the 72nd and the 78th.

The fort has also seen other occupants during its time and in 1795 the permanent garrison consisted of an artillery unit and a company of 'invalids' – men who, although unfit for active service, were capable of garrison duty. Thus ensuring that the guns were always ready, although they were never needed. By the end of the Napoleonic Wars guns were now capable of reaching the fort from the high ground to the east and the effectiveness of the fort was greatly reduced and its use as a barracks was seriously in doubt. Curiously, after Waterloo in 1815, Fort George was considered as a location for the imprisonment of Napoleon, but lost out to St Helena in the end. No doubt to the English government in London, Fort George was considered as remote as an island in the mid Atlantic!

1817 saw an order to dismantle all Highland forts given, then thankfully withdrawn, and this was followed in 1835 with a proposal to convert the fort into a prison – it having held Irish political prisoners for a time – but that too came to nothing. In 1860 a powerful coastal-defence battery was constructed on the sea-facing ramparts and these became the fort's main armament. Within a decade, however, the guns were obsolete and the fort was, once again, quite indefensible. Unwanted and neglected by this time, both Fort William and Fort Augustus were sold soon after the Crimean War. The latter eventually became a Benedictine Abbey whilst Fort William was reduced to being a locomotive depot for the North British Railway.

The guns remained at Fort George until 1881, at which point their purpose became decorative rather than functional. The army reorganisation at this time infused new life into the fort, which remained the Seaforth Highlanders' depot until 1961, when the regiment was amalgamated with the Cameron Highlanders to form the Queen's Own Highlanders. When that regiment left the fort in 1964, they left behind a museum for the Queen's Own and a Regimental Association for the Seaforths. That same year the fort was opened to the public as an ancient monument, but within 3 years once again it held regular soldiers – the Royal Highland Fusiliers. Today the fort is the only ancient monument still functioning as originally intended and is regarded as one of Europe's finest artillery fortifications.

Urquhart Castle

The castle stands on a rocky promontory at Strone Point on the north side of Loch Ness about 2 miles southwest of Drumnadrochit. Once one of Scotland's biggest castles, its dramatic position gives it a commanding view over the loch and the glen, and it is in an ideal position for a fort. People almost certainly lived in this area 4,000 years ago, and nearby Corrimony has a burial cairn dating from 2000 BC. Although there are remains of a settlement from Pictish times, and also evidence of an Iron Age fort, the only written evidence of a castle here is from the 1200's. Columba visited the area in 580 AD when he called at the house of a Pictish holy man called Emchath and converted him and his household to Christianity as he lay on his deathbed.

The people of Moray rose up in revolt against Alexander II in 1228 but were soon overcome and quashed by his army. When Alexander III came to the throne he put his own loyal nobles in charge of the estates in Moray and gave his son-in-law, Alun Durward, the lordship of Urquhart. The earliest parts of the castle date from around that time, so it is likely that he built it. Durward was one of the most influential men in Scotland at that time and was widely recognised as the power behind the throne. After his death in 1275 the castle was given to John Comyn, appointed by Edward I of England, who walled in the upper and lower baileys. The stronghold continued to be of strategic importance throughout the Wars of Independence with England. This was a troubled time in Scotland and after some humiliating defeats, including Dunbar in 1296, John Balliol relinquished his kingship, and all his castles, including Urquhart, fell under English control. Edward reinforced his hold on Scotland by securing forts all across the country. This was the time when the Stone of Destiny was removed from Scone and taken to London, but it was also the time when William Wallace rose up against English dominance. There were uneasy times ahead for Edward, for the Scots were not put down so easily. The castle came under attack from Andrew Moray of Moray in a night-time assault in 1297 but it was doomed to failure, although Sir Alexander Forbes was more successful some time later when he took the castle for Scotland. Wallace moved to Aberdeen and then on to Cromarty and the Highlands were secured from the English once again.

Edward raised a massive army and, alongside a treaty with the French, it marched to the Moray Firth from whence patrols were sent out to quell the surrounding troublemakers. His fierce reputation and the ferocity of his soldiers succeeded in most instances – with the exception of Urquhart castle where Sir Alexander Forbes refused to comply. In 1303 Edward laid siege to the castle in an attempt to starve the occupants. Forbes, realising their position was desperate decided to take his chance and fight the English troops but not before he managed to smuggle his pregnant wife out of the fort disguised as a peasant woman. His poor wife stood on a nearby hill and watched him and his troops fight to the death defending the castle against overwhelming odds. She later escaped to Ireland. The victorious Edward gave the castle into the safe keeping of Alexander Comyn of Badenoch but this only lasted until 1306 when Robert the Bruce annihilated it, and the castle, or what was left of it, was once again in Scottish hands.

The castle was held fast for David II in 1333 against Edward Balliol and Edward II of England, but by 1346 it had passed from the Earls of Moray back to the Scottish Crown. Around this time the castle was refurbished to a fine standard which was probably paid for by the Crown. For 50 years or so, from the end of the 1300s until well into the 1400s, the castle passed back and fore from the clan MacDonald to the Crown. MacDonald of the Isles frequently took the castle only to have the Scottish Crown retake it a few years later, which did nothing for the state of the castle itself, or indeed for the people who lived in the glen nearby. The Lords of the Isles held the castle until 1456 when the MacDonalds power was curbed and it was given to the Gordons of Huntly, although it was the Grants of Freuchie who looked after it for them. In 1509 the Grant's restored the castle principally because it had been a condition of their occupancy. The MacDonalds however were irrepressible and during the 1500s they twice attacked and sacked the castle killing the local inhabitants and laying waste to the surrounding lands.

Urquhart Castle was abandoned by the Grants in the 1600's and the locals, who had suffered so much because of its existence, now reaped a harvest from its timber and stonework, using all they could carry to build houses. This was rectified in the early 17th century when it was fully restored to its former glory. But the glory was short-lived because in 1644 the Covenanters sacked the castle taking everything of value away and leaving Lady Urquhart with nothing but the bare walls. Since Cromwell had a boat patrolling Loch Ness it is likely that he took possession of the castle also.

In 1689 a whig garrison held out for two years against the Jacobites but the castle's end came at that point when it was packed with explosives and blown up to prevent it falling into the hands of the Jacobites. The castle once again lay in ruins and, not for the first time, was plundered for stone and timber, a situation which continued until 1912. The great storm of 1715 blew down the southwest wall, which toppled into the murky waters of Loch Ness. In spite of the fact that the castle has been a ruin for more than 300 years it is still a very impressive sight. Curiously, it was one of the monks from the castle chapel that first reported seeing the Loch Ness Monster, claiming that it had come out of the water and grabbed hold of him, trying to drag him into the water, before he managed to break free from it and escape.

Always a favourite with tourists, the castle had a new, and somewhat spectacular, visitor centre built in 2002 and is now more popular than ever with visitors to the area.

Chapter 13

Inverness and Slavery

One can barely believe that Inverness was, in some way, involved in the slave trade, and that the 'effects' of that involvement reached half-way across the world and are clearly apparent in the City to this day. What involvement did the people of Inverness have in such a despicable trade? Who were they? What remains in the City today as proof of that involvement? These are all questions which, I imagine, are going through the mind of the reader – they certainly went through mine as I started to read about the topic. I attempt in this chapter to outline what part in the slave trade the people of this area played and to show that there was a significant number of families who were heavily involved, some through choice and others through the necessity of their circumstances. I will leave the reader to judge for himself as to whether the descendants of those who gained from their involvement should have a clear conscience or not. Bear in mind, however, that one should never 'judge' history using today's standards – as hindsight is a wonderful thing.

Although I have no doubt that Scots were involved in the slave trade in many parts of the world, my own reporting on the situation is based in what is now called Guyana, South America, where there was a significant connection with Scottish people and particularly Highlanders.

The Dutch colonisation of the area between the Orinoco and Amazon rivers in South America began in the early 17th century and was known as Dutch Guiana. Many small trading posts were set up near various rivers but due to the effects of disease and attacks by natives, these colonies rarely lasted long. In 1621 the government of the Netherlands gave the newly formed Dutch West India Company complete control over the trading post on the Essequibo River. The company established a second colony on the Berbice River southeast of Essequibo, in 1627. Although under the general jurisdiction of this private group, the settlement, named Berbice, was governed separately. Demerara, situated between Essequibo and Berbice, was settled in 1741 and emerged in 1773 as a separate colony under direct control of the Dutch West India Company. Although the Dutch colonisers initially were motivated by the prospect of trade in the Caribbean, their possessions became significant producers of crops. The growing importance of agriculture was indicated by the export of 15,000 kilograms of tobacco from Essequibo in 1623, but as the agricultural productivity of the Dutch colonies increased, a labour shortage emerged. The indigenous populations were poorly adapted for work on plantations, and many people died from diseases introduced by the Europeans. The Dutch West India Company turned to the importation of African slaves, who rapidly became a key element in the colonial economy. By the 1660s, the slave population numbered about 2,500; the number of indigenous people was estimated at 50,000, most of whom had retreated into the vast hinterland. Although African slaves were considered an essential element of the colonial economy, their working conditions were brutal. The mortality rate was high, and the dismal conditions led to more than half a dozen slave rebellions.

Eager to attract more settlers, in 1746 the Dutch authorities opened the area near the Demerara River to British immigrants. British plantation owners in the Lesser Antilles had been plagued by poor soil and erosion, and many were lured to the Dutch colonies by richer soils and the promise of land ownership. The influx of British citizens was so great that by 1760 the British constituted a majority of the European population of Demerara. By 1786 the internal affairs of this Dutch colony were effectively under British control, though two-thirds of the plantation owners were still Dutch. After the Napoleonic Wars in 1814, Britain gained control of the three colonies - Demerara, Berbice, and Essequibo – and at the London Convention of 1814, the colonies were formally ceded to Britain. In 1824, when Demerara presented evidence against emancipation, the secretary of the committee of inhabitants was a Scot, Alexander MacDonnell. He produced reports from five estate managers, four of whom were also Scots. In 1831,

Berbice and the United Colony of Demerara and Essequibo were unified as British Guiana. The colony would remain under British control until independence in 1966, and became a republic (Guyana) in 1970. It is said that history is written by the victors as much in

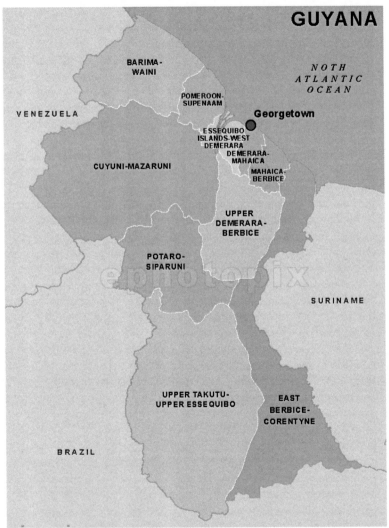

economic as in military struggles and that may well be the case in this instance. The markets in the Caribbean were vital to the growth of the Scottish economy in the 18th century and were, from the 1770s, the most dynamic sector of Scottish overseas commerce. In Chapter 4, I stated that there was a hemp and rope works built beside the site of Cromwell's Citadel. The hemp was initially grown locally before being purchased from the Baltic. Some of it was used to make sacks which in turn were used to transport the cotton, coffee and sugar from the colonies to their worldwide destinations. The impact of this trade was very much felt in the Highlands and often prompted the sons of wealthy families to seek their fortune in the colonies. This is the first group of people who found their way from the Highlands to Guiana and, as their families would have had the money to buy estates in the colonies, they were often the owners of these estates. The agriculture was, of course, very labour intensive, hence the need for lots of slaves. Since the indigenous population was not very 'cooperative' the owners needed to find others to organise and supervise the workforce.

From the 1750s onwards, the forced displacement, or clearances, from the northern Highlands was increasingly common, and these unfortunate souls were forced to find an alternative way to make a living. Often it was left to the younger members of the family to find a way to support the remainder, who otherwise would have been destitute. These were the next group of people who found their way to Guiana. The estate owners wrote home to their families here who, in turn, offered the displaced families passage to Guiana and work when they arrived there. For many it was the only offer they had – so they took it, and ended up working for people they knew, but on the other side of the world. They in turn would then write home and seek brothers, cousins and friends to come and join them, and so the number of Scots in Guiana grew and often developed into small 'networks' of people from particular areas of the Highlands. These men were often employed as overseers by the estate owners. It is reported that the Scots were so close-knit that the people who sold large shrimps called them "Scotchmen" because of the way the shrimps clung to each other and were difficult to separate.

The third group were the sons of families of moderate means who fancied making themselves a fortune abroad, rather than graft for a living in Scotland. I suppose you might call them the "fellow-my-lads" of the time. They too were often employed as overseers. All three groups saw Guiana, and in particular the colony of Berbice, as being a way of making money much faster than they could hope for at home.

Many of those 'speculators' were from the Inverness area – although I also found records of men from Shetland to Perth and from Aberdeen to the Western Isles. In total I found evidence of over 150 families, and their relatives, who emigrated from the Inverness area and worked in Guiana. In particular, the sons of the Baillies of Dochfour, and other family relatives owned many estates in Guiana. The sons and relatives of William Inglis, who was a Provost of Inverness, and after whom Inglis Street is named, all worked on the estates and one was the captain of a slave ship. Many family members of Gordon of Drakies, another Provost of Inverness, were also involved. In fact the sons and families of 4 Provosts of Inverness had connections to estates in Guiana. Also involved were the families of MacKintosh of Ballifeary, Frasers of Belladrum near Beauly, MacDonnell of Milnefield, Frasers of Beauly, Rose of Glastullich, near Tain, and a number of Munro families from Easter Ross. It is recorded that the son (John) of the owner of the Ettles Hotel, which stood on the corner of Bridge Street next to the Town House, died in Guiana of disease in 1814, aged 29 years. This was not uncommon, as the colonies were rife with disease and many of the adventurers who went out there died within a few years of their arrival, some within a few months. One report states that a Duncan Fraser died of yellow fever two days after arriving in the colony and by the following year three more Frasers had also died.

Berbice, the oldest of the colonies, rapidly expanded in the 1730s through coffee production, although the Dutch planters were suspicious of outsiders and Jews, and Roman Catholics were forbidden to settle there. The British involvement there didn't really begin until the 1790s as it was one of the least attractive colonies, subject to sudden changes in weather and epidemics of disease. It still, however, remained a great attraction to young Highland men – particularly those from an area between Inverness and the Dornoch Firth. Perhaps this was helped by Lord Seaforth's report, in 1800, that, contrary to the opinion of the Dutch, " .....drained land on the coast was suitable for growing high quality cotton." The report also provides evidence that, with few exceptions, many of the landowners " ... returned home with larger and some with immense fortunes." At that time, 1801, one of the Frasers of Belladrum is reported to have made " .... £40,000 by his last trip." The equivalent nowadays would be almost £2,500,000 – so one begins to see the attraction. Evan Baillie of Dochfour established himself as a slave trader in West Indian trade before settling in Bristol, which he represented in Parliament from 1802, before succeeding to the family property in Dochfour where he lived until his death in 1835. In 1801, Lord Seaforth was part of a consortium (mainly Scots with Inverness connections) which bought 10 lots of land from the Dutch

Berbice Company during the favourable economic climate of rising sugar, coffee and cotton prices.

The purchase of land could be spread over a few years thus making it more attractive, as a cotton crop could grow in 6 months. Slave purchase could also be spread over a couple of years. Thus the profit from the crop could be used to pay off the debts of any purchases. All was not sunshine and roses, however, because for a period in the early 19th century there was disastrous weather, it being either too wet or too dry, and cotton prices fell and speculators couldn't sell on their land. The Belladrum estate near Beauly had to be sold to cover debts and Seaforth was forced to sell all his slaves to avoid a disaster in Berbice.

In the good times, however, the prospect of rapid fortune depended on the exploitation of slaves. In 1815, in Berbice, the ratio of black slaves to white people was 50:1, and Scottish involvement in the slave trade was significant. A study of the Bristol slave trader, John Rogers, shows that there were numerous Scottish agents that he dealt with in the Carribean area, with names suggesting a strong Highland involvement.

Most slaves bought in Berbice were likely to have been brought from the Gold Coast (Ghana) and were probably from the Ashanti nation. They would most likely have been captured by Arab traders and transported to the African coast to holding areas. Then hundreds would have been crammed into the slave ships for the Carribean slave markets. The crossing would have taken 2-3 months, depending on the weather conditions, and many would have died through self-imposed starvation, abuse and sickness. Those that died

would have been dumped overboard without ceremony. The sailors were not averse to using the female slaves for their own self-gratification and any who resisted would have been beaten.

As soon as possible after the ship arrived in port an auction would have been arranged, as the ship's Captain would not have wanted to feed the slaves any longer than necessary. The men were generally sold first and could fetch anything up to £100 depending on age and fitness. Women were sold next and generally cost between £45 and £75 depending on their looks and their strength. Children under the age of 10 years were usually sold with their mother, older children might be sold separately and parted from their family. Husbands and wives were seldom ever sold together and no consideration whatsoever was given to family units, it just wasn't considered to be important. Immediately following purchase the agents would have the slaves transported to the plantation. No time was ever given to families to say goodbye and it was unlikely that they ever saw each other again.

The life the slaves were brought into was, in most cases, hard and unrelenting. The work in the cotton fields and the sugar plantations was backbreaking. Little consideration would have been given for illness or weakness. The slave either worked or was whipped. If you couldn't work then you weren't fed, it was up to the other slaves to share their food with you or you did without. They were expected to work from dawn till dusk, in many cases, for 6 and sometimes 7 days a week. Not all plantation owners were evil men, however, some did give the slaves a Sunday off and saw that they were reasonably well fed. Clearly, since slaves were expensive, it wasn't good economics to mistreat them too much. Some were allowed to grow their own food and supplement their meagre diet.

Generally speaking, however, life was not easy. Beatings were frequent, especially for men, when they would be whipped by the overseer for some misdemeanour. Women were frequently "used" by the white men who would generally ask the slave for sex. If she refused then she would be beaten and then raped anyway. A male slave had the right to complain to the plantation owner about excessive beating by the overseer, but he had no right to complain if his wife or daughters were abused.

One can imagine that on some plantations the lifestyle the slaves were forced into did not afford them longevity. Most men died young on cruel plantations, they lived longer on better ones, but life expectancy was not great. Women lived longer because most were worked less hard, but even then many still died relatively young. Disease – yellow fever, dysentery and other tropical diseases – was rife, and claimed many slaves and whites alike. The average life expectancy for whites was not high – and many died within a few years of arriving in the colony.

      Flogging was a frequent and daily occurrence in the fields, but also took place as a punishment for misdemeanours. The latter would see the slave tied to the ground, or a tree, whilst the overseer did the flogging – sometimes watched by the plantation owner and his family. A male could expect anything from 10 to 100 lashes as a punishment although in some cases it could be much more. Slaves who were deemed "troublemakers", or those that frequently ran away, were sometimes hanged as an example to the others in order to deter them from similar actions. If a male slave was a troublemaker then sometimes his wife and family would be sold on as a punishment. Similarly, a male slave could be asked to give up his wife and daughter(s) for abuse by the overseer, failure to comply might result in the family being sold on. Women were seldom flogged, but rape was used as a punishment, sometimes in front of their family or other workers in the field, in order to humiliate them. Any slave that lifted their hand and struck a white man was hanged without delay.

It was usual for an overseer to rename the slaves who were purchased at auction and one can often tell where the overseer came from by the names of the slaves on a plantation. In July 1803 a slave ship arrived in Demerara and unloaded its cargo. They were advertised as "Prime Gold Coast Negroes" by the agent, George Baillie, one of several Baillies from around Inverness. Ten men and ten women were bought by Peter Fairburn, acting for Lord Seaforth, Chief of the Clan MacKenzie. The men were all renamed 'Brahan', 'Britain', 'Kintail', 'Lewis', 'Gordon', 'Crawford', 'Ross', 'Sutherland', 'Dingwall' and 'Inverness' and all were sent to Plantation Brahan, in Berbice where the manager, Hector MacKenzie, from near Golspie, was cultivating cotton.

Mackenzie eventually had his own plantation, which he renamed Dunrobin, but died in 1807 after falling ill to one of the many fevers which often swept the colony. He left all his money to his brother Andrew who lived in Canada, both brothers having left Sutherland during the clearances. The twenty slaves were taken to the plantation and joined some 60 other slaves, about 50 of whom were fit for work, the remainder were either ill (one woman had venereal disease) or had absconded. 'Inverness' was about 25 years of age and was fit and healthy. His wife and child had been sold separately at the auction and he never saw them again. By October 1803 'Inverness' and 'Dingwall' had run off to escape the cruelty of the plantation. They were both caught a week later and given 20 lashes each as a punishment for absconding, and in addition they were "masked" to stop them running away again. The "mask" was an iron collar with long hooked spikes on it to prevent them from running through the thick forest if they escaped, thus making their capture more easy.

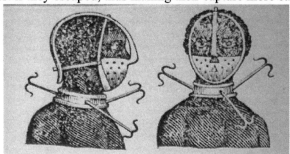

Inverness was given 50 lashes in November for answering back and causing trouble. In April 1804 he ran away again this time with a slave called 'Ross'but both were found hiding a few days later and this time 'Inverness' was given 80 lashes and masked again. In August 1804 he asked the plantation owner if he could marry another slave called Eliza. The owner referred him to the overseer who refused the marriage. The overseer then tied 'Inverness' to a tree and he was forced to watch whilst the overseer and some other whites raped Eliza in front of him. In November of that year 'Inverness' and Eliza ran off and it took two months to find them whilst they hid in the forest with a group of around 50 runaways. They had established a hideaway a few days journey away from the plantation and were growing plantains and rice. 'Dingwall' and another slave from Brahan were also part of the group but evaded capture. His captor was most likely Charles Edmonstone, from Dumbarton, the most successful hunter of slaves in Guyana. On his forced return to the plantation 'Inverness' was given 200 lashes and he died as a result. So, some 16 months after his arrival in Berbice 'Inverness' was dead, having been captured, transported to a foreign land, sold, enslaved, renamed, exploited, severely punished for seeking his freedom and finally killed by Scots from the Highlands.

Is it any wonder that in 1823 the slaves revolted? Some 10,000 slaves either refused to work or ran away. How the revolt was co-ordinated is a mystery but it all happened within the space of a few

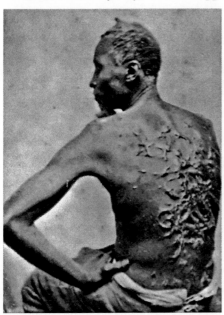

days. The white population must have been thrown into confusion and some degree of fear because it is reckoned that some 2,000 slaves were shot another 250 were caught and hanged and more than 800 were flogged after being rounded up and caught.

By the middle of the 19th century the industry was in serious decline. Slavery was being questioned and debated and many families no longer wanted to be associated with it. This unsettling feeling about slavery affected the industry greatly. The price of land tumbled and fortunes were lost. In 1833 slavery was abolished in the Carribean area and those who still had plantations were forced to free their slaves, some received compensation for doing so. It is reported that Baillie of Dochfour, one of the largest UK slave traders, received the equivalent of £8.5 million in compensation for his slaves in Guyana, which helped to maintain his Highland estates. The slaves, of course, received nothing. Kind owners continued to work the plantations with slaves who chose to stay with them whilst those who had been cruel to their slaves were left with nobody.

That seems to answer the first two questions posed at the beginning of this Chapter, but what of the benefits for the town of Inverness – apart from the money gained by the families involved in the industry? Well, remember Provost Inglis who was always seen as an immense benefactor and fundraiser for buildings in Inverness? He helped to raise large sums of money for a number of important buildings early in their construction – namely the Royal Northern Infirmary, Inverness Academy and the Toolbooth Steeple. Where, I wonder, did he find the donations? No prizes for guessing that all those buildings received large donations from Inverness families who were involved in slavery.

When Provost Inglis sought funding for his projects it was to those who were engaged in slavery, and their families back home,

that he turned, and those who had made their fortune in that way contributed to the building fund – whether through a sense of duty or to promote their own standing is unknown – including his own family. The Inverness Academy, which was built in New Street, (see Chapter 5) had one third of its capital donated from the West Indies, doubtless from the proceeds of slavery. Fortrose Academy had almost half its capital donated by expatriates in India with the remaining half coming from the West Indies and London merchants with interests in the slave trade. A sad reflection indeed. The Royal Northern Infirmary (see Chapter 4) was built at the beginning of the 19th century again from substantial donations from those involved in slavery – probably the same families that donated to the Inverness Academy construction. James Fraser of Belladrum sent subscriptions of over £500 from the colony of Demerara for the Infirmary, whilst £1,000 was sent from Berbice to support the establishment of Tain Academy. Surprisingly, this fact is highlighted by the plaque on the Infirmary wall on Ness Walk which says, "Placed here to acknowledge that this building was erected through donations from the profits of the slave trade and slave plantations of the Caribbean and South America." The only overt admission to the part played by those involved in slavery and how it benefitted Inverness.

In the past, however, there were other ways of 'recognising' that Invernessians were involved in slavery. As I stated earlier, the colonies were populated mainly by men. Few women ventured there, as many of those who did died of disease soon afterwards. Those men, deprived of female companionship, soon turned their attentions to the female slaves and, either by negotiation or force, enjoyed the company of the female population. Most white men took a mistress who would have been a free black woman called a Mulatto, and it was not uncommon for a man to buy an educated black slave as a mistress. The children of such a partnership were generally accepted in the colony, and some were even sent back to Scotland to be educated. Between 1800 and 1815 there were black pupils reported in schools in Cromarty, Fortrose and Tain, and 3 boys and a girl called Inglis, all black, attended Inverness Academy. It is reported that the girl, " ... was clever for a black." Hugh Miller, the famous geologist who went to school in Cromarty, sat next to a black pupil in class. Returning Scots often took their Mulatto wife and the children back with them – although the local population was led to believe they were "housekeeper" and servants. Some white men deserted their Mulatto wives when they returned home and, although they may have left them with some money, never attempted to contact them again. The children of black slaves were seldom acknowledged by white men and

237

were always brought up as slaves although it was often obvious by their colouring that they were of mixed race. Generally, these children commanded a higher price at auction than black children. Hector MacKenzie, however, left £1,000 to his daughter Rose, the child of his slave Nancy to whom he granted freedom, a house on the Dunrobin plantation and a slave of her own. It is clear that there must have been some affection felt for those he left behind.

Further proof of the involvement of Invernessians in slavery can be found in the Chapel Yard. When Roderick MacDonnell arrived in Demerara from Inverness in 1809 he wrote to his father, referring to two Shaw brothers, sons of a 'carrier' in Inverness. They were both overseers on the Golden Fleece plantation. One of these was Edward Shaw, commemorated in the Chapel Yard, where he is described as " .... for many years of the colony of Demerara." He died in 1869, aged 80. The other being his brother David. Their father, commemorated on an adjoining stone, was "David Shaw, farmer, Inverness", who in his will is described as " ..... farmer and horse hirer in Inverness". Phineas MacKintosh, the son of Captain Alexander MacKintosh, was an army surgeon who died in Demerara in 1805. His gravestone can also be seen in the Chapel Yard.

Yet another example can be seen in Rosemarkie kirkyard where Eliza Junor, who died in 1861, is commemorated along with her brother William.. She was a black girl who lived in Fortrose as the free daughter of Hugh Junor and won a prize for penmanship at Fortrose Academy in 1819. There was a Mulatto woman called Henrietta Fraser who lived in Findhorn around 1821 and also the black "housekeeper" of Hugh Ross of Bayfield, Nigg. It was difficult for mixed race people to find a place in Scottish society, particularly as more explicit racist views developed in the mid-nineteenth century, so life for Eliza and the other coloured children who lived in Scotland could not have been easy.

James Baillie Fraser of Reelig took a black slave, called "Black John", back to Scotland with him around 1809. James seemed to be quite the traveller, first heading back to Berbice a couple of times before going on to India, Tehran and Constantinople over the space of 12 years or so. Black John didn't travel with James to Berbice or Constantinople but did accompany him on his other journeys and by all accounts was a trusted servant and companion. James had him baptised in the High Church in Inverness in 1812 and they left for India in 1815 where Black John spent some time. When James was in Constantinople he reported that " .... I miss my faithful John" and that he regretted having to do all the things that John took care of for him. They returned to Britain from India in 1822 but John's health deteriorated and he died a year later. The attachment of John to the family is apparent in letters between them.

On January 20th 1767, the following advert appeared in the Edinburgh Advertiser:

To be Disposed of:

A handsome black boy, about thirteen years of age, very well qualified for making a household servant, serving a table well, etc., of a fine constitution, endured to the climate, and has had the smallpox. Any person inclining to purchase him, may call at Mr William Reid's, ironmonger opposite to the door to the city guard. This advertisement not to be repeated.

It is interesting to note, however, that despite the above advert and for all the involvement Scots had in the slave trade abroad, slavery was abolished in Scotland in 1778, about 55 years before the Slavery Abolition Act which abolished slavery in the British Empire. The Scots ruling came eleven years after the advert appeared in the paper and came about following the very high profile legal case of Joseph Knight, an African slave sold in Jamaica to a Scottish owner, John Wedderburn. Joseph Knight's legal challenge began in 1774 in the Justices of the Peace court in Perth, where he sought the freedom to leave the employment of John Wedderburn of Ballendean in Perthshire. Knight claimed that, although many years earlier he had been purchased by Wedderburn in Jamaica from a slave trader, the act of landing in Scotland freed him from perpetual servitude, as slavery was not recognised in Scotland. The Justices of the Peace found in favour of Wedderburn. However, Knight appealed to the Sheriff of Perth, who found that " ....the state of slavery is not recognised by the laws of this kingdom, and is inconsistent with the principles thereof: That the regulations in Jamaica, concerning slaves, do not extend to this kingdom; and repelled the defender's claim to a perpetual service".

Essentially Knight succeeded in arguing that he should be allowed to leave domestic service and provide a home for his wife and child. In doing so he gave the Court of Session the opportunity to declare that slavery was not recognised by Scots law and that runaway slaves (or 'perpetual servants') could be protected by the courts if they wished to leave domestic service or if attempts were made to forcibly remove them from Scotland and return them to slavery in the colonies.

Appendix 1

Chronological Chart

BC

c.5000   First evidence of human habitation. – probably Mesolithic nomadic hunters.

c.4000   New Stone Age farmers.

c.3000   Passage graves and chambered cairns.

c.2300   Stone circles.

c.2000   Early Bronze Age.

c.1500   Middle Bronze Age.

c.800   Late Bronze Age. Hut circles. Cist burials.

c.500   Iron Age implements and weapons. Timber-laced stone forts.

c.400   Iron Age forts. Crannogs. Duns.

c.200   Celtic speaking peoples.

AD

82   Romans in Northern Scotland. Multi-vallate forts. Caledonians referred to.

297   "Picti" referred to by the Romans.

c.300   Rise of the Pictish power in the Highlands.

c.400   Ninianic mission to Pictland.

565   Columba in Inverness.

Pre 700   Pictish symbol stones.

Post 700   Norse invasions in North and West. Pictish symbol/cross stones.

843   Kenneth, first King of Picts and Scots.

Post 843   Pictish cross stones.

1040   MacBeth, Mormaer of Moray, becomes King of the Scots.

1057   Malcolm Canmore becomes King.

c.1135   Inverness becomes a Royal Burgh.

c.1180   King William the Lyon's Charter.

1228   Inverness burned by the men of Moray.

1233   Monastery of Black Friars (Dominicans) founded by Alexander II.

1249   Vessel built for a French Count to take him to the Crusades.

1303   Inverness Castle captured by King Edward I of England.

1307   Robert, King of the Scots, captures the Castle.

1314   Victory over the English at Bannockburn.

1333	Clan battle at Clachnaharry between the MacKintoshes and the Munros.
1350	The "Black Death" plague.
1369	John, Lord of the Isles, submits to King David II.
1400	Donald, Lord of the Isles, threatens to burn the town.
1410	Inverness sacked by Donald, Lord of the Isles.
1428	King James I at Inverness Castle.
1429	The Lord of the Isles burns the town.
1455	The Lord of the Isles captures the town and takes the castle.
1464	King James III visits the town.
1493	Lordship of the Isles annexed to the Crown.
1508	Alexander Gordon, 3rd Earl of Huntly, Sheriff of Inverness.
1555	The Queen Regent, Mary of Guise, holds court in the town.
1560	Reformation of Scottish Church.
1562	Inverness Castle surrenders to Queen Mary.
1591	King James VI Golden Charter.
1603	James VI of Scotland becomes James I of England.
1607	The castle repaired and strengthened.
1638	National Covenant.
1640	Civil War.
1646	Montrose besieges Town and Castle.
1649	Church built for the Gaelic-speaking community of the town.
1651-60	Cromwellian troops occupy the fort.
1664	The old wooden bridge falls.
1665	"Battle of the Cheese" between the MacDonalds and the townspeople.
1676	New burgh constitution approved and craft guilds recognised.
1685	Completion of stone bridge over the Ness.
1686	Dunbar's Hospital given to the town.
1688	Town besieged by MacDonald of Keppoch.
1689	First Jacobite rising.
1690	The jail steeple rebuilt.
1707	Union of the Scots Estates with English Parliament.
1708	New Town House built.
1715	Second Jacobite rising. Jacobites occupy the Town and Castle.
1718	Castle repaired and enlarged – renamed "Fort George".
1725-26	Wade in Inverness. Castle becomes barracks.
1738	Large extension made to the harbour.
1745	Last Jacobite rising.
1746	Castle destroyed by the Jacobites. Battle of Culloden.
1747	End of Clan chiefs' rights of jurisdiction.

1756	Commencement of New Street – now Academy Street.
c.1760	Improvement in trade and commerce.
1765	Hemp factory opened.
c.1770	First tourists in the Northern Highlands.
1772	Parish Church, Old High, rebuilt.
1773	Dr Samuel Johnson and Boswell visit the town.
1775	Street lighting introduced to the town.
1777	Fire engines and fire-fighting equipment purchased.
1787	Robert Burns visits the town.
1789	New Steeple erected.
1793	Inverness Royal Academy established.
1795	Meal riots and mob fighting in the town.
1800	Expansion of the Town. Population exceeds 10,000.
1803	Royal Northern Infirmary built by public subscription.
1804	Building of the Caledonian Canal commenced.
1807	"Inverness Journal", the town's first newspaper, published.
1816	Annual sheep and wool markets established.
1818	Burgh disfranchised due to election irregularities.
1822	Telford completes Caledonian Canal.
1826	First gas street lights.
1835	Last public execution in the town.
1839	Caledonian Bank founded.
1849	Old stone bridge destroyed by flood.
1855	The Highland clearances. Mitchell's Inverness-Nairn railway opened.
1866	King Edward VII made freeman of the burgh. Cathedral foundation stone laid.
1877	General Ulysses Grant, ex USA President, made freeman of Inverness.
1877	Building of the Cameron Barracks commenced.
1878	New Town Hall foundation stone laid.
1889	General Post Office in Queensgate erected.
c.1890	Depopulation and emigration of the Highlands. Inverness expands and becomes an important fishing port.
1892	Cameron Highlanders Memorial erected in the Station Square.
1898	Inverness-Perth direct rail link.
1901	Lovat Scouts given the freedom of the burgh.
1921	Cabinet meeting held in the Town Hall.
1930	Economic depression in Scotland.
1933	First flight by Fresson's Highland Airways based in Inverness.

1948	King George VI, Queen Elizabeth and Princess Margaret visit the town.
1951	H.R.H. the Princess Royal made a burgess of Inverness.
1953	H.R.H. Queen Elizabeth, Queen Mother, made a burgess of Inverness.
c.1960	Inverness becomes an administrative, commercial and industrial centre.
1961	Freedom of the burgh conferred on the Queen's Own Highlanders.
1961	New Ness Bridge opened.
1962	King Olav of Norway visits the town.
1964	Queen Elizabeth and Prince Philip visit the town.

Reference Books

Adomnan's Life of Columba - A O & M O Anderson, Edinburgh 1961
Ancient Churches and Chapels in Inverness - Dr Alex Ross, Inv Scientific Soc Vol 6
Ancient Wells in the North and Their Folklore - Alex Fraser, Inv Scientific Soc Vol 1
Anderson's Guide to the Highlands Part II - George & Peter Anderson 1863
Antiquarian Notes - Charles Fraser MacKintosh 1897
Armed Figure in Greyfriars' Churchyard - James Barron, Inv Sci Soc & Field Club Vol 2

Boar Stone - D Butter, Inv Scientific Soc Vol 9
Book of the Duffs - A & H Taylor, William Brown 1914
Burgh Court Records - Highland Regional Archive

Caledonian Canal - A D Cameron 1972
Caledonian Canal: Resource Handbook – Sch Lib Resource Service, HELP Publication
Celtic Element in Old Inverness - William MacKay 1914
Chantry Alters and Chaplains of St Mary's - Fraser-MacKintosh, Inv Scientific Soc Vol 4
Chapel Yard Cemetery, Inverness - Schools Library Resource Service, HELP Publication
Chronicles of the Frasers - James Fraser, The Scottish History Society 1905
Clava Cairns - I C Walker, P S A S 1962
Colonisation of Scotland in the 2nd Millennium BC - Sir L Scott, Proc Preh Soc 1951
Concise Bibliography of the Printed and M S Material on the Hist, Topog and Instit of the Burgh, Parish and Shire of Inverness - P J Anderson 1917
Craig Phadrig Interim Rep on 1971 Excavation - A Small & M B Cottam, Univ of Dundee Occ Pap No 1 1972

Dark Ages in the Highlands - Inverness Field Club 1971

Early Ecclesiastical Buildings in Inverness - Sch Lib Resource Service, HELP Publication

Education In the Highlands 1800-1939 - Sch Lib Resource Service, HELP Publication
Emigration From the Highlands - Schools Library Resource Service, HELP Publication
Enchanted Britain - Marc Alexander 1981

Freemasonry in Inverness - Ross 1878
From Drover to Driver (6 booklets) - Schools Library Resource Service, HELP Publication
Further History of a Scottish Voluntary Hospital - Dr T C MacKenzie 1950

Great Highland Famine - Schools Library Resource Service, HELP Publication
Guide to Inverness, Nairn & the Highlands - Alex MacKenzie 1903

Hammermen of Inverness - J A Gossip, Inv Scientific Soc Vol 8
High Court Records - Highland Regional Archive
Highland Communications - Iain Cameron Taylor, An Comunn Gaidhealach 1969
Highland Economy 1750-1900 - Schools Library Resource Service, HELP Publication
Highland Notebook - R Carruthers 1843
Highland Railway - H A Vallance, David & Charles 1953
Highland Railway - O S Nock, Tom Allan 1965
Highland Transport Revolution: Growth of the Highland Railway Network 1725-1920 - Schools Library Resource Service, HELP Publication
Highland Waterway - Francis Thomson 1972
Hist of Inverness & Guide to the Objects of Interest in its Neighbourhood - S & M Douglas 1847
Historic Inverness-Archaeological Implications of Develop - R Gourlay & A Turner 1977
History and Description of Inverness - Douglas, Smith and Fraser
History and Description of the Town of Inverness - George Cameron 1847
History of Inverness - George Cameron 1847
History of Inverness - Murdoch MacKintosh 1939
History of the County of Inverness - J Cameron Lees 1897
Hospital of Inverness and Dunbar's Hospital - Capt Douglas Wimberley 1893

Inverness 1793 - Sir John Sinclair
Inverness and the MacDonalds - Evan M Barron
Inverness Burgh Records - Highland Council Archives
Inverness in the 15th Century - Evan M Barron 1907
Inverness in the 18th Century - Leonella Longmore 2001
Inverness in the Middle Ages - Evan M Barron
Inverness Kirk Session Records - Alexander Mitchell 1902
Inverness Miscellany - No 1 (1983) & 2 (1987), Inverness Field Club
Inverness Royal Academy, A History of 600 Years - Evan Barron 1921

Joseph Cook's Inverness - Joseph Cook 1992

Letter-book of Inverness Harbour Trust 1847-57
Letters From a Gentleman in the North of Scotland - Edmund Burt

Memorabilia of Inverness - James Sutter 1887
Middle Ages in the Highlands - Inverness Field Club 1981
Miscellanea Invernessiana - John Noble 1902

New Statistical Account (1835) XIV - 1845
Northern Highlands in the Nineteenth Century - James Barron
Northern Meeting 1788-1988 - Angus Fairrie 1988
Notes on the Ness Valley - Hugh Barron, Inv Gaelic Soc Trans Vol 43

Observations on a Tour Through the Highlands - T Carnett Vol 2 1811
Old High Church (Pamphlet) - Rev FJL MacLaughlan
Old Inverness - Dr Alex Ross, Inv Scientific Soc & Field Club Trans Vol
2
Old Lords of Lovat and Beaufort - Rev A MacDonald 1934
Old statistical Account 1771-1799
Ordnance Gazetteer of Scotland - Francis Groome 1883

Popular Disturbances in Scotland 1780-1815 - Kenneth J Logue 1979
Port of Inverness - Joseph Cook 1931
Port of Inverness - Schools Library Resource Service, HELP Publication
Presbytery of Inverness 1632 - 1644 - Rev A MacDonald, Inv Gaelic Soc
Trans Vol 9

Queen Victoria in the Highlands - Schools Library Resource Service,
HELP Publication

Recollections of Inverness by an Invernessian - Robert Munro 1863
Records of Inverness - W R MacKay & H C Boyd, New Spalding Club 1911
Records of the Presbytery of Inverness and Dingwall - W MacKay
Reminiscences of a Clachnacuddin Nonagenarian - John MacLean 1886
Reminiscences of my Life in the Highlands - Joseph Mitchell Vol 1 1883
River Ness (4 booklets) - Schools Library Resource Service, HELP Publication
Royal Events in the Highlands - Schools Library Resource Service, HELP Publication

Scotland Farewell - Donald MacKay, Edinburgh, 1980
Seventeenth Century in the Highlands - Inverness Field Club 1986
Sheriff Court Records - Highland Regional Archive
Short Account of the Town of Inverness - Edinburgh 1828
Sketches of Highland Families - John MacLean 1895
Social and Religious Life in the Highlands - K MacDonald
Statutes and Regulations for John Raining's School – 1790

Thousand Tongues to Sing, the story of Methodism in Inverness - Rev TP Addison 1963
Topographical, Statistical and Hist Gazetteer of Scotland - Fullerton & Co, Glasgow 1842
Tour Through the Whole Island of Great Britain - Daniel Defoe 1724 Vol 1-3

United Charities School - Inverness Burgh Library, post 1830

Wade in Scotland - J B Salmond 1934
Witch of Inverness and the Fairies of Tomnahurich - John Noble 1891
Wood's Plan of Inverness 1821

Index